Frolicking Bears, Wet Vultures, and Other Oddities

THE FLORIDA HISTORY AND CULTURE SERIES

Florida A&M University, Tallahassee
Florida Atlantic University, Boca Raton
Florida Gulf Coast University, Ft. Myers
Florida International University, Miami
Florida State University, Tallahassee
University of Central Florida, Orlando
University of Florida, Gainesville
University of North Florida, Jacksonville
University of South Florida, Tampa
University of West Florida, Pensacola

THE FLORIDA HISTORY AND CULTURE SERIES
Edited by Raymond Arsenault and Gary R. Mormino

Al Burt's Florida: Snowbirds, Sand Castles, and Self-Rising Crackers, by Al Burt (1997)

Black Miami in the Twentieth Century, by Marvin Dunn (1997)

Gladesmen: Gator Hunters, Moonshiners, and Skiffers, by Glen Simmons and Laura Ogden (1998)

"Come to My Sunland": Letters of Julia Daniels Moseley from the Florida Frontier, 1882–1886, by Julia Winifred Moseley and Betty Powers Crislip (1998)

The Enduring Seminoles: From Alligator Wrestling to Ecotourism, by Patsy West (1998)

Government in the Sunshine State: Florida Since Statehood, by David R. Colburn and Lance deHaven-Smith (1999)

The Everglades: An Environmental History, by David McCally (1999), first paperback edition, 2001

Beechers, Stowes, and Yankee Strangers: The Transformation of Florida, by John T. Foster Jr. and Sarah Whitmer Foster (1999)

The Tropic of Cracker, by Al Burt (1999)

Balancing Evils Judiciously: The Proslavery Writings of Zephaniah Kingsley, edited and annotated by Daniel W. Stowell (1999)

Hitler's Soldiers in the Sunshine State: German POWs in Florida, by Robert D. Billinger Jr. (2000)

Cassadaga: The South's Oldest Spiritualist Community, edited by John J. Guthrie, Phillip Charles Lucas, and Gary Monroe (2000)

Claude Pepper and Ed Ball: Politics, Purpose, and Power, by Tracy E. Danese (2000)

Pensacola during the Civil War: A Thorn in the Side of the Confederacy, by George F. Pearce (2000)

Castles in the Sand: The Life and Times of Carl Graham Fisher, by Mark S. Foster (2000)

Miami, U.S.A., by Helen Muir (2000)

Politics and Growth in Twentieth-Century Tampa, by Robert Kerstein (2001)

FROLICKING BEARS, WET VULTURES, AND OTHER ODDITIES

A NEW YORK CITY JOURNALIST IN NINETEENTH-CENTURY FLORIDA

Edited by Jerald T. Milanich

Foreword by Gary R. Mormino and Raymond Arsenault

University Press of Florida
Gainesville Tallahassee Tampa Boca Raton
Pensacola Orlando Miami Jacksonville Ft. Myers

10 09 08 07 06 05   6 5 4 3 2 1

Library of Congress Cataloging-in-Publication Data
Cummings, Amos J. (Amos Jay), 1841–1902.
Frolicking bears, wet vultures, and other oddities : a New York
City journalist in nineteenth-century Florida / edited by Jerald T.
Milanich; foreword by Gary R. Mormino and Raymond Arsenault.
p. cm. — (The Florida history and culture series)
A collection of twenty articles written by Amos Jay Cummings.
Includes bibliographical references and index.
ISBN 0-8130-2848-5 (acid-free paper)
1. Florida—Description and travel. 2. Natural history—Florida.
3. Florida—History—19th century. 4. Florida—Biography.
5. Cummings, Amos J. (Amos Jay), 1841–1902—Travel—Florida.
6. Journalists—New York (State)—New York—Biography.
I. Milanich, Jerald T. II. Title. III. Series.
F316.C95 2005
917.59'04—dc22   2005042290

The University Press of Florida is the scholarly publishing agency
for the State University System of Florida, comprising Florida A&M
University, Florida Atlantic University, Florida Gulf Coast University,
Florida International University, Florida State University, University
of Central Florida, University of Florida, University of North Florida,
University of South Florida, and University of West Florida.

University Press of Florida
15 Northwest 15th Street
Gainesville, FL 32611-2079
http://www.upf.com

Contents

Series Foreword

Frolicking Bears, Wet Vultures, and Other Oddities is the 33rd volume in a series devoted to the study of Florida history and culture. During the past half century, the burgeoning population and increased national and international visibility of Florida have sparked a great deal of popular interest in the state's past, present, and future. As the favorite destination of hordes of tourists and as the new home for millions of retirees, immigrants, and transplants, modern Florida has become a demographic, political, and cultural bellwether.

A state of vast distances and distant strangers, Florida needs more citizens who care about the welfare of this special place and its people. We hope this series helps newcomers and old-timers appreciate and understand Florida. Unfortunately, the quantity and quality of the literature on Florida's distinctive heritage and character have not kept pace with the Sunshine State's enhanced status. In an effort to remedy this situation—to provide an accessible and attractive format for the publication of Florida-related books—the University Press of Florida has established the Florida History and Culture Series.

As coeditors of the series, we are deeply committed to the creation of an eclectic but carefully crafted set of books that provide the field of Florida studies with a fresh focus that will encourage Florida researchers and writers to consider the broader implications and context of their work. The series includes monographs, works of synthesis, memoirs, and anthologies. And, while the series features books of historical interest, we encourage authors researching Florida's environment, politics, and popular or material culture to submit their manuscripts as well. We want each book to retain a distinct personality and voice, but at the same time we hope to foster a sense of community and collaboration among Florida scholars.

Frolicking Bears, Wet Vultures, and Other Oddities is pure delight, a story within a story. Jerald Milanich's detective story of how he managed to track down the protagonist and identify a bizarre cast of gator hunters, mule-skinners, and murderers—with the aid of tireless graduate students and modern computers—is as compelling as the original material he brings to life.

Milanich, an archaeologist and scholar of the original inhabitants of Florida, introduces to twenty-first-century readers tales from the late nineteenth century. It is largely a story of one remarkable figure and his curious wanderings.

Printer, filibusterer, gourmand, Civil War hero, Tammany boss, U.S. congressman, and journalist, Amos Jay Cummings compressed several lives into one. Between 1873 and 1893, Cummings made repeated trips to the eastern coast of Florida and the interior, writing essays for various northeastern newspapers, most notably the *New York Sun*. Milanich perfectly characterizes Cummings as "a great American chronicler," one of the first of what we would call today human-interest reporters.

When Cummings first encountered Florida in 1873, gloom and despair hung over the Sunshine State. "The great drawback," wrote the visitor, "is the State Legislature." Military Reconstruction and civil discord characterized political life in Tallahassee, but Cummings preferred to explore the natural wonders of the desolate east coast and the wild hinterland. For twenty years, Cummings—whom a protégé acknowledged as having a "sulphurous vocabulary"—dispatched reports on the tropical paradise and eccentric characters found in places of which few Americans had ever heard. He described a bountiful frontier that is hard to fathom: so many green turtles and loggerheads that farmers routinely fed their eggs to their mules and pigs; schools of mullet so vast and loud that settlers could not sleep at night; and gators so large and numerous that it seemed as if a man could walk across the Ocklawaha on the gators' backs. His descriptions of the old Dummitt grove sandwiched between the Indian River and Banana Creek; Indian River wreckers with their "winged phaetons" (cat-rigged sailboats); Lake Worth before it became a saltwater body; and mosquitoes—"Tongue can neither exaggerate their numbers nor their ferocity"—are classics.

In *Lonesome Dove*, the grizzled Augustus McCrae exclaims upon first seeing Montana, "I can't think of nothing better than riding a fine horse into a new country." So, too, the modern reader appreciates the wonderment in Cummings's accounts of Florida between 1873 and 1893.

Raymond Arsenault and Gary R. Mormino, Series Editors
University of South Florida, St. Petersburg

Introduction

Amos Jay Cummings and His Florida Adventures

NOT ONLY WERE there bruins and buzzards, there were rascals and racists, as well as sea turtles and music-loving cows. There were political flacks and suicidal fleas; murderers and mosquitoes; rich soils and poor souls. The Florida that New York journalist Amos Jay Cummings saw and wrote about from 1873 to 1893 was mysterious, quaint, horrible, exotic, and every adjective in between. It was a wonderland that drew northerners in droves; it was a harsh land that brought misery to local residents.

Like a modern-day Carl Hiaasen, Amos Jay Cummings stripped away the veneer painted by land speculators and tourist home operators eager for northern investors and tourists and found another Florida. The underlying result was not always pretty, and Cummings pulled no punches. He was an outlander who was at times enthralled and other times repelled by what he saw. As a foreigner he could ask questions and record scenes that a local journalist or writer might or could not.

Cummings's articles stand in contrast to much of the literature published about Florida during the last third of the nineteenth century. Books like Daniel Brinton's *A Guide-Book of Florida and the South for Tourists, Invalids, and Emigrants* (1869), Rambler's *Guide to Florida* (1875), Sidney Lanier's *Florida: Its Scenery, Climate, and History* (1875), George M. Barbour's *Florida for Tourists, Invalids, and Settlers* (1882), and Silvia Sunshine's (a pseudonym for Abbie M. Brooks) *Petals Plucked from Sunny Climes* (1880) tended to extol Florida's virtues. Cummings, on the other hand, wrote it as it was.

A century after the naturalist William Bartram traveled down the St. Johns River and into North Central Florida, Cummings covered some of the same territory. But where Bartram found a wilderness that was home to Seminole Indians, Cummings found a land being settled by a host of characters, many of whom were not gentle in their attempts to wrest a living from Florida's natural resources.

Bartram, a visitor from the North, marveled at Florida's wildlife. Many of the northern visitors Cummings encountered spent their waking moments shooting at every animal that moved. Others were busily importing an Eden of nonnative plants, species that still vex the state today.

I was not born in Florida, but I have lived in the Sunshine State pretty much continuously since my second birthday. Florida things interest me. I love the novels of Carl Hiaasen, Randy Wayne White, Elmore Leonard, and Harry Crews—authors who look beyond and under Disney World, Silver Springs, and the press releases of local chambers of commerce to pen prose pictures of an extraordinary state and its people. In the nineteenth century, Amos Jay Cummings did much the same thing, though he wrote newspaper articles rather than fiction.

I first met Amos Jay Cummings in 2001 just after the new millennium dawned and nearly a century after his death. James Cusick of the University of Florida's P. K. Yonge Library of Florida History sent me a copy of a newspaper clipping dated April 23, 1873. Cut from the *New York Weekly Sun*, the clipping had been among a collection of Floridiana donated to the library by the family of Thomas and Georgine Mickler, owners for many years of Mickler Books of Chuluota, Florida.

Unsigned, the article described the author's visit to Turtle Mound, an archaeological site in modern Volusia County, just south of New Smyrna Beach. Today the mound, actually a shell heap—perhaps the largest in Florida—is designated a State Archaeological Site and lies within Canaveral National Seashore. Along with Turtle Mound, the article described a number of other archaeological sites in East Central Florida, from the St. Johns River to Merritt Island. The article conjured some colorful characters, such as Old Cone, the gator hunter, and it offered some marvelous accounts of Florida scenes, all written only fifteen years after the Third Seminole War. One thing that drew my attention was the descriptions of the destruction of archaeological sites and the wholesale attacks on the land, especially the fauna. Less than a decade after Robert E. Lee surrendered to U. S. Grant, Florida's natural history also was involved in a civil war, one being waged by its new residents.

I was fascinated. Who wrote that article? What else did he or she write? I headed across campus to the University of Florida library, walked up to a computer terminal, and began a search.

Identifying Amos Jay Cummings

The dateline of the March 20, 1873, newspaper article read "De Soto Groves, Florida," which I quickly learned was in East Central Florida, not too far from modern-day Cape Canaveral and the launch pads from which the National Aeronautics and Space Administration sends satellites and shuttles into the future. The text made it seem likely that the author was a visitor to the region. It was also clear that my unidentified scribe could write. His second sentence, which described Turtle Mound as "a day's ride from civilization," captivated me. Had the author written other articles about Florida in the 1870s?

Ensconced in the P. K. Yonge Library, I flipped through book after book looking for clues. The first came from John Eriksen's 1994 book *Brevard County, A History to 1955*, in which there is mention of a British baronet named Sir Tatton Sykes who had a hunting camp on the Indian River in 1857. Almost certainly that was the same individual referred to as Sir Francis Sykes in the 1873 *Weekly Sun* article on Indian sites. But that lead took me nowhere.

Worn out from the day's hunting, I traipsed back across campus to my office, where I decided to pull out some nineteenth-century references on Florida's natural history to see if anyone else had written about Turtle Mound. I reasoned that since academicians often follow the old adage that "something worth saying is worth saying more than once," my mystery author might also have used that same visit to Turtle Mound in some other article.

By blind chance, the first book I pulled from the shelf was *Guide to Florida*, written by Rambler, an obvious pseudonym, and published in 1875. My copy, a facsimile printed in 1964, literally fell open to page 131 and a long undated quote about Florida's Indian River region taken from the *New York Sun*—a companion newspaper to the *New York Weekly Sun*—and said to have been written by "Ziska." What caught my eye were three of Ziska's phrases. One referred to bears hunting turtle eggs on the beach, another mentioned Sir Francis Sykes, and the third noted that Turtle Mound "looms on the horizon like a pillar of Hercules." All three of those elements also appear in the 1873 *Weekly Sun* article. Ziska most likely was my missing author. But who was Ziska?

My search for Ziska took me on some wild adventures using electronic databases, which I chronicled in an article entitled "The Historian's Craft," published in 2002 in the *Florida Historical Quarterly*. To make a long story short, I spent a lot of time chasing a British avant-garde woman writer who in 1897 had published the novel *Ziska: The Problem of a Wicked Soul*. But ultimately, John Edward Haynes's slender and dusty 1882 volume *Pseudonyms of Authors, Including Anonyms and Initialisms* took me from London to New

Much to my surprise, I found this photograph of Amos Cummings on e-Bay while I was doing online searches. It is cut from a biographical dictionary or similar publication that, according to the e-Bay information, was published in 1895. Despite diligent searching by myself and librarians at the University of Florida and the New York Public Library, I could never find the original source.

York. On page 103, Haynes told me that Ziska was a pseudonym used by Amos Jay Cummings, a New York journalist! I had my author.

Biographical information from various sources filled out some of the details of Cummings's life. He had been a journalist, war hero, politician, and, yes, he had visited Florida and had written under the pseudonym Ziska. I soon learned that there were four scrapbooks belonging to Cummings in the New York Public Library. A visit to the old handwritten catalogue in the Rose Reading Room at that venerable institution turned up eleven more. I believe the fifteen scrapbooks were discarded after Cummings died, perhaps after the death of his spouse in 1916 (Cummings and his wife had no children). In May 1927, a sharp-eyed New York Public Library employee spotted the scrapbooks at the Bargain Book Shop in Manhattan and acquired them for the library. Pasted on the pages of those scrapbooks was Cummings's journalistic and legislative literary oeuvre, including numerous yellowing newspaper articles he had written that had appeared in the *New York Sun*, *Weekly Sun*, and *Semi-Weekly Sun* newspapers. Among them was the 1873 article on Turtle Mound.

Who Was Amos Jay Cummings?

Over the next week, I browsed through all fifteen scrapbooks and perused any number of biographical dictionaries and the like. As I learned more and more about Amos Cummings, he and I became friends. Most biographical sketches and literary citations (including his obituary in the *New York Times*) give May 15, 1841, as the day he was born in Conklin, New York, a small town in Broome County southeast of Binghamton (some accounts state the town was "Conkling" in "Boone" County). A few sources give 1838 and others 1842 as his birthday. On a small footstone on his grave in Clinton Cemetery in Irvington, New Jersey, the birth date is May 15, 1838, as it is on the larger monument erected above his grave and that of his second wife, Frances Caroline, née Roberts, whom he married on March 6, 1869.

Clearly Cummings lied about his age during his adult life. Even official biographies surrounding his government service as a congressman and military hero list 1841. It is likely that the small grave marker was inscribed under the auspices of his second wife, while the larger monument was put up after her death in 1916. His wife knew his true birth year.

I found a bit about Frances Cummings in various sources. According to the burial marker in Clinton Cemetery, she, like Amos, was born in 1838. But that date does not jibe with the 1870 federal census, which suggests that she was born in 1834 or 1835. On the date that she and Amos were counted in that census (July 20, 1870), her age was thirty-five. Did she, too, maintain a fiction about her age, one recorded even after her death?

In the 1870 census, Frances is listed as Amos's spouse. Her occupation was "keeping house," while Amos was said to be a "printer." I have not found any information about Cummings's first marriage, other than a note that his first wife had died.

That Cummings subtracted several years from his age by altering his date of birth also is verified by his federal census entry for 1900. (HeritageQuest, whose software provides a transcript of that census, mistakenly records Amos J. Cummings as "Annas J. Cummings.") In the 1900 census, compiled in June, Cummings's birth date is listed as May 1838, and his age is given as sixty-two years. His occupation at that time was "Congressman."

As a young teenager, Cummings began his career in journalism working in a print shop that printed, among other things, local religious newspapers (the *Christian Herald and Messenger* and the *Palladium*) written by his father, Reverend Moses Cummings (his mother was Julia Ann Cummings, née Jones). Some biographies state that he started as an apprentice printer (setting type) when he was only twelve, though that may have been a story he promulgated.

Apparently seeking wider pastures, Cummings left home at age fifteen (or was he eighteen?), traveling about the country and working as a compositor—at the time such people were referred to as "tramp printers"—for several newspapers before moving to New York City, where he was hired as a reporter on the *New York Tribune*, whose editor-in-chief was Horace Greeley. That he had set type in every state in the Union, as one biography notes, may also be a story Cummings spread about himself.

Another biographical sketch says that Cummings joined the 1858 expedition of William Walker to Nicaragua, one of several Walker organized to try to overthrow political regimes in that Central American country. Though it is recorded that Cummings traveled to Nicaragua, that also may be a made-up story; Walker, who sailed from Mobile in 1858, never got beyond the mouth of the Mississippi River on that trip because he was arrested for violating United States neutrality laws and tried (in New Orleans, where he was acquitted). Still another story is that Cummings was on Walker's earlier 1857 expedition, while a third places him on Walker's 1860 expedition to Nicaragua and Honduras. If so, Cummings indeed reached Central America. On that 1860 expedition, Walker was arrested, turned over to Honduran authorities, and shot. From a review of historical accounts, I think it most likely that Cummings joined Walker in 1858 in Mobile and never made it to Central America.

With the outbreak of the Civil War, Cummings enlisted in the U.S. Army. In 1861, he was serving with the 26th New Jersey Infantry and was promoted to the rank of sergeant major. He saw action at both Fredericksburg (late 1862) and during the Chancellorsville campaign (April–May 1863). After the war, probably in the early 1870s, he found newspaper articles recounting the engagements in which he had been a participant, cut them out, and pasted them in one of his scrapbooks with his own comments in the margin. On an article from the *New York Herald* dated June 28, 1862, and datelined "Battle Ground near Charleston (West Virginia)," he wrote, "The first battle in which my reg't was engaged." He also collected other articles about the Civil War, as well as the assassination of President Abraham Lincoln and the subsequent arrest of John Wilkes Booth. Those, too, are pasted in one of his scrapbooks.

Cummings apparently was wounded in 1863 in Virginia and mustered out of the service. His unspecified war-related infirmities would continue to bother him his entire life.

Returning to New York City, he was rehired at the *New York Tribune* as a night editor. One of his tasks was to condense news articles for publication in the *Weekly Tribune*. Several biographical notes, including his obituary in the *New York Times*, have him helping ward off a mob of military draft protestors who raided the *Tribune*'s offices.

A strike by the paper's printers cost Cummings his job, and he went to work briefly for the *Law Transcript*, which was published in New York City. When Horace Greeley offered him an editorship at the *Tribune* in 1866, he returned to that paper first as a city editor and then as a political editor. In late 1868 (or early 1869), Cummings moved to the *New York Sun* to become managing editor. According to Frank M. O'Brien's *The Story of the Sun*, Cummings told Charles Anderson Dana, the *Sun*'s owner, "I am leaving the *Tribune* because they say I swear too much" (241).

In late 1872 or early 1873, Cummings, besieged by health problems, resigned his editorship and headed south, stopping in Savannah, Georgia, on his way to Florida, where he stayed for two months (March and April). Though not a full-time *Sun* editor, he certainly was a correspondent for that paper. Several of the *Sun* stories reprinted here are from that 1873 visit. He returned to New York City, apparently by train, and then almost immediately embarked on a seven-month odyssey across the continent to San Francisco, traveling with his spouse. I do not know if she was with him earlier in Florida.

From New York, Cummings traveled mainly by rail to Cincinnati and St. Louis, and then to Colorado, where he visited Denver, Caribou, Boulder, Manitou, and Spanish Bar. Then he moved on to Cheyenne, Wyoming, and Salt Lake City, always writing articles for the *New York Sun* about what he saw and whom he spoke with. The stories apparently were wired back to the newspaper, where they were published as "Correspondence of The Sun."

Cummings's stay in Salt Lake City included an interview with Brigham Young, about whom he wrote an article. A short note in the *Salt Lake Daily Herald* on September 2, 1873, recorded that "Mr. Amos J. Cummings of the *New York Sun* and Mrs. Cummings left for the west after a pleasant stay of six weeks." I suspect Cummings wrote the piece himself. In some of the scrapbooks there are "Letters to the Editor" that I am certain he wrote so that, as editor, he could answer them to make some point.

The published articles that Cummings wrote in Florida and on his trip to the West, along with related clippings such as the one from the Salt Lake newspaper cited above, were not very carefully cut out of newspapers and pasted in his scrapbooks. Some of the clippings are without titles or subheadings, and almost none have the date or name of the newspaper in which they were published.

From Salt Lake, the two Cummings traveled to San Francisco, leaving there in early November 1873. A clipping, certainly written by Cummings and pasted in a scrapbook, records their departure. Dated November 4, 1873 (but with no newspaper attribution), the clipping states: "Amos J. Cummings, managing editor of the *New York Sun*, accompanied by his wife sailed on the steamer Constitution yesterday for home. . . . [Cummings is an] accomplished angler as well as a brilliant and vivacious writer." He apparently enjoyed a great deal of trout fishing in California.

The stories that Cummings wrote on his transcontinental trip are an extraordinary view of a large section of the country a century after independence. They certainly deserve to be republished, and Cummings should be given his due as a great American chronicler.

Once back in New York, Cummings again packed his bags and headed south. The datelines on articles pasted in the scrapbooks place him in Columbia, South Carolina, in late December 1873, then in Augusta and Savannah, Georgia, in January and February 1874. By March, he was back in Florida, again writing articles that were published by his New York newspaper. This time, however, the articles for the most part bore his pseudonym "Ziska," as did the bylines of some of the articles he wrote in 1873 on the way to California.

On the way back north from Florida in May and June 1874, he stopped off in Charleston and Florence, South Carolina, where he wrote more stories. The 1873 and 1874 journeys to Florida apparently were neither his first nor his last. In a letter to the editor of the *Sun* (himself), writing as Ziska, he states he had "spent five winters averaging four months each in Florida." Judging from its placement in one of the scrapbooks, that letter was probably written in 1873 or 1874. One biographical sketch also notes that he wintered five times in Florida, including in 1875 and 1876. On the other hand, in the several pages attributed to Ziska in Rambler's *Guide to Florida* (137), Cummings mentions spending only two winters in the Indian River area. Perhaps he was in other parts of Florida at times before or shortly after 1873 and 1874.

From the fifteen Cummings scrapbooks, I gleaned more information about his life as a journalist. He also wrote under the pseudonym "Uncle Rufus Hatch" while he traveled to England and Paris, penning articles that were sent back to the *Sun*. And, as Uncle Rufus Hatch, he frequently wrote about Wall Street and the deals being made by financiers like Jay Gould.

Writing under a pseudonym may seem a bit peculiar to us, but the practice has a long literary tradition, especially in the nineteenth century. For instance, in the early part of the 1800s Charles Lamb wrote as "Elia," while in midcentury "Boz" was a pen name for Charles Dickens. Similarly, the names of two well-known contemporaries of Amos Cummings, the authors Lewis Carroll and Mark Twain, both were pseudonyms (for Charles Dodgson and Samuel Clements, respectively).

Cummings made a second trip west of the Mississippi River, to Colorado, Nevada, Utah, and California, probably in the later 1880s. In 1888, Cummings visited the Black Hills to check out reports of tin mining, but I am uncertain if that journey took place during his second western trip or was an independent adventure.

During the late 1870s, the 1880s, and into the 1890s, he continued to publish articles in the *Sun*, at times under the name Ziska. In later years, his articles were signed with his own name.

For a short time (at least during a portion of 1876), he edited the *Evening Express* in New York, though he continued to have ties to the *Sun*. In 1887, he founded and ran the *Evening Sun*, another newspaper. Among other things, he is known for reporting several notable murder trials during the period 1877–86, and he reported on the national political party conventions in 1880, 1884, and 1888.

As a journalist, Cummings was something of a legend. In his book *Adventures of a Tramp Printer, 1880–1890*, John Hicks, another itinerant printer, encountered Cummings in New York City about 1889. He describes Cummings as a "newspaper genius" who had a "terrible temper" and whose "sulphurous vocabulary had caused [Horace] Greeley to ask him to leave the *Tribune*" (270). O'Brien (in *The Story of the Sun*, 241) notes that "Cummings was the best all-round news man of his day. He was the first real human-interest reporter." In his *New York Times* obituary, Cummings is described as "versatile, energetic, and gritty," and "a humorist of no mean type."

Cummings, a fierce proponent of the typesetters union, was very popular with his fellow New York journalists, serving as president of the New York Press Club in 1885–86. Articles about the scrumptious repasts shared by Press Club members with detailed menus often found their way into the *Sun*. Fishing also played a large role in his life, and he wrote about fishing-related exploits as well. Pasted in one of the scrapbooks are two fortune cookie-sized pieces of paper (about 1½ x ⅜ inches). On one is printed, "Hon. Amos Cummings of the *Sun*, eats shark chowder for his Sunday dinner," while the other reads "Hon. Amos Cummings of the *Sun*, is very fond of Jamaica Bay trout." (Jamaica Bay is just southwest of John F. Kennedy International Airport within New York City.)

That his colleagues must have enjoyed razzing Cummings about his fish-catching and fish-eating exploits also is evident in a short poem pasted next to the two small pieces of paper. Accompanied by a pen-and-ink sketch depicting a fisherman sitting on a dock with numerous empty glasses around him, the poem, entitled "Hon. Amos Cummings of the 'Daily Sun' Fishing for Bagalls[1] at Rockaway Beach," reads:

In the hot sun
   Sat he and wondered!
From morn till mid-day
   Sat he and wondered!
The mosquitoes be fit not,
   The bagalls, well, they bit not,
While roasted he sat there;
   Sat there and wondered!
He baited with bull frog,
He baited with egg nogg,
   And sat there and wondered!
Glasses to the right of him,
Glasses to the left of him,
   Still he roasted and wondered!
Eight mortal hours sat he!
Nary a bite got he!
   But the waiters ne're blundered;
Though melted and wasted,
And in the sun roasted,
   While he sat there and wondered.

Pasted in two of Cummings's scrapbooks are newspaper articles about the activities of the New York "Ichthyophagous Club" (Fish-eating Club), written with tongue in cheek. One reports on the "first annual dinner" of the club

This is a clipping pasted into scrapbook 4 (of four) in the New York Public Library. The clipping, perhaps from a program or magazine (not a newspaper), shows Amos Jay Cummings with seven other men. *Top row, left to right:* Roswell P. Flower, Cummings, S. S. "Sunset" Cox, Warner Miller. *Bottom row, left to right:* C. S. Fairchild, William M. Evarts, Daniel S. Lamont, and William C. Whitney. There is no label or date, but I believe the clipping is from 1887; it depicts important New York City political figures. At that time, all eight were either U.S. congressmen representing districts in the city (Cox, Cummings, and Flower), New York senators (Evarts and Miller), or members of President Grover Cleveland's administration (Fairchild was secretary of the treasury, Whitney was secretary of the navy, and Lamont, formerly a private secretary to President Cleveland, was named secretary of war in 1887). Courtesy of New York Public Library.

whose "object is to test the edibility of unappreciated fishes." Included on the menu were shark fin consommé, tartlets of horseshoe crabs, and sea robins. I suspect he both participated in the club and wrote the articles.

Cummings, according to biographical information, also was known for his authorship of a book or pamphlet titled *Sayings of Uncle Rufus* (1880), which I believe was a political tract, and at some point his Ziska "letters" may also have been collected and published. I was not able to locate copies or library citations for either of these two publications.

In 1886, Cummings ran for office as a Tammany Hall Democrat and was elected to the Fiftieth Congress, representing New York District 6 around Wall Street in lower Manhattan, serving during 1887–89. In 1888, he chose not to run for his House seat, opting instead to found the *Evening Sun* newspaper.

However, during the Fifty-first Congress he was appointed to an open legislative seat for District 9 in New York City, which he held until 1893, running successfully for election once. Later, from 1893 to 1895, Cummings represented the 11th District. Then he ran for the 10th District seat, a post he held from 1895 until his death in 1902.

In 1894, while a U.S. congressman, Cummings belatedly was awarded a Congressional Medal of Honor in recognition of his bravery in battle in Virginia thirty-one years earlier, specifically his charging a Confederate artillery battery at Salem Heights on May 4, 1863, during the Chancellorsville campaign. Such were the perks of a U.S. congressman. Another perk was travel. A trip to Florida in April and May 1893 resulted in three articles about the state that are reprinted here as chapters 18–20.

Many of the speeches Cummings gave on the floor of the House were published in the *Congressional Record.* They and various newspaper clippings about him are pasted in his scrapbooks. Some of the clippings in which he is mentioned are from newspapers well outside New York City.

Cummings's political stature is reflected in his being chosen as a delegate to the Democratic National Convention in Chicago in 1896. Representing New York's 8th District, Cummings appears only twice in the *Official Proceedings of the Democratic National Convention,* once when he is listed as a delegate, and again when he took the podium to read a telegram from Joseph C. Sibley withdrawing Sibley's name as a nominee for the vice-presidential slot on the Democratic ticket. As he took the podium, Cummings was introduced to the convention as a "member of the famous Tammany Society of New York."

As a politician, he drew national attention. In 1890, his name was tossed about as a possible running mate for William Jennings Bryan. In that election, Bryan was running for the second time for the United States presidency against William McKinley. Instead, Adlai E. Stevenson—grandfather of the Democratic nominee Adlai Stevenson who was defeated twice by Dwight D. Eisenhower—served as Bryan's running mate. McKinley, of course, won the election.

Cummings's political interests and activities began as early as 1872, when he wrote the sixty-four-page pamphlet *The Sun's Greeley Campaign Songster,* which was published and distributed by the newspaper. Years later, while a congressman, he authored *The Political Handbook; Political Information for Present Use and Future Reference* (1896). A copy of the former exists in the Library of Congress, while the latter is in the New York Public Library. In addition, the Library of Congress has four lengthy speeches that he wrote while a congressman and that were published through the Government Printing Office. A fifth short speech in the Library of Congress dealing with municipal elections in New York City (1898) and attributed to Amos G. Cummings (1898) may also be by Amos J. Cummings.

Florida, the United States, and the World in Cummings's Day

When Cummings first visited Florida in 1873 during Reconstruction, much of Central and South Florida was a frontier area, while the northern portion was a rat's nest of post–Civil War politics and racism. As Cummings relates it, corruption was a way of life as politicians and other residents vied for power, money, and land.

Travel from Jacksonville to Tallahassee, the capital, was by horse and buggy or by train. A portion of the overland route was via the Bellamy Road, itself an approximation of the seventeenth-century *camino real* and other roads used by Spaniards and mission Indians. Elsewhere in the state there were steamships, feet, and the backs of horses, along with an occasional train, to transport people. Given those options, travel by water almost always won, and the St. Johns River proved to be an entry into the Indian River area of East Central Florida. There were no electric lights, automobiles, or air conditioning when Cummings visited Florida in 1873 and 1874, and Remington and Sons had only begun to mass produce the manual typewriter.

It was only a handful of years prior to Cummings writing about people traveling on steamships on the St. Johns River that the first riders had descended into a New York City subway (1870; the subway was only a block long). Charles Darwin's *Descent of Man* appeared in print in 1871, and George Armstrong Custer, sporting a shorter hairstyle than in the past, had his last stand at the Little Bighorn in 1876. In that same year, Alexander Graham Bell patented the telephone, and in the next, Thomas Alva Edison received his patent for the phonograph. Two years later, he topped that with the electric lightbulb. In much of the Western world, it was the time of the Victorian Age, and the Industrial Revolution was well under way. In Florida the same year, federal troops left over from the Civil War still were occupying the state.

Between the time Amos Cummings wrote about Florida's orange groves (1873) and her sugarcane fields (1893), Sheriff Pat Garrett plugged Billy the Kid (1881), and Jesse James went to his final rest (1882). The Coca-Cola label was registered in 1887, while women were first given the right to vote in 1893 (in New Zealand; it would be three more decades before the United States followed suit). Amos Jay Cummings saw it all.

The *Sun, Semi-Weekly Sun,* and *Weekly Sun* Newspapers and the Fifteen Cummings Scrapbooks

The *New York Sun*, the *Weekly Sun*, and the *Daily Sun* were sister publications put out on different schedules by the same publisher. The January 5, 1874, issue of the *Sun* gives the following subscription information:

Weekly Sun, eight pages, fifty-six columns, $1.00 per year.

Semi-Weekly Sun, same size as the *Daily Sun*, $2.00 per year.

Daily Sun [also the *Sun*], twenty-eight columns, daily circulation over 120,000, $0.02 per copy, $0.50 per month, $6.00 per year.

The *Weekly Sun*, published once a week on Wednesdays, began as the weekly edition of the *Sun* in 1836. It became the *Sun Weekly* in 1840 and then the *Weekly Sun* in 1851. It ceased publication in 1894. For a short time, there was a steamer edition (prepared for transatlantic ship crossings), a national edition, and a European edition. As far as I can determine, the *Weekly Sun* published only articles that also appeared in the *Sun*. Type was not reset; the same typographic errors appear in the same stories in both editions.

The short-lived *Semi-Weekly Sun*, published Tuesdays and Fridays, was another sibling publication of the *Sun* and also contained articles that appeared in that daily. Records indicate that it probably began in 1869 and ceased publication in June 1873. Copies of the newspaper are rare.

The *Sun*, sometimes known as the *Daily Sun* to differentiate it from the other editions, was published daily except for Sunday from 1833 to 1875, when it went to seven days. The paper merged with the *New York Press* in 1896 and continued to be published as the *Sun and New York Press* until 1916. To confuse the issue a bit, there also was an *Evening Sun* in 1852, and again from 1887 to 1916.

In 1873, the articles that Cummings wrote about Florida appeared in various combinations of the *Sun, Semi-Weekly Sun*, and *Weekly Sun*. Some were published in two of the editions; I did not find any published in all three, but it is possible that did occur. The New York Public Library's holdings of the *Weekly Sun*—now all on microfilm as are the sister editions—are incomplete. I was told that when the microfilming was done, probably in the 1950s, the original copies of the papers were discarded.

Each of Cummings's Florida articles shares the same basic layout—the same as other *Sun* articles of the time. Each has a headline printed in all capital letters in a 14-point font. A linear dingbat (a symbol used in typography, often to separate one section or paragraph from another) separates the headline from a subhead, also in all uppercase letters, but in italics and in an 8-point font. Another, slightly smaller linear dingbat separates the subhead from a readout, usually (but not always) consisting of section headings taken from the text of the article, which follows. The readouts served as teasers to draw the attention of readers. Each article also has a dateline consisting of a city or place name in Florida, followed by the date (month and day). Most, but not all, of the articles have "Correspondence of The Sun" as a separate line in 6-point type between the readout and the dateline.

Threading my way through Cummings's scrapbooks and the microfilm copies of the newspapers was an interesting task, and ultimately I was able to find at least one newspaper issue containing each of the Florida articles that I found in the scrapbooks and that are reprinted here. On the other hand, I also found Florida articles in the print editions (on microfilm) that were not in the scrapbooks. In each case, those latter articles are "companion pieces" to those in the scrapbooks, mentioning some of the same places and people, and I am certain they were written by Cummings. In one of those articles, he identifies himself as a *New York Sun* correspondent. The other articles not in a scrapbook all are signed by Ziska or by Amos J. Cummings. It also is reasonably easy to recognize Cummings's writing style, especially when he was writing about Florida, people, and nature. There is no doubt that he wrote the twenty articles reprinted in this volume.

My use of the fifteen Cummings scrapbooks in the New York Public Library has barely sampled their contents. The four earliest of the scrapbooks are catalogued as "Cummings, A. J. Scrapbook of newspaper clippings" and given call number "*CZ+." The catalogue notes that the four volumes are "on miscellaneous subjects [New York? 1872–88]." They contain articles written by Cummings for the *Sun* and its sibling publications and may have been assembled by Cummings himself. As noted above, the articles are not always carefully cut out, and there is little or no information on where and when they were published. Volume 1 contains the articles written on Cummings's 1873 tour cross-country to California and articles on his trip south in late 1873 into 1874. Volume 2 contains a number of articles about Florida, including the ones reprinted here, from that same latter trip. That particular scrapbook has deteriorated to the point where it should not be used. The third and fourth scrapbooks feature more articles, some from London and Paris, along with published speeches written by Cummings.

Each of these four scrapbooks also contains articles and tidbits of information on a variety of subjects that were clipped from newspapers and magazines, including *Harper's New Monthly Magazine*. Small clippings range across a variety of topics, from spiders to coffee to sport dogs to Civil War battles fought in 1862 on James Island near Charleston, South Carolina.

There are also pamphlets and the like inserted into the bindings of the scrapbooks. My heart skipped several beats while reading the third scrapbook when I came across the February 4–11, 1723, edition of *The New-England Courant,* a paper published by Benjamin Franklin's older brother for whom young Ben served as an apprentice. But I calmed down when I read the last line on the bottom of the last page; the issue was an 1856 reprint of the original.

More authentic is an undated four-page program for a concert by "Hampton Colored Students" that was held in conjunction with an appeal for monetary support for the Hampton Normal and Agricultural Institute. Included in the program is a history of the Institute (today Hampton University) and an essay titled "From Bondage to Freedom" written by a "Hampton boy."

One of my favorite clippings, in scrapbook 4, is a printed version of a speech Congressman Cummings gave on October 14, 1888, when he awarded the pennant to the New York "National Base Ball League" champions coached by James M. Murtie. The team was shortly to play against the American League St. Louis team in the playoffs. Cummings made a number of handwritten changes to the speech presumably before he gave it.

There are a number of empty pages in that same fourth scrapbook. Evidently, about the time Cummings was elected to Congress, he began to use other scrapbooks. Those new scrapbooks are the eleven attributed to Cummings and catalogued as "Scrapbooks of newspaper articles, pamphlets, etc., [1927]" in the New York Public Library. They received catalogue number "AN+." There are clippings of articles written by Cummings as early as 1884 contained in those scrapbooks as well as copies of congressional speeches he gave. There also are clippings of articles from a variety of U.S. newspapers that mention him, most from his days as a U.S. congressman. The second of the eleven volumes contains clippings of the three 1893 articles reprinted here. His death and funerals are chronicled in volume 11.

For the most part, these volumes are neater and more systematically organized than the other four. It is likely that his staff kept them, especially after he was elected to Congress. Cummings probably subscribed to one of the many newspaper clipping services that were in vogue at the time, and that allowed his staff to collect clippings of articles from around the nation.

In the first two of the four early scrapbooks, there are clippings of several articles on Florida that I chose not to include in this volume. One, datelined "September 4, St. Augustine," relates the disaster that befell the steamship *Vera Cruz* on a voyage from New York City to Havana when the ship hit a hurricane on August 28–29, 1880, off the Atlantic coast of Florida. From September 4 through September 15, 1880, the *Sun* carried a series of articles about the disaster and the fates of the seventy-eight crew and passengers, twenty-two or twenty-three of whom survived. I believe that Cummings wrote the articles from his office in New York. For at least one of the articles he relied on firsthand information wired him by a friend he first had met on his earlier trips to East Florida.

In the September 10, 1880, issue of the *Sun*, a slow news date regarding the wrecked Vera Cruz, Cummings published a short article he authored (as Ziska) entitled "A Florida Typhoon. A Graphic Description of a Hurricane near Mosquito Inlet." The article is a brilliant account of a Florida hurricane, though no specific storm is indicated. Cummings must have experienced at least one such storm when he was in Florida.

Slightly longer is another article in the same scrapbook (with no dateline or byline): "Life in a Florida Colony." The story relates the unhappy lives of people at a cooperative colony eighty-five miles south of Jacksonville. I suspect the article also was written by Cummings, though I never found the original in the *Sun*.

Still another short piece in that scrapbook is quintessential Cummings. Datelined "March 2, Jupiter Inlet" (but with no year), "A Coon and a Commodore. Surprising Adventures of a Well-Known New York Gentleman" recounts a humorous encounter aboard a boat involving a raccoon, dogs, and the "well-known," but unnamed, "Commodore."

A Note on Transcribing, Annotating, and Organizing Cummings's Articles

Though I have no qualms about editing someone's prose in draft—I've been doing it for students for years—I truly hate messing around with someone's published writing, especially when that person is not around to tell me what he or she intended. Spelling rules have changed over time, as has the spelling of specific words. For instance, Cummings, or perhaps Cummings's editor, apparently had no reservations about spelling Mosquito Inlet as "Musquito" in one place and "Mosquito" in another, or spelling pompano as "pompaneau" in one article and "pompino" in another. And in the typesetting at the *Sun*, "menatee" is used instead of "manatee." I have made no attempt to correct such quaint spellings. I did correct double words (for example, I eliminated one "the" when "the the cow" appeared); and I also corrected very obvious typos (for example, "the" spelled erroneously as "teh"). When I wasn't certain if something was a typo or a unique spelling, I left it as it was and inserted "*sic.*"

Terms that are little used today and that may appear strange to readers (for example, Cummings's "gad" is a "goad") drew annotations. When I could find more information about people and places or could further identify them, I added annotations. Sometimes, however, I could not find any information. Some of my readers certainly will have more information about the people and places Amos Cummings encountered and wrote about. If you do, please send it to me.

Many of the names found in Cummings's articles still can be found on Florida's landscape if you look at the right map. DeSoto Grove is still there, as is Pepper Hammock. The names of early Floridians whom Cummings met and wrote about also are etched on the landscape, assigned to various natural features. There is still a Dummitt Grove, as well as a Dummitt Creek and a Dummitt Cove. There is even a Futch Point.

For each of seventeen articles, I have written a brief introduction, putting places and, sometimes, people in context or attempting to make another point or two. I did a single introduction for chapters 4–6, all of which are about an "incident" in Lake City in 1873. I also added an epilogue to that triad.

I agonized over the order in which to present the articles, as did several other individuals whom I consulted. In the end, I took the easy way out and put them in the same chronological order in which Amos Cummings presumably wrote them, as indicated by the date he placed on each.

Acknowledgments

James Cusick of the University of Florida's P. K. Yonge Library of Florida History deserves credit for my initial foray into the world of Amos Jay Cummings. Few researchers and librarians are as unselfish with their time and expertise. When my scheme to scan Amos Cummings's articles and convert them to text failed miserably, Andria Kuzeff—at times working with some pretty bad prints made from worn microfilm and photocopies of torn clippings—transcribed them the old way. She has earned my eternal gratitude. Rebecca Gorman, my research assistant and a University of Florida graduate student, helped organize the annotations. Lawrence Harris, Robert Jay Malone, Gary Mormino, and Gordon Patterson each reviewed a draft of the manuscript, providing me with ideas (and corrections). Scott Mitchell drafted an exact copy of Cummings's map of Lake Okeechobee and helped with other of the images reproduced here; N. Adam Watson, Florida State Archives, and John L. Knaub, University of Florida Office of Academic Technology, helped me assemble the images used in the book. University of Florida journalists Ralph Lowenstein and Jon Roosenraad helped me with newspaper terminology.

Along the way, a number of librarians at the University of Florida (especially those in the P. K. Yonge Library of Florida History) offered assistance, as did librarians at the New York Public Library at Forty-second Street and Fifth Avenue (in the Rose Reading Room, the Microforms Room, and Room 121, home to the Irma and Paul Milstein Division of United States History, Local History, and Genealogy). I thank them all.

Many of those librarians showed me how I could use electronic databases to find information. As a result, I learned a great deal and developed a more than passing acquaintance with HeritageQuest, GaleGroup, ProQuest Historical Newspapers, and www.politicalgraveyard.com. As an archaeologist used to delving in the dirt, I will never cease to be amazed that I can fall out of bed, log on my laptop, and while still in my bathrobe learn about people whom Amos Jay Cummings wrote about more than a century ago.

———

Wouldn't it be nice if we all had an opportunity to have spent time with Amos Jay Cummings? I'm betting he could have told some incredibly entertaining stories about Florida in the nineteenth century. But at least we have these twenty articles. I hope you enjoy reading them as much as I did.

Oranges and Dummitts

Think of Florida and it is difficult not to think of oranges. Today one can enter any grocery store in the United States and buy a quart of Florida orange juice or a bag of fresh Florida oranges or other citrus. In March 1873, when Amos Cummings wrote about East Florida's growing orange industry, the citrus boom was just gathering steam, fueled in large part by the famed groves of what would later be marketed as Indian River fruit. Twenty years later, orange groves would be ubiquitous throughout East Florida, only to be slapped farther south by devastating freezes in the latter part of the 1890s. Even so, during a large part of the twentieth century orange groves were seemingly everywhere in most of peninsular Florida.

I recall driving south along U.S. Highway 441 from Gainesville to Orlando in the 1960s and smelling orange blossoms from just below Ocala all the way past Leesburg to Orlando. Groves literally blanketed the rolling hills of Central Florida. But in the 1980s, a series of killing freezes again dealt the groves a blow, pushing the northern edge of orange production farther south. Even so, I can't help but think that Amos Cummings would be astounded at Florida's orange industry today.

What I love about Cummings's articles is that though each may focus on a subject he thought would be of interest to his nineteenth-century New York City readers—in this case, oranges—it's often other information, little tidbits, that draws my attention. In this article, it is the people living in the Indian River area, many of whom appear in other of his articles on Florida. Some must have become friends whom he visited on at least several occasions. Others, like Douglas Dummitt (or Douglass Dummett, as the name is sometimes spelled) are fascinating for what they tell us about Florida at the time. Ethnically and racially, Florida's was a complex population.

Douglas Dummitt was a son of slave-owning Barbadian plantation owners who moved to East Florida. The 1870 federal census for Volusia County lists Mr. Dummitt as seventy years of age at that time and gives the West Indies as his place of birth. A collection of documents collected by Ianthe Bond Hebel in her 1968 study "The Dummetts of North East Florida," a copy of which is housed in the

University of Florida's P. K. Yonge Library of Florida History, provides additional background information on the family.

Dummitt, whose first wife left him for another man, began living with a Barbadian former slave, with whom he had three daughters, Louisa, Kate, and Mary, ages twenty, eighteen, and sixteen at the time of the 1870 census. That same 1870 census lists two women named Dummitt living in St. Augustine, both natives of Barbados. One, Annie, was fifty-two at the time, while Mortiwood(?) was seventy. I am not certain of their relationship to Douglas Dummitt, who died March 27, 1873, shortly after Cummings visited him. In his will—his estate was handled by Henry T. Titus and Mills O. Burnham, two men who also figure in Cummings's articles and in the history of the local region—Douglas Dummitt acknowledged his three illegitimate daughters.

Daughter Kate married Andrew L. Jackson, a black man whom Cummings mentions in this article. In 1879, Louisa married Robert Sanchez of St. Augustine. She would have been twenty-nine at the time. Daughter Mary moved north, "went white," and married a man named Anderson.

A report written just after the Civil War by Col. George F. Thompson, an agent for the Freed Men's Bureau, a federal agency, wrote of "an old man by the name of Dummett, who, in addition to the raising of oranges has tested the experiment of miscegenation, the results of which may be seen running about his place, with complexions of a color midway between charcoal and chalk" (quoted in Eriksen, *Brevard County*, 61). Apparently Thompson was referring to the Dummitt daughters.

The presence of Campbells in Volusia County's Laughing Waters cemetery with the Jacksons and Dummitts suggests that the "smart looking colored man" named Doctor Campbell whom Cummings writes about ("Doctor" is listed as Campbell's given name in the 1870 census) may also have been married to a Dummitt daughter at some point. Perhaps one of the daughters was married more than once.

If Cummings were to visit Florida today and find the orange industry amazing, imagine what he would think of the sleepy settlement of Sand Point and the relatively isolated Merritt Island region, which he wrote about in 1873 and 1874. Today he would find Titusville, Cocoa Beach, Cape Canaveral Air Force Station, and the John F. Kennedy Space Center. Would any of it be recognizable to him? I hope so.

The Cummings article that follows appeared in the *New York Sun* on March 24, 1893, and in the *Semi-Weekly Sun* on March 25.

1

FLORIDA'S ORANGE GROVES

❖

A MAN WHO RAISES 1,500,000 ORANGES IN ONE YEAR.

❖

A Visit to Capt. Dummitt's Great Indian River Grove—An Industrious Negro
Planter—An Idle Floridian—New Yorkers who Raise Oranges in Florida—
What It Costs Them—Harriet Beecher Stowe's Grove.

TITUSVILLE, FLA., MARCH 1.—Over forty years ago an English gentleman named
Dummitt[1] entered Florida. He was a man of refinement and education. He
passed through St. Augustine, went down to Matanzas Inlet, crossed into Bulow's Creek, went down the Halifax river, through Musquito Lagoon, and
entered the Indian river. This placed him among the savages,[2] far away from
civilization. The Indian river is a long salt water bay, similar to Barnegat bay,[3]
running down the eastern coast of Florida for over 200 miles. The eastern
shore, dividing the river from the ocean, is from 100 yards to five miles in
width. Its soil is sand as pure as the sand at Coney Island, but covered with a
saw palmetto and scrub oak so thick that none but experienced hunters can
force their way through it. The saw palmetto grows to the height of a man's
head. The scrub oaks are no higher. The former is called saw palmetto, because the three-square stalk bearing the fanlike leaf is ridged with teeth as
sharp as the teeth of a saw, and quite as difficult to break. It frequently grows
so dense that no man can make his way amongst it. Such is the eastern shore
of the Indian river, but the ridges of palmetto scrub alternate with what are
termed savannas—low, sandy spaces running for miles at the sides of the
ridges, and covered with a coarse saw and wire grass. Occasionally plots of
rich black sand covered with live oak, palmettos, bay and wild orange trees[4]
rise above the scrub, especially on the shores of the river. These are what are
called hammocks. They vary from ten to 300 acres, and undoubtedly contain
the richest land in the United States.

CAPT. DUMMITT'S DISCOVERY.

Capt. Dummitt discovered the richness of these hammocks, and settled in one
upon the shores of Banana creek, which connects the Indian river with Ba-

nana river. The war with the Seminoles came on, and Capt. Dummitt went upon the warpath. While he was looking for the Indians he discovered an extra rich hummock bordering both Mosquito Lagoon and Indian river. At the close of the war he and the rebel Gen. Hardee[5] preempted this hammock, and planted an orange grove. This grove is now the finest grove in the United States, and probably the world. Your correspondent visited it on the 2d of February. The weather was as hot as a July day in New York. The trees were covered with foliage and filled with birds of brilliant plumage. I landed at Andrew Jackson's Grove,[6] a mile and a half north of Dummitt's.

AN INDUSTRIOUS COLORED PLANTER.

Andrew Jackson is a gentleman as black as the Rev. Henry Highland Garnet,[7] with double that gentleman's energy. He bought his little grove for $500 from a "poor white" named Futch,[8] who was either too proud or too lazy to cultivate it. It contained about five hundred orange trees. Andy has cleared about $1,000 from it during the present season. Many of the trees were still loaded with oranges when I was there. The ground was heaped with piles of the golden fruit. A Capt. Bennett from Savannah was loading a little schooner with the oranges, for which he had paid two cents a piece unpicked. The Indian river oranges retail in Savannah at five cents a piece. Their flavor and juiciness are unequalled, and they are in great demand throughout the South. Very few, if any, reach the Northern States.

Andy had cultivated the grove for three years. He lived in a little board shanty in the midst of his orange trees. His place was entirely free from weeds. He was fencing it in from the thick scrub. He was still clearing up the hammock and was planting a small grove of a hundred trees to the south of the main grove.

THE POOR WHITE.

I entered the road leading from Andrew Jackson's to Capt. Dummitt's. It was cut through the dense saw palmetto and scrub oak. After leaving the hammock the road was ankle deep with white sand. Less than a mile north of Dummitt's I passed Futch's residence. Futch and his two six-foot sons were lounging around the house. The dwelling was a curiosity. It was a rough board affair, thatched with palmetto. It was so old that the sides of the house in two places had rotted away, leaving holes large enough for a man to enter. With characteristic Floridian energy the female members of Futch's family had slapped a couple of small water casks against the inside of the holes. Even these casks looked as though they would fall to pieces from age. There were no windows in the house. An old-fashioned rifle stood outside near the door. Futch and his sons wore dirty jean breeches and dark-colored shirts without collars. Each man had a leather belt which held a large knife. They were well built, and had long hair and sallow complexions. Noticing about a hundred pounds of alligator meat drying in the sun, my guide asked Futch what he was going to do with it.

"Eat it," was the response.

Turning to me, the guide remarked: "Why, that 'gator must have been a regular old bull. He was so rank that I can smell him clear here. He must have been fifteen or sixteen feet long."

"Is it customary," I asked, "for people down here to eat alligator meat?"

"I never saw anybody eat any of it before," the guide replied, "and I have seen a great many astonishing things on this river."

A line loaded with faded calico ran out to one side of Futch's house.

"That's racked calico," said a boy who was accompanying the guide.

"What is racked calico?" I asked.

"Calico taken from a rack," answered the boy, scratching his leg with one of his black bare feet. "Didn't you never hear of the rack of the Ladona? She was a ship from New York. She lays right over thar, about twelve mile, I reckon," pointing to the southeast.

THE FUTCH FAMILY.

Meantime the ladies of Futch's family, four in number, crowded the door to look at me. They all wore dresses made of the same faded calico. They wore dresses, but that was all—no bustles, no stockings, no corsets, no hoops, no neckerchiefs, no bows—nothing but calico dresses. They were good looking, however, though they apparently had no life in them. The whole family seemed to be steeped in the essence of laziness. They breathed as though it was work to breathe, and when they talked their words ran into each other in such a manner that it was almost impossible to understand them. This was the family that had sold Andrew Jackson the orange grove. They had bought a fine sailboat with the money, but were too lazy to take care of it. The boat lay upon the beach near the house, warped and cracked by the action of the sun, and good for nought else but firewood. While I was looking at the boat four gaunt dogs, with great mournful eyes, ran from behind the house and followed me to the Indian river beach. A school of mullett broke from the water and flashed in the light of the sun. The dogs went into the water like shot, and each reappeared with a fish in his mouth. They ate the raw fish as though they had had nothing to eat within a month.

DUMMITT'S GROVES.

I reached Dummitt's groves about noon. They contain 3,000 orange trees, and are surrounded by a thick scrub. No fences separated them from the scrub, and it is a common thing for deer, and even bears, to be seen in the groves. Possums and coons are plentiful, and even wild cats and panthers make their appearance at intervals. The groves are about a mile long and a quarter of a mile wide. The trees are about twenty-five feet apart. The ground beneath them is kept entirely free from any vegetation. It is of a rich sandy formation. The whole grove was cool and shady. Hardly a fleck of sunlight fell upon us while we were in it. The land was naturally curved like a parenthesis, thus keeping it entirely free from swampy moisture. The first tree that attracted my attention as I entered the grove was a lemon tree. The lemons were thin-skinned and of an extraordinary size. In some places I found lemons and oranges growing upon the same tree, and in one case lemons, oranges, and limes upon the same branch. Some of the orange trees were in blossom, others were loaded with dark green fruit in various stages of development, but the most of them groaned under the weight of large, ripe yellow oranges. The climate and the soil are such that Capt. Dummitt says that he has raised oranges every month in the year. The Captain's black razor-backed hogs appeared to have a good time of it, for they roamed about the grove fattening upon the ripe oranges as they fell from the trees.

A MILLIONAIRE'S HOUSE.

As I approached the Captain's house, the trees grew thicker and the shade became more dense. The most lovely spot in the grove was occupied by the Captain's hogpen. This pen was made of palmetto logs, and was ten or twelve feet in height. It was shaded by the most thrifty growth of orange trees. The leaves were so fresh and hardy that they looked as though they were made of green wax. I asked why the Captain made his pig pen so high, and was informed that he was much troubled because it was not high enough. His long-snouted razor-backs would go up the logs and over the pen as easy as a coon or a possum could go up a persimmon tree.

The Captain's house was a few yards south of the pig pen. One of his daughters stood in the door. The mansion was built of unplaned boards. They had neither been painted nor whitewashed, and had become black from the action of the weather. The house contained but one room. The Captain's bed, well protected by mosquito bars,[10] stood in the southwest corner. Another bed was in the other corner. Opposite the door was the fireplace, surmounted by a rough mantelpiece. A well-bound copy of Byron and numbers of the *Gentle-*

man's *Magazine*, ranging from 1790 to 1801, stood upon the mantelpiece. Two or three wooden chairs were scattered about the room, and a hen was laying her egg on a sort of a work bench in the corner nearest the door. Everything was as clean as a pin, thanks to the Captain's daughter. The walls were neither lathed nor plastered, and streaks of daylight could be seen beneath the side boards. There were no windows in the house. Light was admitted through a square hole, which was covered with rough wooden shutters.

GRAVES IN AN ORANGE GROVE.

I seated myself upon a wooden bench at the door. Nothing was to be seen in any direction but orange and lemon trees, limes and guavas. Dr. Campbell, a smart looking colored man with gray hair,[11] who has started a grove on Mosquito Lagoon, handed our party a dozen oranges and told us to help ourselves. After resting and taking a drink from a well which had been sunk in the soft rock underlying the soil, we went through the upper part of the grove. The trees were the same. Oranges, lemons, limes, guavas, tamarinds, bananas, and other tropical fruits all grew in great abundance. A half dozen graves were stretched beneath an orange tree. Wooden headstones told the names of the persons buried, but no fence surrounded the mounds.

On the east side of the grove the hummock had not been fully cleared; though another grove, equal in extent to the one we visited, lay upon the other side of the hummock.

DUMMITT'S INCOME.

Dummitt's Grove has produced 600,000 oranges this season. He says he will raise a million next year. Three or four years ago the trees were nearly destroyed by insects, but they have fully recovered and look finer than ever. This grove is celebrated throughout the State. It is looked upon as a kind of Mecca by the orange producers of Florida. It costs Capt. Dummitt not quite $1,000 a year to keep his magnificent grove in order. Six hundred thousand oranges at two cents apiece on the trees would give him a nett [sic] income of $11,000 a year, and one million oranges would give a nett income of $19,000. But a first-class grove, fully developed, ought to average 3,000 oranges to the tree. Many trees yield 5,000, and one tree in the old Eaton Grove, near Enterprise,[12] is said to have produced 10,000 oranges in one year. Dummitt's Grove, in the hands of a shrewd Yankee possessed of Dummitt's experience, would turn in an income of from $50,000 to $70,000 a year, provided the oranges could be sold at their present price.

Frost has been seen at Dummitt's, but it is very rare and never was known to injure the guavas, let alone the oranges. The reason is that the grove is situated upon a stretch of land between two bodies of salt water. The water of both Musquito Lagoon and Indian River is much more salt than the water of the ocean. This is owing to the action of the sun and the shallowness of the water.

Capt. Dummitt is nearly 70 years old. He is a thin man, with gray hair and a gray beard. He cares but little for money and is contented so long as he makes a living. If anybody wants his oranges they must go to his grove and buy them on the trees. The Captain never looks for a purchaser. The purchaser must look for the Captain.

THE CHARMED NEW YORKER.

Just after the close of the war a New York captain named Curtin ran a cargo of Yankee notions down to St. Augustine. He got rid of his cargo, but was unable to secure any return freight. In this dilemma he heard of the Indian river orange groves. He ran his schooner past Smyrna down Hillsborough river[13] to a point now known as Swift's encampment.[14] This was twelve miles from Capt. Dummitt's Grove. As the water was too shallow to go nearer the grove, he ran his small boats to the Captain's wharf and landed. Capt. Curtin was charmed. "Heavens," said he, "this is a perfect paradise. This State is the garden of the world, and the only wonder to me is that every foot of the land is not under cultivation. I could live and die here as happy as a king."

Here he asked Capt. Dummitt if he had any oranges to sell. The Captain said yes.

"How many will you sell me?" inquired Capt. Curtin.

"Well, I'll sell you all that there are on the trees," Capt. Dummitt replied. "I reckon there must be about 200,000 of them."

"I'll take them," said Capt. Curtin, "and furthermore, I'll take all the oranges you can raise, at the same price, for the next five years."

Here Capt. Dummitt introduced Capt. Curtin to Capt. Burnham[15] who owns a celebrated grove within five miles of Cape Canaveral Light.

"How many oranges have you got?" inquired Capt. Curtin of Capt. Burnham.

"About 100,000," answered Capt. Burnham.

Capt. Curtin—Do you want to sell them?

Capt. Burnham—Yes. I'll sell them if you want to buy them at the same price as you pay for Dummitt's, though I believe they are better oranges.

Capt. Curtin—Well, I'll take all the oranges you can raise, Capt. Burnham, for the next five years at the same price.

Here Capt. Curtin turned to Capt. Dummitt, saying, "I suppose there'll be no difficulty in getting men to pick these oranges for me?"

Orange grove landing on the Indian River in the 1870s. Courtesy of Florida State Archives.

"Well," responded Capt. Dummitt, drawing his words and his pipe from his mouth at the same time, "I don't know. I don't speak for anybody else than myself; but as for me, I wouldn't pick a damned orange for you if you would give me two million dollars a minute."

The answer is characteristic of the man. Nobody who knows him believes that he would pick oranges for another man if a third party stood by to put two millions of dollars into his hands at the end of two minutes. "Dummitt works for no man—not even himself," is a common saying on Indian river.

THE NEW YORKER AWAKE.

As nobody lived within twenty miles of Capt. Dummitt at that time, Capt. Curtin had to depend upon his own resources to secure his oranges. He immediately put his crew to work gathering the fruit. When night came, and the full moon poured a flood of silvery light upon the gold-bespangled trees, and a million fire-beetles danced upon the palmetto scrub, Capt. Curtin went to bed, declaring that the scene reminded him of scenes in the Arabian Nights. He was up at daylight. But what a change. Both eyes were nearly closed, and his head was as big as a water cooler. Millions of mosquitoes had paid him their respects during the night. Meeting Capt. Dummitt, he said, "How many oranges have my men picked?"

"About 17,000," said Capt. Dummitt.

Capt. Curtin—Well, that's enough. I don't want any more. Here, men, get the oranges into the boats and let's get out of here.

Capt. Dummitt—It appears to me that you're in a hurry to leave this Paradise of the World.

Capt. Curtin—Yes, I am. I wouldn't pass another night here if you would give me your grove, and I could raise 16,000 bushels of doubloons to the acre.

That was the last of Capt. Curtin. He never appeared in Florida again.

THE MOSQUITOES.

Dummitt himself acknowledges that the mosquitoes are the great drawback to the enjoyment of his grove. Tongue can neither exaggerate their numbers nor their ferocity. In summer they penetrate the thickest nettings, and it is almost impossible to sleep, day or night. At one time Capt. Dummitt got an idea that if he could build a little shanty out in the middle of the lagoon he might be able to sleep. So he built a pier about 600 feet in length and placed a shanty at the end of it. He slept in it one night, and never went there afterward. The mosquitoes attacked him with such fury that they nearly carried away the house from over his head.

ORANGE GROVES OWNED IN NEW YORK.

So much for Dummitt's Grove. Many others have planted groves, but none, so far, have done as well as Capt. Dummitt. There are many beautiful groves on the St. John's river, but none of them are so large or so fine as Dummitt's. The soil is not the same, and the oranges are not so sweet. The soil on the St. John's river is composed mainly of white small shells.[16] These are so thick that in many places a man may walk on shells for rods. It is said to be very good soil for oranges, but the men who say this have never visited the Indian river groves. Probably the finest of the St. John's groves is one owned by H. L. Hart[17] of New York. This grove is situated three miles below Pilatka. It contains twelve hundred bearing trees, but the fruit is inferior to the Indian river oranges. This grove is visited by hundreds of people every winter. Mr. Hart is a brother of A. H. Hart, dealer in twines and yarns at 90 White street, New York. He can live in Florida in his old age, and reap thousands of dollars a year from his orange groves.

Another fine grove is owned by Charles S. Brown, a produce commission merchant at 44 and 46 Pearl street, New York. Mr. Brown's grove is situated a few miles below Pilatka, on the opposite side of the river. He has 1,200 trees,

Orange groves on the St. Johns River, 1887. Courtesy of Florida State Archives.

and they are just beginning to bear fruit. A beautiful little cottage situated in the centre of the grove is Mr. Brown's residence in the winter. His wife takes a great interest in the grove, and probably understands the cultivation of the orange better than any woman in Florida.

THE LITTLE FRENCH GENTLEMAN.

Back of Enterprise, over two hundred miles south of Jacksonville, I found two or three acres of land just outside of a hammock, surrounded by a new board fence. A large glass hot house was squatted in the centre of the lot. While standing at the gate I saw a little man with a gray beard digging among some half burned stumps. He was a little French gentleman from New York city, named Dubois.[18] He is a well known jeweller, and is suffering from the orange fever. He invited me into his hot house. This is the only hot house I have seen in Florida. Miniature orange groves, from one inch to three feet in height, were ranged in boxes within Mr. Dubois's conservatory. There was also a hot house within the hot house. It was hot enough outside to blister a man's face and hot enough inside to roast him.

"Now," said Mr. Dubois, "zis eenside conservatoire I close up at 4 o'clock. In it is orange seed planted. It came up in two weeks."

"What kind of seed is it?" I asked.

"Well," said he, "if I buy one orange in ze city of New York, and agreeable to me is ze flavor, ze seed I plant, an ze orange I eat. I plant ze seed in my conservatoire in New York, in ze city. Now zees trees you see (pointing to the little trees in the boxes), I plant zem in Novembare in ze city, and I brings zem wiz me to zees place. Two weeks more, and I plant zem in ze fields."

Mr. Dubois was forcing the growth of his trees while they were very young, intending to plant them in his grove after there was no possibility of frost. Whether the trees will grow as hardy as trees raised from the seed in the grove, is a question. If they do, Mr. Dubois gains two years through his conservatory. In other words his trees will be loaded with fruit in six years instead of eight. He does his own planting, and every day he is to be seen hoeing among his stumps, and dragging the dirt around his tiny green trees.

MR. DE BARRY'S GROVE.

Mr. De Barry, the Champagne King of New York[19] has started a magnificent grove three miles below Enterprise. He has cleared up the most of the land, planted nearly 2,000 trees, erected the finest residence in the State, and spent altogether about $60,000 upon the place. Most of the trees are very young, and none of them have borne fruit. His house resembles a rich gentleman's country seat on the Hudson. It is beautifully furnished, and lighted by gas manufactured on the place.[20] The view from the grove is very fine. The eye reaches across Lake Monroe into Orange county. Mr. De Barry has a magnificent sulphur spring,[21] surrounded by private bath houses, but a few rods from his mansion. His overseer is a Mr. Rossiter,[22] who is the finest specimen of a native Floridian that I have seen in the State. Although young, he appears to have had much experience in planting oranges and profits by his mistakes in the past. He does not believe in trimming the trees when they are very young, and he believes that they should have as much shade as sunlight. His heart seems bound up in this grove. The ground, however, is not like the soil of the Indian river hammocks, and the oranges will never thrive as they do nearer the sea coast. Indeed I hear that Mr. De Barry is already disgusted, and offers to sell out for $10,000.

THE KENT AND SANFORD GROVES.

At Mellonville, opposite Enterprise, a Mr. Kent has a very fine grove, containing probably 800 trees. They are all thriving, and are dotted with the yellow fruit.

Gen. Sanford, formerly United States Minister to Belgium,[23] has several thousand acres of land near Mellonville. He has imported a colony of Swedes, who agreed to work for him a specified time without wages, after which each one was to receive two acres for a homestead. Some of the destitute Italians who recently landed in New York have found their way to Sanford's grove, and are said to be doing good work. The General has planted several thou-

Frederick de Bary's house, 1885. Courtesy of Florida State Archives.

sand trees. I did not visit his place, but I was told by the neighbors that his trees were not doing well. I was also informed that many of the Swedes have broken their contracts and deserted him, because they had been offered better inducements by parties in other portions of the State.

Capt. Brock,[24] Mrs. Summers,[25] and a gentleman named Stark,[26] have very fine groves at Enterprise, but they are small and the fruit lacks flavor. Capt. Henry Peters of London is clearing up a beautiful grove near the Brock House, but his operations have been terribly impeded by a petrified cypress log, which was swept upon his building spot during high water.

Mr. J. W. Harvey[27] and a Mr. Feaster[28] also have fine young groves at Sand Point,[29] about a mile from the Indian river. Their groves, though small, are in fine condition.

At Orange Bluff, a gentleman from Michigan has started a young grove that promises fairly. He has about a thousand trees, and gathered fruit for the first time this year.

Col. Dancy,[30] formerly of the United States army, who built the sea wall at St. Agustine [sic], has a beautiful grove at Orange Mills, a few miles above Tocoi. The Colonel has lived there for thirty years. His grove is a small one, but as he understands cultivating oranges the fruit is excellent.

HARRIET BEECHER STOWE'S GROVE.

Mrs. Harriet Beecher Stowe's grove at Mandarin, a few miles above Jacksonville, is a small affair. She has probably one or two hundred trees. Her cottage is partly hidden beneath some fine live oaks. It is an unpretending mansion, and I was told that it was for sale.

The principal orange groves of St. Augustine are owned by Dr. Anderson[31] and U.S. Senator Gilbert.[32] They are small groves, but are much talked about by those who have not seen larger ones. While I was in St. Augustine Mr. Nathaniel Johnson of Wellsville, Allegany county, New York, bought a small grove in the city for $10,000. The land will be worth more to him hereafter than the oranges.

Mr. James Peterson, a well-known Toronto lawyer, owns the beautiful De Soto groves on the Banana river, ten miles north of Cape Canaveral. He saved his life by purchasing this grove, and living upon it. He has 800 fruit-bearing trees, and has recently set out several hundred more. His hummock is large and rich, and in a few years his groves will be second only to Dummitt's grove. Unlike the old settlers, Mr. Peterson has erected two beautiful cottages upon his place, and entertains his visitors with old English hospitality. It cost him more to get his lumber to his house than it did to buy the lumber originally. He is literally out of the world, being over twenty miles from a post office, forty miles from a doctor, and fifty miles from a church. There is no public road within twenty miles of his place, and his only way of travel is in cat-rigged sail boats. The climate, however, is delightful all the year round.

One of the finest groves in the State was the Eaton Grove, on Lake Monroe. It was not large, but the trees were remarkably prolific. It is now going to ruin. It was planted by an old man named Eaton, who left it as his monument. Eaton never wore a shirt in his life. When he was out of clothing he made a pair of breeches out of corn sacking. For a shirt he cut three holes near the bottom of a corn sack, and ran his head and arms through the holes. He lived and died without eating a beefsteak, drinking a glass of lager, or handling a shirt collar.

ADVICE TO NORTHERN FARMERS.

If the Florida orange groves prosper, the price of oranges must go down, and those who have put their all into orange groves in anticipation of making fortunes will find themselves mistaken. Still the man who owns a good grove will be able to live without work, despite the condition of the orange market. The Indian river groves are never in danger from frost. This is not the case with those on the St. John's river. Capt. Brock saved his grove from the effects of cold weather by building large fires between the trees on frosty nights. This is not uncommon on the St. John's. Even if the groves escape the frost they are apt to suffer for years from the ravages of an insect which attacks the bark of the trees. Florida is a good place for invalids, but a farmer in good health can do better raising wheat and corn in the North than he can planting orange groves in the Land of Flowers.

An advertisement for Jacob Brock's steamboats taken from Rambler's *Guide to Florida* (1875). Many of the guidebooks about Florida from that era contained advertisements for hotels, transportation, and other services.

Florida Wrecks and Wreckers

Where the space shuttle blasts off today, Floridians once stashed loot salvaged from seagoing ships that were unfortunate enough to wreck on the coast of Cape Canaveral. Though Key West is well known for its nineteenth-century "wreckers"—people who salvaged shipwrecks as a source of livelihood—the wreckers of the Indian River area are less prominent in the writings of historians. In this 1873 article, Cummings gives them their due, using words to paint an engaging portrait of some truly colorful individuals. (Though dated March 3, the article did not appear in the *Sun* until May 5 and in the *Semi-Weekly Sun* on May 6.) The wreckers of Key West had nothing over their Indian River–area counterparts.

Shipwrecks were a windfall for the residents of Florida's Atlantic coast. Their arrival must have been similar to having the rear doors of a speeding armored car spring open on your street with hundreds of twenty dollar bills spilling out, only to be scooped up by your normally law-abiding neighbors. Salvagers must have known the items they collected were not really theirs, but no one stopped to ask questions. In 1873, even the local tax assessor showed up for a look.

"Old Harris" and the Seminole Indian "Young Tigertail," both wreckers about whom Cummings writes, were certainly not the first salvagers along Central Florida's Atlantic coast. Wreckers have a long tradition there, one that no doubt began as soon as the first Spanish or French ship met the shore or a reef. Local residents—the Ais Indians and their neighbors—saw them as windfalls, just as the local populace did in 1873.

One little-known salvaged wreck is that of the *Trinité*. Though few residents of the Indian River area today would recognize the name, the fate of the *Trinité* was pivotal to the history of the United States. In late August 1565, a small fleet under the command of the Frenchman Jean Ribault anchored at the mouth of the St. Johns River on the Atlantic coast of Florida. Ribault had come to reinforce and resupply the beleaguered settlement at Fort Caroline, a French colony established the year before several miles upriver.

As luck would have it, Ribault's fleet arrived only a week ahead of a Spanish fleet sent by the Spanish sovereign, Philip II, to oust the French colony. Sighting the Spaniards, Ribault and his men cut their anchor ropes and sailed out into the

Atlantic to escape. The Spanish commander, Pedro Menéndez de Avilés, pursued, but he soon gave way and sailed south, landing at a place he christened St. Augustine. There he set about establishing his own settlement.

Learning of the Spanish camp, Ribault decided to attack. On September 10, the French fleet carrying about six hundred soldiers and sailors set sail for St. Augustine. As luck would have it, a hurricane struck, scattering the French fleet. Four vessels were blown ashore, three near Ponce de Leon Inlet and the fourth, the *Trinité* with Jean Ribault aboard, near Cape Canaveral.

Meanwhile, Menéndez traveled overland to attack Fort Caroline. He captured it with little difficulty. Florida would be a Spanish colony, not a French one.

We might guess that the local Indians made good use of whatever they could salvage from the *Trinité* (the wreck of the ship has never been located) and its sister ships. That Indians were indeed Florida's first wreckers is certain. Items, especially metals, taken from Spanish ships have been found in numerous Florida Indian sites of the sixteenth and seventeenth centuries. Only recently archaeologists have uncovered French artifacts most likely from the *Trinité* in a site just north of Cape Canaveral.

There is also, of course, the account penned by Jonathan Dickinson, a Philadelphian who was aboard the *Reformation*, a ship wrecked in 1696 just north of Jupiter Inlet. Dickinson's narrative of the wreck and what befell him (see the Andrews' edited volume *Jonathan Dickinson's Journal; or God's Protecting Providence*) includes a marvelous description of the local Indians salvaging the ship's carcass and collecting the cargo and furnishings that washed ashore. Had he known of the Dickinson account, Amos Cummings might well have marveled at the similarities between those late seventeenth-century Indians and the wreckers he wrote about 180 years later.

2

THE FLORIDA WRECKERS

*THE WINGED WAGONS OF THE INDIAN RIVER
AND THE GULF STREAM.*

A Storm—News of the Wreck—Cat-Rigged Buggies—A Wrack! A Wrack!—Descent of the Bull-Drivers—Old Harris's Dodge—The Loss of the Ladona—Midnight Scenes—Col. Titus's Ruse—An Ignorant Methodist Minister's Copper Nails.

PEPPER HAMMOCK, MERRITT'S ISLAND, FLA., MARCH 3.—The eastern coast of Florida is always strewn with wrecks. Though the shore lines the path from the Gulf of Mexico to the north, but two lighthouses rear their heads to the sky between St. Augustine and Cape Florida, a distance of four hundred miles. Even at Smyrna and Indian River inlets there are no lights. The coast is unusually dangerous. Below Canaveral it is fringed with broken coral rocks, which are only visible at low tide. A dozen lines of breakers crash over these rocks. A coral reef runs north and south ten miles east of Canaveral. Beyond that rushes the Gulf Stream. There is a passage inside the reef, but it requires an experienced pilot to navigate it. On such a coast the sailor is frequently driven by the terrible storms that suddenly burst upon him in these southern waters.

WINGED WAGONS.

The beach varies from fifty yards to five miles in width. It separates Musquito lagoon and Indian river from the ocean. The lagoon and river are connected by a short cut, or canal, hewn through a bed of soft coquina rock during the Seminole war. This canal, or "haulover,"[1] as the natives call it, is about a mile from Dummitt's celebrated orange grove and is nearly four hundred yards long. The main land, with its vast growth of pines, stretches beyond the lagoons.

The Indian river is a sort of public highway. Not more than fifteen families live upon its banks. Each family owns a winged wagon, or cat-rigged sailboat.

There are but few land roads, and all the travel and business are done in these centre-board buggies. Some of the inhabitants are compelled to sail two hundred miles to reach a store or a church. Others go as far for a doctor. The dead are buried in the garden in home-made coffins. There are no schoolhouses within a week's journey. In some cases it takes four days to go to a post office and return. Everything depends upon the wind. People look for the course of the wind the first thing in the morning. "When do you think the wind will shift?" is a common question. Instead of "How's the weather?" you hear, "How's the wind?" I found a Swede[2] living upon an island in Lake Worth, who was in the habit of sailing two hundred miles to borrow a book or a newspaper. He usually returned it within a month. As this necessitated two trips, he actually traveled eight hundred miles for the sake of a little reading.

NEWS OF A WRECK.

Such are the people who look upon a wreck as a godsend. It furnishes them with shoes, muslin, calico, buttons, hooks and eyes, and a thousand little necessaries of life which they can get in no other way. A storm arises, and a vessel is driven ashore. The sailors wander across the beach to Indian river. They hail some straggler, and are forwarded north in the little cat-rigged wagons. The news of the wreck spreads like wildfire. As the country is flat, the spars of a stranded vessel can be seen at a great distance. "A wrack, a wrack," is the cry, and within twenty-four hours Indian river is dotted with winged phaetons, all striving for the nearest point to the ship. The wreckers fight their way through the almost impenetrable palmetto scrub to the beach, and pick up whatever they can find. When the dead bodies become bloated and offensive, they are buried in the sand. Each wrecker piles his plunder in a heap. Some hunt in couples. One man watches the pile, while the other adds to it. Occasionally whole parties club together. A part of them operate upon the wreck, one of them guards the store, and the others tote the booty through the sand and scrub to the boats, which may be miles away from the wreck. Thus a pathway is opened, which is used by all. At times the water is so shallow that the fleet of cat-rigged sailboats are compelled to anchor a quarter of a mile from shore, and the wreckers have to wade out to them with their plunder on their backs. As fast as the boats are loaded they put for home, and return for a second cargo as soon as possible. Some men are weeks in securing all their booty. Occasionally parties build a shanty upon the sand from the driftwood of the ship. They occupy it until the last vestige of the cargo has disappeared. Then they strip the vessel of all the brass and copper they can reach, and leave her for good.

WHERE THE BULL DRIVERS COME IN.

Those living on the Indian or Banana river generally get the first chance at the wreck, but after three or four days the news spreads among the bull drivers of the vast cattle ranges on the main land, and they flock to the beach like hungry crows. Knowing that the tidbits of the cargo will be picked up long before their arrival, they bring with them all their ringboned and spavined nags, and barter them for wrecked goods. They are sharp at a trade, and make curious bargains. When the Ladona[3] was wrecked a bull driver swapped a mare to a man named Summelin for 125 pairs of brogans, a peck of buttons, a half bushel of spool thread, and a pint of fish hooks.[4] Summelin thought he had made a big bargain, but the mare died within a week for want of something to eat. The bull drivers generally bring with them a lot of provisions, which they trade with the wreckers, who are nearly famished, for articles that strike their fancy.

Water is usually very scarce in the vicinity of the wreck. An old cove[5] named Harris turns this scarcity into money. On the announcement of a wreck he arms himself with a two-gallon jug filled with water, jumps into his boat, hoists his sail, and puts for the ship. On his way over the beach he meets a dozen men in the hot sun bending under the weight of plunder which they are toting to the boats. Some of them have not tasted water for twenty-four hours. As Harris meets them he kindly offers them a drink. They drop their loads, and gladly seize the jug and turn its bottom to the sky. Meanwhile Harris steals the most valuable part of their booty, receives the thanks of the thirsty victims for his kindness, and travels on. If he is caught stealing, he coolly says, "Well, Tom, you've got more of this than you want, an' I reckon you won't miss this here roll of flannel, so I'll jest confiscate it." In nine cases out of ten, the victim, in gratitude for the water, will say, "All right, Harris, take it along." Should Harris meet a man bearing a load not worth stealing, he will turn away his head as if intensely interested in something beyond him, and not see the thirsty wrecker. Harris and his jug turn up at every wreck. The old man's peculiarities, however, have become well known, and his business is falling off.

THE LOSS OF THE LADONA.

The steamship Ladona drove ashore during the terrible gale of Aug. 17, 1871. She struck the beach in a bight twelve miles north of Canaveral light. Every soul on board, twenty-three in number, perished. The Ladona was freighted with dry goods and Yankee notions. She was bound from New York to New Orleans. She struck the beach at night. Not a star was visible. The wind was blowing a hurricane. For hundreds of feet above the ocean the air was filled with blinding spray. The mist was so thick that the powerful light at Cape Canaveral could not be seen 300 feet from the lens. All the trees were stripped of leaves, and the ragged palmetto scrub was whipped into strings. Orange groves were prostrated and houses were blown down. Bears and wild cats ran about the clearings crazy with terror. The birds of the air vainly sought shelter in the forests. They could not live in the wind, and many of them were killed in the branches of the trees. Pelicans, cranes, and ducks were so frightened that they were picked up by scores. Even the seagulls were unable to breast the tempest. The man-of-war hawk or frigate pelican alone sailed upon the wings of the hurricane. It has been known to cut through the sky for hours without flapping its wings. It has a body about the size of a turtle-dove, and wings measuring from seven to nine feet from tip to tip.

Daybreak revealed the situation of the Ladona. The first wrecker reached her before noon. She lay fifty feet from shore, and had dragged half a mile in the sand. The wind had gone down, but the waves were dashing high over her stern. The beach was covered with dead bodies and merchandise. Before night there were a half dozen eager men at the wreck. They worked like beavers. There was such a variety of articles dashing upon the beach that the first comers were rather dainty in the selection of their booty. They preferred gold watches and silks and laces to bolts of muslin or Kentucky jean. They made blazing fires upon the sandhills from the siftings of the wreck, and continued their work through the darkness. Throughout the night there were fresh arrivals. All pitched in for themselves. Fresh bales of merchandise and fresh boxes of dry goods were heaved upon the shore. The wreckers waded and swam to the ship, overhauled whatever they could reach, and pitched it overboard. Men stood in the breakers, and drew the floating treasure to the beach.

OFF FOR THE WRECK—STARVING.

The news reached New Smyrna on the following day. In a half hour the place was deserted. One man swam his horse over Mosquito lagoon to the beach, and then swooped down upon the wreck like a pelican on a mullet. He went to work with a will, and soon had a stack of plunder awaiting the arrival of his partner, who came in a boat by way of Banana creek.

By the evening of the second day there were nearly seventy-five persons at the wreck. All had left home at a minute's notice, without provisions and without water. They began to suffer through want of food. It was a struggle between ailmentiveness and acquisitiveness. Capt. Frank Sams[6] and Dr. Fox[7] of Smyrna told me that they saw some acquaintances frying onions on the beach. They were invited to the feast. "I asked them where they got the on-ions," said Dr. Fox, "and they said that they had picked them up on the beach. I noticed that there was a peculiar taste about the onions, and I told Sams that I thought it was the salt water. Then Sams asked them where they got the grease in which to fry the onions, and they said that it came from the wrack, that they had found it all nicely packed away in sound wooden boxes. Then Sams asked them to show him the boxes, and I'll be hanged if it wasn't wagon grease."

The majority of the wreckers stood it out. Some of them went three days and nights without food, and worked all the time like steam engines. When they were totally exhausted they would drop upon the sand in the shade of the ragged scrub and sleep for hours.

WHAT THEY FOUND.

One man carried home over five hundred pairs of shoes of all sizes; another had two hundred gross of razors. A negro was freighted with hair oil and cotton batting, while a Methodist minister was lugging off about three hun-dred yards of leather pipe,[8] which he afterward burned for the copper nails it contained. The pipe was worth about $2.50 per yard, but the minister was ignorant of its value. "Dug Scovey," a well-known cracker, had a half bushel of pocket knives and a barrel of fine-toothed combs. One of his comrades loaded his boat with chignons, and sailed for home. He had heard that human hair was worth its weight in gold, and he thought his fortune was made. His wife opened his eyes. The chignons were jute, and had been ruined by the action of the salt water. The wrecker had brought them over eighty miles, and they were "not even good enough for manure," he said. One man had a small pyramid of rat traps, and another was loaded down with lip salve. A man from the Hillsborough river bagged several thousand yards of printed calico, and another, who was unmarried, fell upon five hundred pair of women's stock-ings. A third man found a boat load of garters, and a fourth sailed away with tooth brushes enough to stock a wholesale store. As a general thing, the more useless the article the more eager the finder to retain it. A negro had a thou-sand sticks of whisker pomade. He refused to trade any portion of it for valu-able articles of clothing.

COL. TITUS'S RUSE.[9]

Early on the morning of the fourth day a man rushed down the beach shout-ing that Alden,[10] the Collector at Smyrna, had landed near by, and was de-scending upon the wreckers. This caused great excitement. The wreckers be-gan to tote their piles into the saw palmettos and hide them. Harrison and

Dug Scovey,[11] who lived near the wreck, had accumulated immense piles of goods. They were so frightened that they gave them away to whoever wanted them. It afterward turned out that the announcement of Alden's arrival was untrue. The report was started by Col. Titus, of Kansas and Nicaragua memory. The Colonel had got to the wreck at a late hour, and he adopted this ruse to secure his share of the plunder. It succeeded admirably. The Colonel is said to have bagged property valued at a thousand dollars. He declares that he earned it, and laughs at the Indian river people who fled from their booty on the mere rumor of Alden's arrival. A day afterward, however, Alden really did put in an appearance, but nobody paid any attention to him. He fretted and stormed, but the wreckers smiled at him, and when he threatened them with United States cavalry the idea was so absurd that they fairly hooted him from the beach. Finally, it is said, Alden turned wrecker himself. He began operations upon a firkin[12] of butter which he found rolling in the surf, and ended by sending home a boat load of Yankee notions. The natives accuse him of taking stuff away from them and turning it in to the account of the Collector instead of to the account of the Government. Alden is a carpet-bagger from Michigan.

I have said that each wrecker had his pile of goods upon the beach. Some of these piles were watched, and some were not. If one man saw anything in another man's pile that struck his fancy, he watched his opportunity and stole it. The owner made himself square by stealing from his neighbor, and so the thing went round. An old corduroy pair of breeches changed owners at least a dozen times.

THE DEAD PURSER.

On the fifth and sixth days the bodies of the dead became so offensive that the wreckers turned in and buried them. They were scattered along the sand for miles. By the light of a lantern Dr. Fox discovered the body of the purser. "I saw from his clothes," said he, "that he was something more than a common sailor; so I dug a grave high up on the sand and buried him. I found in his pocket a letter from his wife. So I took his watch, his knife, his keys, and a comb from his pockets, and sent them to her. She lived somewhere in Connecticut. I have forgotten where. But I got a letter from her afterwards thanking me for sending the things, and asking me if I could not pick out the spot where her husband was buried, as she wanted to send for the body. Well, I went down to the wreck again, but I couldn't find the grave. You see I had buried him by the light of a lantern, and the waves had washed out all the landmarks. I might have looked for fifty years, and never have found him. So I wrote his wife, and that was the last of it."

A WRECK. A BLESSING.

Two weeks rolled away before the wreckers stripped the Ladona, and left her. I visited the steamer last month. There was nothing left but her prow, and the water was pouring through her hawse holes. Her cabin seemed to be hidden away under the sand and waves. Immense timbers lay upon the shore and a small shed stood at the foot of a nest of sand hills half buried. The sand was so white that the little hut seemed to be sunk in the snow. While prowling about the sandhills I found a keg of white lead, which had been forgotten by some careless wrecker. Ancient shoes and old hats peeped from under the sandy ridges, reminding one of an old battle-field.

In talking with a native to-day he said that a good wreck was very much needed in this part of the country just now. The people were out of clothes, whiskey, and other necessaries of life, for which they depended on stranded vessels. He said that he hoped the next wrecked ship would carry a better stock of goods then the Ladona. "They were the poorest stock of goods that I ever saw, sir," he said, bringing his fist down upon the railing of a stoop. "The Yankees don't make nigh as good goods as the Inglish. We're really a sufferin' for an Inglish wrack jis now."

FLORIDA PHILOSOPHY.

Most of the inhabitants here wear wrecked goods. Even their hats and shoes come from stranded ships. Their wives and daughters have dresses and aprons made of wrecked calico, their tables are covered with wrecked linen, and their beds are spread with wrecked muslin. A good wreck will supply an economical family for years. The ship ashore is regarded as legitimate prey. The people are honest and passably industrious, but they will go for a wreck like gulls after a dead fish. They reason like philosophers. A vessel freighted with merchandise runs ashore. The goods drift upon the beach in a sandy wilderness, miles away from any residence. Before the authorities can take any action, everything will be ruined. The people declare that they might better secure what comes ashore than leave it upon the beach to rot. So they take what they can find. They look upon it as a gift of Providence. The difficulties of transportation are such that it will not pay the underwriters to secure a ship's cargo unless it is unusually valuable and imperishable. In nine cases out of ten a Government official will help himself to the booty, and consequently the wreckers seem to think it a duty they owe themselves and the country to get ahead of him. They are kind-hearted and generous to ship-wrecked passengers and sailors, and unhesitatingly peril their lives to save them. They will go miles out of their way to forward them on their way north, feeding and clothing them without asking a cent in return. They throw out no false lights; but calmly await whatever the wind and the Lord may send them. They bury the dead in the sand, and regard the cargo as common property. Ministers, deacons, Freemasons, Christians, and sinners all run a race for the plunder. They do not call it stealing, but simply saving an immense amount of property from being wasted. A man would be safe among them with a million of dollars in his pocket—much safer than he would be in New York city, but they would plunder a wrecked bumboat[13] without a qualm of conscience.

MARINE INSURANCE.

The Government officials, however, do not entirely forget their duty. When a worthless vessel is wrecked they are wide awake and on the make. Some time ago a schooner ran ashore below Cape Canaveral. She was freighted with fifty dollars worth of shingles. The Government officers promptly sailed in and rescued the property. They saved the shingles, but it cost the people of the United States $4,000 to do it. Nevertheless the officers acted with praiseworthy alacrity.

There is but little doubt that the Florida coast is turned to good account by dishonest shippers and captains. When a vessel gets old and unseaworthy, it is an easy matter to load her with a nominal cargo, and insure both vessel and cargo double their value. She can be scuttled or run ashore on the Florida coast miles away from any habitation, and the insurance companies are none the wiser. It is said that one-third of the wrecks are caused by rascally captains. Col. Titus gave me the name of a steamer which went ashore near Lake Worth in January last, which he places in this category. I have forgotten her name, but she came from New York, and Titus declared that he could prove what he said.

INDIAN WRECKERS.

The Indians secure all valuable cargoes that go ashore below Jupiter light. They are unusually bright. Last year a British ship freighted with silks and linens went ashore above Biscayne Bay. Young Tiger Tail[14] and his band got the plunder. They traded the linens with the Crackers and wire-grass population on the Eastern shore and the interior, but they carried the silks to Tampa and Cedar Keys, on the Gulf coast, which points are visited from steamers from New Orleans and Havana. There they sold their booty at a fair price, and returned to the borders of the Everglades with plenty of money.

The inlets at Smyrna and Fort Capron, being without lights, are dotted with wrecks. Some of them now lay half a mile from the water, acres of sand having filled in behind them. At Cape Canaveral all the dogs and cats came from wrecked ships. While I was at the light-house a crew came ashore from a Prussian vessel loaded with iron, which had been abandoned at sea. They brought with them a wrecked cat, which was duly added to the living curiosities at Cape Canaveral. The vessel came from Cardenus, and the Prussian Consul in New York was said to be a part owner.

I have written of the folks on Indian river as wreckers, though they are not so, strictly speaking. The real wrecker lives near Key West, and operates among the Bahama Islands and Florida Keys. He has a government license, and looks to the owners of the vessel and cargo for his salvage.

Alligators and Steamboats

It's not easy being a Florida alligator. Sure, various government regulations offer some protection, but every year there is an alligator hunting season when people with headlamps, shotgun-sticks, sharp skinning knives, and a variety of boats take to Florida's waterways, intent on turning the reptiles into restaurant hors d'oeuvres and pocketbooks. Even the large-as-life mascot alligators—Albert and Alberta—who prowl the sidelines of University of Florida football games occasionally get pummeled by Tigers, Ibises, or whichever other mascot is representing the opposing team that particular fall day.

Today's alligators, however, have little to complain about (okay, I didn't mention insecticides and other water pollutants). They may not have it as good as did their distant ancestors—the alligators who provided meals for many generations of Florida Indians—but they certainly are better off than their relatives of Cummings's day. The reason is simple: alligators lived in rivers; steamboats traveling the rivers brought people; people brought guns and pointed them at the alligators. Unable to surrender, hundreds, thousands, tens of thousands of alligators gave up their hides, teeth, and lives. The carnage must have been horrific.

I have never understood what would make people want to steam up and down the St. Johns River and its chain of lakes, shooting at every alligator in sight. "Sportsmen" from the North came to Florida in 1873 just for the opportunity to shoot at animals, especially alligators. At least the Florida crackers who shot alligators to collect their hides did so to support their families. But either way, being a Victorian-age alligator in East Florida was hazardous duty.

This article appeared in the *Sun* on April 8, 1873, and in the *Semi-Weekly Sun* on April 11. We will return to the topic of alligators later in this book.

THE FLORIDA ALLIGATORS

AN INTERVIEW WITH AN OLD ALLIGATOR HUNTER.

How Frank Kerns Killed a Monster—Judge Emmons's Good Shot—Taming a Young Alligator—The Largest Alligator in Florida—An Enormous Alligator Hole.

ENTERPRISE, FLA., MARCH 4.—About a week ago I got aboard the little steamer Volusia, in Sand Lake. This lake is forty miles above here, and is one of the thousand little lakes or ponds that hitch themselves on to the St. John's river, through innumerable creeks or bayous. The Volusia runs from Sand Lake to Jacksonville. It takes a week to make the trip, running night and day. Formerly the lagoons and lakes, as well as the river itself, above Enterprise, were filled with alligators. They are thicker there now than on any other part of the St. John's. About four o'clock in the afternoon, while running through what is known as Snake Creek, the steamboat was overhauled by a row boat. It contained two men. They tied their boat to the stern of the steamboat and came aboard. The row boat was provided with a small sail which was used when the wind permitted. One of the men tossed a dozen alligator hides upon the deck, consigned to a firm in Jacksonville. He wore a pair of dirty pantaloons, a butternut colored woollen shirt, an old fashioned coat, and a black slouched hat. His face was much bronzed, but he had a pair of blue eyes brimful of good nature. He was about six feet high, and he carried a double barrelled rifle proportioned to his height. I asked Capt. Lund[1] of the Volusia who he was.

"Cone, the 'gator hunter," was the reply.[2]

THE OLD ALLIGATOR HUNTER.

I told the Captain that I had some whiskey down in my stateroom, and if he would ask Mr. Cone to join us, I would bring it up to the Captain's room. The whiskey was brought and introduced to Mr. Cone. The alligator hunter took about four fingers, smacked his lips and "reckoned that it was right smart whiskey." I learned that Cone was in the habit of boarding the Volusia and going upon the Captain's deck where he watched the passengers, who invariably spend the day in shooting at alligators which sun themselves in the maiden cane and other marshy places surrounding the lakes and lagoons. If a passenger killed an alligator, Capt. Cone marked the spot. Occasionally three or four alligators would be killed inside of three miles. Capt. Cone would then cast off his little boat, retrace his course and skin the animals. He gets seventy-five cents a piece for the hides delivered in Jacksonville. At this time he was filling an order from a London firm, through a Jacksonville merchant for 3,000 hides.

After taking a second drink he came out on the left of the pilot house, went through his old rifle to see that "she was ketched jest right," as he called it, and then entered into conversation with your correspondent. We were running through a creek, as crooked as a ram's horn, about twenty-five feet wide. Almost as far as the eye could reach, on either side, there was nothing but marshes covered with grass and rushes. Some of the rushes were over thirty feet high. Millions upon millions of ducks, white and blue cranes, white curlews, marsh hens, herons, water-turkeys and blue-peters were feeding in these marshes.

A TALK WITH THE OLD PROFESSIONAL.

"Now," said Capt. Cone, pointing to a spot where the coarse grass was beaten down into the mud at the side of the creek, "thar's a 'gator belongs to lie right thar, but he aint thar. I done made up my mind I'd ketch him this here trip."

"How large a one was he?" I asked.

"Well, right smart of twelve feet long, I reckon. He's liable to be taken for twelve feet for sure," Cone replied.

Correspondent—How long have you been hunting 'gators?

Capt. Cone—Since the 1st of November.

Correspondent—How many have you killed?

Capt. Cone—Well, these here skins make three hundred and forty odd 'gators, I reckon. You see huntin' 'gators haint what it used to was. There haint the number o' 'gators in the first place, and the big 'gators is more skeery. I reckon they know more than they knowed oncet. Now, I can remember three or four year ago when 'gator hides was wuth from two to four dollars apiece in Jacksonville. Now they hain't wuth a quarter as much.

Correspondent—How large was the biggest 'gator killed by you this season?

Capt. Cone—Not over ten feet. The 'gators is little this season, I reckon, or the big uns is too plaguey skeery. But it's all the same on the hides. One hide's wuth as much as t'other.

Alligator hunters, 1870s or 1880s. Courtesy of Florida State Archives.

Correspondent—How long does it take you to skin an alligator?

Capt. Cone—Well, I done peeled the bark from a 'gator in twelve minits. I'll everedge fifteen minits, I reckon.

THE DIE-HARDS OPEN FIRE.

At this point two passengers saw an alligator on the right of the boat, and opened fire. The old 'gator hunter straightened himself up, grabbed his rifle and rushed on the other side of the pilot house just in time to see the slimy black animal slide into the water.

"Now," said Capt. Cone, on his return, "the heap o' lead that is thrown away on 'gators by these here die-hards who come down to Florida every winter, is more than any man 'ud reckon on. Yesterday a die-hard signified to me that he thought he saw a 'gator with his head out of the water, and he went to pitchin' bullets into that here 'gator. He had one of these rifles that shoots eighteen times one after another without stoppin', and I'll be dog-goned ef he didn't put eighteen bullets into the 'gator, and the 'gator stood it. T'want nothing but a sunken log sticking out of the water after all."

Alligators and Steamboats

"How far up the river have you been looking for 'gators?" I asked.

"Clean up into Lake Washington," he replied.

CAPTURING A YOUNG ALLIGATOR.

Lake Washington is about 320 miles south of Jacksonville. It is opposite Cape Malabar, on the coast and about eight miles from the Indian river. The old 'gator hunter said that he had killed a few alligators by moonlight. Occasionally he found them in the night time away from the river, prowling for food in the pine woods. Indeed the pine woods in Southern Florida are filled with alligators. I found them thicker there than in any other spot. The woods are frequently cut up into swamps and savannas, and water stands in these places all the year round. The alligator makes large holes in these swamps and savannas. He covers the holes with dried cane, grass, and what ever he can find of a similar nature. This covering is raised like a cone, and is two or three feet in height. There is a hole in one side of the covering, through which the 'gator crawls out and in. In these holes the female alligator raises her family. In Turnbull swamp, near New Smyrna, I saw an alligator hole which seemed to be filled with young ones about eight inches long. I was hunting deer with Mr. A. J. Alexander of Woodburn farm, Kentucky, and Capt. Frank Sams,[3] a prominent Indian river hunter. Sams was about to put his hand in the hole to pick up one of the little 'gators when Mr. Alexander shouted, "Hold on, Sams, there's an old she one in that hole, and she's watching you. I can see her head." Mr. Alexander then drew a bead on the old she one, and fired. There was a thrashing of the water as if a tiger had fallen into a cistern. Mr. Alexander had hit the old 'gator but had not killed her. In her agony she had thrown one of the little fellows near the mouth of her nest. Sams snatched it up and put it in his pocket. The little fellow was very lively, and his eyes were as bright as diamonds. We took him to Lowd's Hotel at Smyrna[4] and tied him on the mantelpiece. He became quite tame and would amuse himself by catching flies. He was very pugnacious and would croak and snap at little sticks on the slightest provocation. About Smyrna there are thousands of alligators. The people there say that it does not pay to kill them for their hides, as Smyrna is too far from a market.

THE ALLIGATOR FEVER.

It was sundown when Capt. Cone prepared to leave the boat. He said he knew where there were two 'gators in a marsh near an old Indian mound, and he was going after them. As he entered his boat I asked him what was the length of the largest 'gator he had ever killed.

"Fifteen feet and two inches, I reckon," he shouted back. He then hoisted his sail and we soon lost sight of him in the tall maiden cane.

Crowds of Northern men flock to Enterprise during the winter, and many of them employ their time in hunting alligators. The guests sit upon the verandah of the hotel hour after hour polishing alligator teeth with sandpaper and buckskin. Every day somebody brings in an alligator which has been shot in the vicinity. After killing the alligator, the men hitch him to the stern of their boat with a chain and tow him to the beach in front of the hotel. They then hire a negro to cut off his head and skin him. After the head is cut off it is buried for two weeks. This is necessary to secure the monster's teeth. It is amusing to see eminent bankers, ministers, judges, and others watching a spot in the ground, near the hotel, where they have buried an alligator's head. Occasionally some gentleman gets hold of the wrong head, and then there is a row. Everybody seems crazy on the subject of alligator teeth. They sell from two dollars apiece up to five dollars. I saw one tooth five inches long sold to Capt. Tom Reeves[5] for twenty dollars. Some negroes make a fair living by carving flowers and curious figures on the teeth.

FRANK KERNS'S ALLIGATOR.

The largest alligator brought in since I have been at this place was eleven feet in length. Two or three days ago a man named Kinney went up the river at the head of Lake Monroe. It was a beautiful, sunshiny day. About noon he saw a 'gator stretched in the sun, on the edge of a marsh. He was lucky enough to send a ball crashing through its brain. He rode up to the body and measured it. It was thirteen feet and one inch in length. After measuring it, Mr. Kinney rode to a little clump of Palmetto trees some distance from the spot, for the purpose of cooking a cup of coffee and taking dinner. Meantime a little steamer called the Pannasoffkee approached the spot where the 'gator lay. She was freighted with Frank Kerns,[6] a well-known New York minstrel, and a party of his friends and acquaintances, who were going up the St. John's river on a hunting expedition. They sighted the 'gator, and great excitement followed. "My God, what a big one he is!" shouted Kerns. Every man rushed for his rifle, and all began firing at the 'gator. Three or four balls went into him, and about one hundred balls glanced from his back as though he had been an iron boiler. The steamer stopped, and the party went for the 'gator. Of course, every man claimed to have killed him. With great difficulty they got him on board and drew lots for him. It took four gallons of carbolic acid to cure him. The party stuffed him and sent him as a present to the proprietor of a museum in Indianapolis. When Kinney had finished his dinner and returned he was astonished to find that his 'gator had disappeared. It was not until to-day that

Drawing of alligator shooting from a steamer on the Ocklawaha River, ca. 1874. Courtesy of Florida State Archives.

he learned what had become of him. He now threatens to sue the party for the value of the 'gator. He claims that the teeth alone are worth $100, and the injury to his feelings he estimates at double that sum. It will be a queer suit if it is ever brought to trial.

CAPT. TOM REEVES'S ALLIGATOR.

This morning Capt. Tom Reeves went 'gator hunting. He returned about an hour ago in a very bad humor. It seems that about two weeks since, Capt. Tom discovered a very large alligator on a marsh fronting Mr. de Bary's[7] boat house. The old captain kept his discovery to himself. Every morning he has risen with the sun, taken his rifle, and sneaked off alone in his little boat in hopes of securing the big alligator. He tells his story as follows:

"Well, this morning I got down opposite de Bary's boat house just after the sun popped up, laid down in the marsh flat on my belly and waited for the 'gator. I laid there about two hours. Then I heard a noise, and the big cuss began crawling up out of the water. He was only about twenty feet from me. When he got his shoulders up on the mash he began to smell around and growl to himself as if somebody had told him that old Tom Reeves was there looking for him. By and by he got out of the water, turned around two or three times like a dog just before he lays down, and stretched himself out in the hot sun with his tail toward me. He opened his mouth as though yawning two or three times, and then shut his eyes and went to sleep as though he had a nice soft thing all to himself. I let him lay there about five minutes and then I raised up and made up my mind to give it to him. I aimed at his left eye and pulled the trigger. Just my luck. The cap didn't go off. But the old cuss didn't stir and I pasted another cap on the tube and went for him again. The cursed cap was good for nothing. I tried four caps on him and all were bad. Then the 'gator shook himself up, looked at me as much as to say, 'Well, you're the worst I ever saw,' and wriggled himself into the water."

Tom then filled the perfumed Florida air with a choice selection of oaths, and said that he had discovered that the lock of his gun was broken and that she didn't have power to snap a cap. As it is known that Tom has at least six 'gator heads buried in the garden fronting the hotel, nobody has much sympathy for him.

JUDGE EMMONS'S ALLIGATOR.

While I was at Lake Jessup I went 'gator hunting with Judge Emmons[8] of Jacksonville. We found a twelve-foot alligator sleeping on top of the water about twenty feet from the shore, near a small grove of palmettos. The Judge put a rifle ball directly through the alligator's skull. The ball made a terrible hole. The 'gator was as dead as a mackerel. We slipped a rope around his shoulders and towed him ashore. While the monster lay in the water and we were debating as to how we would get his head off, I jabbed a stick through the bullet hole down into his brain. A colored man who was passing by said: "Boss, you done be careful with dat ah gaitah. He no done gone dead yet. You better stick you knife in he fore paw to see ef he dead. He done do you some mischief. Boss, suah, if he no dead." I took my knife out of its sheath and ran it into the alligator's fore paw. The monster lashed the water with his tail, almost knocking the Judge into the lake, and nearly putting out my eyes. When I recovered my eyesight, I saw the Judge, but not the alligator. The animal had sailed off, stick and all, and left no track behind him.

THE LARGEST ALLIGATOR IN FLORIDA.

The largest alligator in the State of Florida can be found near Pepper Hammock on Banana creek, and the head of Merritt's Island. This animal is known all along the Indian river. Capt. Dummitt[9] told me that this alligator is certainly over twenty feet long. Dummitt says that he has seen him in his present quarters, off and on, over twenty-five years. The Captain thinks him [*sic*] is at least 100 years old, and probably more. Over a dozen hunters have spent days in trying to kill him, but though some have got shots at him none have been successful. His hide turns the bullets as a duck sheds rain. His hole is under a high bank and covered with a growth of moss and rushes. I camped four days at Pepper Hammock, and this alligator's roar kept me awake at night. It sounded like distant thunder. One morning Dr. Fox,[10] my companion, ran a wounded deer into the shallow bay fronting the alligator's hole. A large yellow dog called Buster was on the trail of the deer, and ran into the water after him. When the alligator heard the baying of the dog he gave chase. The Doctor reached the bank and took in the situation. As he had wounded the deer, and was chasing it, and expecting it every moment to drop, his rifle was not loaded. He began to shout loudly at the dog, and then ran into the water after the alligator. The monster heard the Doctor coming, dropped the chase, and fled to his hole. The Doctor was much excited. He thought the world of his dog, and said that he had almost rather have lost a leg than have lost Buster.

WHAT AN ALLIGATOR LOVES.

If there is one thing in the world that an alligator loves more than any other one thing it is a dog. The bark of a dog will frequently bring a dozen alligators to the surface of the water. Hunters occasionally tote their dogs on horseback while crossing shallow water or very swampy places. When an alligator hears the baying of a hound he always puts for a ford, if there is one in the vicinity, hoping to catch the dog when he comes that way. Young colored children are also said to be rare dainties for alligators.

The greatest alligator hole in Florida is on the ocean side of the Indian River, about twenty miles above Fort Capron. It is situated in a fresh water swamp, back of a dense growth of mangroves. This hole is about sixty feet wide at the mouth, but it extends a great distance under the ground, and appears to be a paradise for alligators. It is about a mile from a little Palmetto hut, where a Georgian, named Estes, has lived alone for over fifteen years. Estes protects these alligators and will allow no one to shoot them.

OLD MR. WATSON'S NARROW ESCAPE.

Some years ago the father of Capt. Watson[11] of this place visited a marsh at the lower end of Lake Monroe to hunt stray hogs. The captain is a little man, with sharp, gray eyes, and quick of foot. While roaming about over the marsh and hallooing for the hogs he was suddenly seized by an enormous alligator and hurled in the mud. The alligator caught him by the leg and stripped the flesh to the bone. The old man was terribly wrenched, and for a long time his recovery was doubtful. It was six months before he left his bed. This is the only well authenticated case that came to my notice in which an alligator attacked a man. Some people think that while Watson was walking over the marsh he took the alligator for a log and jumped on him. It is certain that the animal seized Watson by the leg and nearly broke the old man's back by a blow from his tail.

HOW ALLIGATORS GET THEIR LIVING.

Alligators frequently fill their stomachs with ducks. They find the spots in the marshes where the ducks huddle together at night and make a descent upon them. Frequently, while flocks of great fat raft ducks are swimming in the deepest part of a river or lake, an alligator will glide under the ducks and select those that suit him best. They are drawn under the water so quietly that the flock is not startled for some time, and the alligator manages to secure a square meal before he is suspected.

On summer nights the alligator crawls to a chosen spot in the marshes. The air is filled with millions of mosquitoes. The monster opens his enormous mouth and keeps his jaws apart until the inside of his mouth is black with the insects. Then he brings his jaws together with a snap, runs his tongue around the inside of his mouth and swallows his winged visitors. He will keep this up until his appetite is satiated.

Reconstruction Politics Florida Style

On one hand were Grant Republicans; on the other were Democrats, a few of whom also were members of the Ku Klux Klan. It was the *body politique* in Columbia County, Florida, during the administration of President Ulysses S. Grant (1869–77), and it was not pretty. The Civil War had ended, the African-American slave population of the South had been emancipated, and great social changes were underway. Corruption—stolen elections, embezzled public funds, attempts to intimidate citizens, even murder—was common not only in Lake City, Florida, but elsewhere as well. Graft stretched from the office of the governor down to the level of local officials.

Cummings, with his eye for news and his willingness to turn over rocks to report on the slugs underneath, offers an extraordinary account of life in North Florida in these three articles titled "The Trouble in Florida." The three appeared, respectively, in the *New York Sun* on March 17, 1873, and in the *Semi-Weekly Sun* on March 18; in the *Sun* on March 18; and in the *Sun* on March 19, and in the *Semi-Weekly Sun* on March 21 (the second article was not published in the semi-weekly newspaper, probably because of the publication schedule). Cummings, himself a Democrat, takes aim at the "negroes and carpet-baggers" from Georgia who were "flocking to the land of flowers" (that is, Florida), where they would vote "against honest government" (that is, vote as Republicans). But he certainly did not think much of the tactics of the Democratic opposition, either.

In North Florida in 1873, political clout could be turned into real dollars. Reconstruction was a time of economic realignment, a time of illegal schemes to make money when residents did not hesitate to organize to force their way into the political catbird's seat. Brute force and the threat of force were means of discouraging Columbia County newcomers who threatened to wrest power from local people who had had things their way for many years.

In the first article, Cummings notes there were only "a few Northern men and but a thin sprinkling of colored men" in Columbia County in 1873. Several days later, however, he made his comment about carpetbaggers and African-American people "flocking" to Florida. The 1870 federal census of Columbia County certainly invalidates Cummings's contention that there were few "colored men" in the county. Perhaps African-American families were living outside of town, and he simply did not see them.

A review of a sample of two hundred heads of households from the 1870 Columbia County census (I looked at the first one hundred and the last one hundred entries in the alphabetically organized census list) revealed that 39.5 percent of the families were African-Americans, 5 percent were listed as mixed race, and 55.5 percent were white. About half of the people designated as mixed race in the census were natives of Florida. The remainder came mainly from Georgia, South Carolina, and North Carolina. The percentage of African-American heads of households who were natives of Florida was even lower: 32 percent. Twenty-nine percent of the African-Americans in Columbia County were born in Georgia and 34 percent in South Carolina (smaller numbers were from North Carolina, Pennsylvania, Virginia, Alabama, and Africa). These numbers do support Cummings's contention that African-Americans were moving into Florida in large numbers.

It is interesting to compare these census data to the 1870 census data from Fort Capron, Florida (then in Brevard County), at the time the southernmost settlement on the Atlantic coast of Florida. In Fort Capron, only 2.5 percent of heads of household were African-American; the remainder were listed as white. Certainly the demographic structures of North Florida and of the southern Florida frontier, at least at that time, were very different.

When we look at white heads of households, there also are differences. Only 11 percent of the white heads of household in Fort Capron were native-born Floridians. The vast majority were from Georgia (54 percent), South Carolina (19 percent), and Alabama (12 percent), with the remainder from Virginia, Louisiana, and Tennessee. In Columbia County, on the other hand, 23 percent of white heads of household—twice the percentage of Fort Capron in Brevard County—were Florida-born. Forty percent were from Georgia, 16 percent from South Carolina, 5 percent from North Carolina, and the remainder from other southern states, northern states, and elsewhere (for example, Virginia, Tennessee, South Dakota, and England). Fort Capron was a frontier that drew new settlers; Columbia County had a long-term resident population, but it, too, was drawing newcomers in droves, threatening the status quo and leading to conflicts like those Amos Cummings wrote about.

A comparison of census figures from 1860 and 1870 bears out the status of Florida as a frontier to which both whites and African-Americans from other southern states were moving. An article ("Lessons of the Census") in the *New York Times* on March 10, 1873—the same time Amos Cummings was in Lake City—lists Florida as the second-fastest-growing southern state (behind Texas). During the decade before 1870, Florida's population had grown 33.7 percent. For the same period, Virginia had a population loss of 23.25 percent (although West Virginia had taken part of that number), while South Carolina had increased by less than 1 percent, Louisiana by 2.67 percent, Alabama by 3.4 percent, North Carolina by 7.9 percent, and Georgia by 12 percent. From 1860 to 1870, Florida's African-American population had grown by 46.3 percent. People were indeed flocking to Florida in droves.

A fourth article about the troubles in Florida was published in the *New York Sun* on March 20, 1873. Entitled "The Lake City Outrage," datelined "Jacksonville, March 15," and appearing in the "Correspondence of The Sun," the article is much shorter than each of the three Cummings wrote. I have not included this article here because I don't think it was written by Cummings. It is not his writing style, and I believe he already had gone south from Jacksonville to the Indian River area. I believe that the article was written by a local reporter and sent to the *Sun* at Cummings's behest. Cummings might well have given him information, though. I have summarized this article in an epilogue at the end of Cummings's articles.

Did the outrage in Lake City draw national attention? Barely. It may have been all too common in the South. In the March 14, 1873, *New York Times*, there was a very short article entitled "Trouble in Florida," which read:

Washington, March 13. The Attorney-General [of the United States] has received the following telegram: Jacksonville, Fla., March 11.

Hon. Geo. H. Williams: A serious affray at Lake City, Fla. Postmaster and county officer driven from town. Am making all investigation in connection with District-Attorney, United States Marshall, and Commissioner. Ringleader arrested. Will report in a few days. (Signed.) H. O. Whiteley, Chief United States Secret Service.

The outrage, however, was reported in a Jacksonville paper. The *Tri-Weekly Florida Union* published articles on March 11, 13, 15, 18, and 20, with follow-up stories on March 25, 27, and 29, and April 1, 3, and 8. (I obtained the microfilmed articles from the Library of Congress on interlibrary loan.)

Interestingly, on March 25, the *Union* reprinted Amos Cummings's second article titled "The Trouble in Florida" (reprinted here as chapter 5). In that issue of the paper, the *Union* editor notes: "We re-publish to-day, on our front page, a long letter from the New York *Sun*, relative to the troubles in Lake City. The writer (whom, we presume, was the managing editor of that paper, lately in this city), interviewed various persons connected with the troubles, and gives a long report of these interviews, stating, very minutely, the several explanations of the cause of the trouble."

The "Lake City Outrage," as the incident has come to be known, did not escape the analytical eyes of two generations of Florida historians. Jerrell Shofner, in his 1974 book *Nor Is It Over Yet: Florida in the Era of Reconstruction, 1863–1877*, reported on the outrage, relying in part on the articles in the Jacksonville newspapers (229). More recently, Canter Brown, in *Ossian Bingley Hart: Florida's Loyalist Reconstruction Governor,* mentions the Lake City incident (283–84). His book also highlights the actions of Governor Hart that so enraged some of the residents of Lake City and puts the outrage in the context of Florida politics of the Reconstruction era. It is, however, in large part thanks to the *New York Sun's* correspondent, Amos Jay Cummings, that history now has the livid details of this incident. All of these writers, historians, and journalists have given us a better understanding of Florida in 1873.

4

THE TROUBLE IN FLORIDA

REPUBLICAN KU-KLUX IN COLUMBIA COUNTY.

A County Under the Control of Desperadoes—Houses Assaulted at Midnight—Defenseless Women and Children Shot At—The Adjutant-General Calls Out the Troops.

JACKSONVILLE, FLA., MARCH 10.—W. S. Bush,[1] Sheriff of Columbia county, has been arrested under the Enforcement act, and is now in custody in this city. Singular as it may seem, he is a Grant man,[2] and so is the man who made the complaint against him. The Sheriff is also Tax Collector, and a Representative in the Legislature from Columbia county. As it is reported that a Klu-Klux [*sic*] outrage lies at the bottom of the arrest, your correspondent has ascertained the following facts:

ORIGIN OF THE TROUBLE.

When Harrison Reed[3] was elected Governor of Florida, Dr. Day[4] of Lake City was given the certificate of election as Lieutenant Governor. His opponent was Bloxham,[5] who ran as the Greeley candidate for Governor last fall. Day was counted in by the grossest frauds, and Bloxham contested his election in the State courts. Meanwhile, Gov. Reed was impeached, and Day assumed the Governorship *ex officio*. Day resided in Lake City, the shire town of Columbia county. After assuming the Governorship he remained at the State capital for some time, and then came down to this city, where he owned valuable real estate. Gov. Reed was in Jacksonville at that time. Hearing of Day's arrival, Reed sped back to Tallahassee, and through the connivance of Gibbs,[6] then Secretary of State, obtained possession of the State seal. He next issued a proclamation declaring Day a usurper, on the ground that the State Senate had failed to promptly act upon the articles of impeachment. Reed then filled Tallahassee with State troops, and bade defiance to Day. Soon afterward the State courts decided that Bloxham was really elected Lieutenant Governor, and Day was forced to retire to private life.

Drawn portrait of Governor Harrison Reed.
Courtesy of Florida State Archives.

In this State the Governor has the power to appoint all Sheriffs, County Judges, and Tax Collectors and Assessors. In fact, no county officer is elected, unless a constable may be termed a county officer. The Governor's appointments, however, have no force unless they are confirmed by the State Senate. Gov. Reed, in accordance with this provision, appointed A. P. Holt, a native of North Carolina, County Judge; Keight S. Waldron, a Floridian, Clerk of the Circuit Court;[7] and W. S. Bush of South Carolina, Sheriff and Tax Collector of Columbia county. These appointments were confirmed by the State Senate. The county officers, it is fair to suppose, looked out for their own interests during the trouble between Reed and Day.

THE COUNTY OFFICERS DEFIANT.

There are few Northern men and but a thin sprinkling of colored men in Columbia county. Bush, though a Grant Republican, was once an active member of the Ku-Klux Klan. He seems to have been easy in his collection of taxes, and to have aimed at a personal popularity that would send him into a still higher position. Dr. Day, who is a Southerner and a Grant Republican, is also said to have once been a prominent member of the Ku-Klux Klan. He endeavored to retrieve his fallen fortunes. Of course he could do nothing under Reed's administration. Last fall he supported Hart[8] for Governor. Hart was an old personal friend, and it is fair to presume that Day was certain that he could influence him to a great extent in the distribution of the county offices. Bush, though Sheriff and Tax Collector, aspired to the Assembly. Columbia county was entitled to two members. Day effected a combination with Bush, and placed a colored man with Bush upon the Grant Assembly ticket. While this strengthened Bush with the colored men, it also strengthened the colored candidate with Bush's friends. To secure his election Bush promised the county offices to his supporters. It is probable that Day deluded him with the idea that this would be allowed, for both men supported Hart for Governor, and Bush and the colored man were elected to the Assembly. The session passed over without a sign of a change in the county officers. After the members had dispersed, however, Gov. Hart reappointed Judge Holt, County Judge, and Keight S. Waldron, Clerk of the Circuit Court, but at the same time appointed Tax Collector W. W. Moore, a Floridian, and Postmaster of Lake City,[9] and George G. Keene,[10] a Georgian, Sheriff. All these men were friends of Dr. Day. Bush and his friends were in arms at once. Bush refused to give up the office of Sheriff, declaring the Governor's action to be unconstitutional, and alleging that he could not lawfully be removed unless charges were preferred against him and his successor was confirmed by the State Senate. His friends claim that he intended to resign the office of Tax Collector while clinging to the Shrievalty, and Moore's friends assert with equal positiveness that Moore means to resign the office of Postmaster as soon as he is installed Tax Collector. The fact is that nearly every Grant member of the Legislature holds two or three offices, either State or Federal.

THE MIDNIGHT ASSASSINS.

On the night of March 5, the difficulty began to come to a head. A gang of a dozen men visited the houses of Holt, Moore, Keene, and Waldron, between midnight and 4 A.M., and riddled them with bullets. They endeavored to entice Moore to the door, but failing in that poured volley after volley into the house. Moore's invalid wife and his children were in the house at the time. The assassins then visited Judge Holt's house, and sent a shower of balls into his bedroom window. The Judge's wife had but recently been confined with twins, and was quite feeble. She will not soon recover from the shock. The

Executive Department.

In the Name and under the Authority of the State of Florida.

Whereas, *George G. Keen* hath been duly appointed by the Governor according to the Constitution and Laws of said State to be *Justice of the Peace in & for the County of Columbia to hold his office during good behavior subject to removal by the Governor at his own* Now, Therefore, Reposing especial trust and confidence in the loyalty, patriotism, fidelity, and prudence of the said *George G. Keen*

I, HARRISON REED,

Governor of the State of Florida, under and by virtue of the authority vested in me by the Constitution and Laws of said State, Do Hereby Commission the said *George G. Keen* to be such *Justice of the Peace* according to the Laws and Constitution of said State for the time aforesaid, and in the name of the People of the State of Florida to have, hold, and exercise said office and all the powers appertaining thereto, and to perform the duties thereof, and to enjoy all the privileges and benefits of the same in accordance with the requirements of Law.

In Testimony Whereof, I do hereunto set my hand, and cause to be affixed the Great Seal of the State, at TALLAHASSEE, the Capital, this *23* day of *May* A. D. 18*70* and of the Independence of the United States the *94* year.

L. S

By the Governor. Attest:

Jonathan C. Gibbs
Secretary of State.

Harrison Reed
Governor of Florida.

Commission appointing George Keen as justice of the peace in Columbia County. Dated 1870, the document is signed by Secretary of State Jonathan C. Gibbs and Governor Harrison Reed. Courtesy of Florida State Archives.

desperadoes then visited Keene's house. The windows of his sitting-room and bedroom were shattered with bullets, and the sides of his residence were honeycombed with flattened balls. His life was only saved through the pluckiness of his wife. The villains then attacked Waldron's house. His wife is a feeble woman, with a child, a mere babe. They riddled the door with bullets, some of which splintered it on the inside. Several balls were picked up from the floor. The gang then again visited Moore, and again poured a terrible volley into the house. Again Holt suffered, and again the Keene family were placed in deadly danger. Poor Mrs. Waldron shouted to them, declaring that her husband was away from home, and asked them if they meant to murder her and her baby. They answered by discharging a pint of bullets into the roof. The deadly round was made a third time before the murderers separated. Lake City contains probably 1,200 inhabitants. They were cowed. Not one of the whites and only one or two of its colored citizens went out to see the cause of the shooting. The assassins were not disguised in the least, but approached the windows, and blazed away as unconcerned as though they were firing at so many dogs. Yet the citizens appear to have made no effort to find out who they were, though the firing continued for three hours. It having been reported that Dr. Day was away from home, he was not molested.

On the following day, Moore, Holt, Keene, and Waldron fled to Jacksonville, leaving their families entirely unprotected. Colored citizens, however, enrolled themselves and guarded their houses at night. Though terrible threats filled the air, and it was even intimated that the houses of the absent men would be burned over the heads of their families if they did not leave the town, their lives have thus far been spared.

MEETING OF CITIZENS.

Mayor Baya[11] immediately called a meeting of the citizens, to be held in the City Hall at 11 A.M. on Friday, "to express their condemnation of the outrage perpetrated in the town on Wednesday night last, viz.: the shooting into the dwellings of several citizens at midnight in different parts of the town by persons unknown." The Mayor presided, and S. S. Niblack, brother of the ex-Congressman,[12] was requested to act as secretary. The meeting appointed Dr. Hunter,[13] Dr. McLaurin,[14] J. E. Young,[15] J. H. Mickler,[16] Dr. T. C. Griffin,[17] A. Davidson,[18] G. J. Jones,[19] and Mayor Baya a committee "to be attended by some officer qualified to administer oaths, to call before them any and all persons in the community to testify concerning the outrage, taking the testimony in writing of such persons as should be called or voluntarily testify, and report their acts at an early day to the Mayor." The meeting then contented itself with passing the following resolution:

Resolved, *That we, as citizens of Lake City, publicly condemn the outrage, and feel it our duty to do all in our power to bring the perpetrators to justice.*

The meeting then adjourned, subject to the call of the Mayor. Of course this meeting was partly composed of the very men who were concerned in the attempted assassination, and some of the members of the committee are known to be friends of the suspected parties. One of the committee is a colored man, whose mental calibre is exceedingly small.

ARREST OF THE SHERIFF.

On Saturday Moore appeared before the United States authorities, declaring that he was obstructed in his duties as Postmaster. He backed up his complaint by an affidavit implicating Bush as one of the assassins. Deputy Marshal McMurray[20] was despatched to Lake City with orders to arrest Bush and bring him to Jacksonville. McMurray and Bush seemed to be old friends. The Marshal allowed the Sheriff the freedom of the city, and the Sheriff used it with a vengeance. He met Dr. Day on the street and deluged him with profanity. The Marshal took a ride out in the country with Bush in the afternoon, ate supper with him in the evening, and slept in his house all night. He brought him to this city last night. Bush appears to have the freedom of the city here, as he is under no restraint except his word to appear for examination to-morrow afternoon. Dr. Day is also here, it being unsafe for him to remain in Lake City.

Last night your correspondent visited Lake City. The town is pleasantly situated in the midst of the turpentine farms on the line of the Jacksonville and Tallahassee Railroad, sixty miles from this city. Two lovely fresh water lakes add to the beauty of the place. It would undoubtedly be a fashionable summer resort were it not for the terrible name that it bears. Murder seems common, and the murderers appear to overawe the respectable citizens, who find it unsafe to attempt to bring them to justice. The desperadoes having, in a certain measure, had the control of the county authorities, naturally affiliate with Bush, though, as all the parties are Southerners, it is possible that the new appointees failing in legal measures, may be able to bring a desperate gang to their defence. I left this city at 7 o'clock on Sunday evening, and arrived in Lake City at 11. Moore, the Postmaster and new Tax Collector, went up in the same train. A covey of assassins from Ellisville, a town thirteen miles from Lake City, known as a paradise for murderers, were in hiding at the depot for the purpose of shooting down any anti-Bush man who might return. Moore scented danger in the air, and jumped from the train before it reached the depot. He was met by some colored men, who informed him that his house was watched by Bush's friends, and that his life would not be worth a rush if it was known that he was in town. Under these circumstances he concealed himself, and left on the 4 A.M. train from Tallahassee. Your correspondent stopped at a hotel opposite the depot. He recognized there as a fellow guest, Mr. Newcomb, of Col. Whitely's United States detective force. Newcomb had probably been sent up from Jacksonville by the Colonel to obtain evidence in substantiation of Moore's affidavit. It was evident that the Federal Government had a finger in the pie, but it was thought that that finger would be withdrawn when Grant men alone were found to be in the conspiracy. The Administration organs attempted to dress up the outrage in Ku-Klux garments, but the facts were so put that the scheme received no countenance from either the State or Federal officers.

ARRIVAL OF COLORED TROOPS.

At 4 A.M. I heard cheers at the railroad depot. The cheers announced action on the part of Gov. Hart. Gen. Varnum, the State Adjutant-General,[21] had arrived from Tallahassee, with five days' rations, eighty stand of arms, and six colored soldiers! It is understood that the Governor instructed the General to call out the military in Lake City and arm them, so as to prevent a further breach of the peace, and save the homes of the fugitives. As there were no organized military companies in Lake City, this was nonsense. The effect of the Governor's action is to place within the reach of the Bush faction eighty rifles of the most approved pattern.

After breakfast I began to question the proprietor concerning the outrages. He was sorry to say he knew nothing about them. He had heard guns, and had heard that the houses had been fired into, but he didn't know anything about it, and it was none of his business. He was anxious, however, that I should ride out into the country with him, and look at a turpentine farm. The land could be bought cheap, and if I was going to settle in Florida he was sure that I could not find a place in the State that would suit me better. The society was excellent, and Northern men were welcomed everywhere. He then pointed out Mr. Keene's house, which was a few yards distant. Mr. Keene was not at home, but Mrs. Keene, who was a comely lady weighing about 140 pounds, received me cordially. The house was dotted with bullets both inside and outside. A hallway ran through the centre from north to south. The firing first began at the dining-room on the east of the hallway. There were two windows to this room on the east. There were four bullet holes through the right window, and two through the window to the left. Those holes, however, were not indicative of the number of balls that had been thrown into the room. A table sat in range of the left window. A massive gilt-edged Bible lay upon the table. A large-sized ball had passed through it endwise, cutting many of the leaves and destroying its covers. A ball had also passed through a violin box near by, and another ball remained in the back of a wooden chair which stood in range of one of the windows. I counted six bullets scattered over the wall, and seven more in the siding of the house, making sixteen shots in all fired into the sitting-room alone. I then examined the west side of the house, and particularly Mr. Keene's bedroom. There were three shots through the bedroom window. One of these balls destroyed the lamp which sat upon the bureau, and another entered Mr. Keene's pillow. A third ball entered a chair near the bed. Several balls were imbedded in the window casing. Bullet marks also appeared on the walls. I should think that a dozen shots in all were fired at or into the bed-room. In the dining-room adjoining the bedroom were the marks of four balls. Another ball smashed a plate which sat upon the table, while still an-other was buried in the back of a chair. Altogether nearly fifty bullets were fired into Keene's house. The escape of the family was miraculous. The assas-sins seemed to be aware of the situation of the inmates. Two strangers from Georgia occupied a bedroom adjoining that of Mr. Keene. Not a shot was fired into their room. Mrs. Keene told her story to the correspondent as follows:

MRS. KEENE'S STORY.

We knew there was going to be trouble. Threats had been repeatedly made against us. Mr. Keene came home about sundown. He said that he had met Bush but a few minutes before he came, and that Bush had warned him to get out of town. Mr. Keene asked him what for. Bush said that Tressay Bathay[22] was coming into town that night, and had threatened to shoot both Bush and Keene and burn their houses.

Correspondent—Who is Tressay Bathay?

Mrs. Keene—A man who has a bad reputation, but who never fails to let a person know when he is an enemy, and who is a true friend. When he is an enemy you know it, and when he is a friend, you know it. Bush said that he was going to get out of town, and he advised Keene to clear out also. It hap-pened that Mr. Keene knew Tressay Bathay to be his friend. He knew that Bush lied, and I know that Bush did not leave town that night, because a certain clerk can testify that Bush came to his store between 12 and 1 o'clock, and bought two boxes of cartridges of different sizes. My husband went over to Waldron's, and told Waldron his fears. On his return I drew down the curtains of the sitting room. It was then dark, and more dangerous to attempt to leave the house than to remain in it. We went to bed early, and between 12 and 1 o'clock I awoke with the noise of the firing. It was some time after the train for Tallahassee had gone. I could hear them talking and jumping over some lum-ber in the yard. They shot fast—just as fast as they could. I couldn't have counted the number of the shots if I had tried. We next heard them shooting into Mr. Waldron's house, next door. I reckoned then that they had gone for good, and went back to bed. I was asleep when they returned the second time, and began firing into the bedroom window. I saw from the direction of the shots that they intended to shoot Mr. Keene while in bed if possible. I lighted the lamp and got him out of bed, and made him lie down upon the floor where I thought it would be safer. They saw the reflection of the pillow on the curtain as I was getting it for Mr. Keene, and gauging its position, put a bullet into it. Then a bullet smashed the lamp, which was standing on the bureau. I then went to this left window and looked out. There was a man standing at the picket fence only twenty feet away. I went to Mr. Keene and asked him to let me have his repeater, so that I could kill the scoundrel. I am sure that I could have put a bullet through him. Mr. Keene said that if I did it would only be a random shot, and he thought he had better keep the repeater for his protection in case they came into the house. They then went away, and we heard them firing into Mr. Waldron's house. About 4 o'clock they came back to the house again, and fired into the dining room. That was the last of them. I counted eleven shots while they were firing into the bedroom. They were near the window, as I could plainly see the flashes of their pistols when they fired. The flashes were like flashes of lightning.

I then asked Mrs. Keene what she thought was the cause of the difficulty. She replied that Bush wanted to run the county, and that he was angry because her husband had been appointed Sheriff. It was an attempt to drive men that Bush didn't like away from Lake City. She did not recognize the man at the fence.

MRS. WALDRON'S STORY.

I next visited the Waldron house, the next one north of Keene's. It was a rough board dwelling, without plastering, but it looked very neat and comfortable. Most of the shots seemed to be directed to the front door and the roof. There were five bullet holes low down in the door. The inside of the door was splintered. Some of the bullets went clean through the door which was apparently an inch and a half thick, and were picked up on the floor. Mrs. Waldron is a thin, feeble woman, with a hectic flush, and eyes indicating consumption. She had a baby in her arms. She was apparently much frightened. She said that Mr. Keene first informed her husband of the anticipated trouble. Her husband didn't believe that any attack was intended. "He went out doors to wash his hands," said Mrs. Waldron. "I was afraid he would be shot, and I went out ahead of him. I saw two men going slowly by the fence. They stopped at the corner, and seemed to be watching for Mr. Waldron. We then went into the house, and I shut all the doors. Soon afterward I heard a noise at the door.

It was a man from Dr. Day's, who said that the Doctor's son had gone away, and that the Doctor was at home alone. He was afraid of his life, and wanted Mr. Waldron to come and pass the night with him. My husband said that he didn't think I would be in any danger if he was out of the house, and if there was danger he would go where there was the greatest danger. He then went to Dr. Day's with the colored man who called for him. After Mr. Waldron had gone I began to get frightened. I sent to Mr. Keene's, where a friend of Mr. Waldron's, named Michael King[23] was stopping, and he consented to come and sleep in our house. I made him a bed behind the front door. The shooting began at our place and Mr. Keene's at about the same time. I was alarmed for the safety of my baby. The firing was at the front door, and the bullets were pattering almost at King's head. They fired probably twenty shots and then went away. Mr. King said that if I would light a lamp and give him some matches to make a fire, he would go to the woods and stay for the remainder of the night. He said he thought they would not be so apt to trouble me if I was alone. After King had been gone about an hour they began to shoot into the house again. I held my baby tight to my breast, and shouted to them. I told them that I was alone, and asked them if they wanted to murder me and my baby. They didn't say anything, but began to shoot into the roof. I told them that if they shot me or my husband, there would be trouble. We had many friends, and they would have revenge. They were not here, but they were where they could be got at and where they would be got at. They didn't make any answer, but after a time went away. They fired into the roof once after that, but they shot more the second time that they came to the house than the first time."

JUDGE HOLT'S HOUSE.

Judge Holt lives fronting the public square over a drug store. It is a large building, painted white. He has been accustomed to sleep in a bedroom fronting the square. A day or two before the attempted assassination he had changed his bedroom. The windows of his former sleeping apartment were perforated with bullets. Since Holt has left town Judge Long,[24] his father-in-law, has taken charge of his wife and her twin babes. Mrs. Holt is represented to be a spunky little woman with snapping black eyes, and as brave as a lioness. It is thought that she may hurt some of the assassins before the trouble is over.

MRS. MOORE'S STORY.

Moore lives in a house owned by State Senator Johnson,[25] who also holds a second office. Johnson is a friend of Bush, and is believed by some to be implicated in the attacks upon the new appointees. The house is a neat Gothic cottage, painted a dull yellow color. Moore slept in a bedroom on the northeast corner. His bed was in the southeast corner of the room. The desperadoes had his bed gauged to a nicety, for they fired eight shots catacornered through the northeast window. The most of these shots struck in the wall just above Moore's head. Two of them landed not two inches from his pillow. Mrs. Moore is a delicate woman. She is very much alarmed. Moore and Holt had received not the slightest warning of an attack, and of course their households were taken by surprize.

Just after the Tallahassee train left there was a knock at the kitchen door, and calls for Mr. Moore. The Postmaster refused to go to the door. Failing to draw him into the trap the murderers crept around to the northeast corner of the cottage, and began to hammer the clapboards with a heavy stick. Then a deadly volley was poured through the window. Mrs. Moore and another lady barely escaped with their lives. The bullets struck articles that they were carrying in their hands, and Mrs. Moore picked up five flattened balls on the floor. Chairs and other furniture bear marks of pistol balls. The second visit to the house was devoted to the parlor windows. A fine piano bore marks of bullets, a music book was ruined, the parlor chairs were slugged, and the walls looked as if they had been through the old Indian war. The third visit of the ruffians was paid to the kitchen, where the same scene of destruction was witnessed. I counted in addition to the marks of bullets in the bedroom, parlor, and kitchen, eighteen marks on the outside of the house, showing that nearly fifty shots were fired into Moore's house alone.

A VISIT TO THE MAYOR.

I next called upon Mayor Baya, the leading dry goods merchant of the place. I found him in his store, and was cordially received. He was a young man of quick perceptions. He apparently wanted to do what was right, but didn't know how to do it. He said that no complaint had been made to the Mayor's Court, and he was as yet unofficially informed of the outrage. He had called a meeting of the citizens, however, and a committee of investigation had been ordered. The cause of the trouble was a fight between two Republican factions, and the only interest the Conservatives had in the matter was the injury that the town would receive on account of the bad reputation it would acquire through such outrages. Lake City was a pretty place, and if it were not for its bad reputation it might be filled with winter boarders. The climate was superior to that of Jacksonville. It was surrounded by beautiful lakes filled with fish, and it possessed every advantage over places on the seashore and gulf. As for society, that was unsurpassed. In no place in Florida was a lady treated with more politeness, and the Mayor was sure that if I had a desire to settle in the South, I could find no place more agreeable than Lake City. All this was pleasing information. The Mayor added that the committee would meet at 10 A.M., and they would undoubtedly be pleased to have a New York reporter present, as it was important that the world should know that the people of Lake City emphatically condemn the dastardly outrage.

MEETING OF THE COMMITTEE.

The committee met at the appointed hour in the town hall. The town hall is an old unpainted and unplastered building on the public square. The floor was covered with three inches of coarse sawdust, and a man could easily count the shingles in the roof while listening to the debates of the Common Council. A platform about a foot and a half high extended across the eastern end of the room. It contained two small wooden tables and an old-fashioned unpainted desk, evidently of Lake City manufacture. A long table covered with a glazed cloth stood below the platform, and beyond this were thirteen planed wooden benches, with legs like capital Ms. A half dozen chairs were ranged along the wall on the left. On the left of the platform was nailed a piece of pine wine box. It was nailed there because it contained a knot which was used as a hat-rack. The board bore the word PORT upon it. The Mayor called the committee to order by nominating Dr. Hunter for chairman. Dr. Hunter is the proprietor of the leading drug store in Lake City. He is a long man with a long face and a long head. He was apparently a man of good judgment, and his laughing blue eyes indexed a man who had few enemies and plenty of friends. The Doctor was elected chairman of the committee and Mayor Baya was chosen secretary.

The first question that came before the committee was whether the investigation should be public or private. It was quickly apparent that some of the gentlemen who were participants in the outrage were present, and that they had friends among the committee. It was voted that the sessions should be public, and that the witnesses should be sworn. If they preferred to testify in private, the committee would hear their evidence in private and suppress their testimony, only using it as the basis of their report to the next meeting of the citizens. It was at first suggested that every citizen should be made to prove an *alibi*. As a precedent for this course the Mayor said that when Mr. Abby was assassinated on the board sidewalk some time ago the citizens met, and every citizen was required to prove an *alibi*. Dr. Hunter was understood to say that one of the citizens who proved an *alibi*, afterward owned up on his deathbed that he was the man who committed the murder. The *alibi* proposition being disposed of, citizens were requested to step forward and give any evidence they might have regarding the criminals. A colored man known as Dan,[26] with two immense plain brass rings on the little finger of his left hand, was then dragged forward. He said when he was going home that night he saw three white men going up the street locked arms. They were forty or fifty yards from him, and one of them wore a shawl. The moon was shining dull, and he could not recognize them. They were going in the direction that he afterward heard the firing. Fifteen minutes afterward the shooting commenced. That was all he knew about it.

A member of the committee here said that he had heard that a colored blacksmith, James Hightower, had said that he saw the firing, and that he recognized some of the parties who were blazing into Moore's house. A man was sent after Hightower, but the blacksmith refused to come, saying that the United States Marshal had advised him to pay no attention to the committee. The Mayor then threatened to arrest Hightower and bring him before his court, but as it was suggested that no complaint had been preferred in his court and he had no official cognizance of the outrage, he changed his mind. It was stated that Hightower had got to Moore's house before the parties left, and that Mrs. Keene had said she had recognized some of the assassins. Messengers were then sent for Mrs. Keene and Mrs. Waldron.

INTERESTING STATEMENTS.

Isaac Stevens,[27] Dr. Day's colored gardener, was then brought before the committee. Isaac had his hair plaited in two tails and fastened behind his ear. During his examination he amused himself by chewing a pitch-pine toothpick. He was sworn and testified as follows:

"Dun know who do de shootin'. Hear de shootin' when I was in Morris's house. I said 'I don' like to hear dat shootin'. It don' soun' right.' I reckon it was about fifteen minits from de time I heard de fust shootin' fore I hear de secont shootin' down to Mr. Holt's house. Dan Watson an' me an' Hightower an' John Anerson[28]—we hears de shootin' down to Misser Keene's. An' Hightower he say, 'Less go an hear what dat' shootin' means.' By de time we got up to my house de shootin' hab quit. Hightower, he libed quite close to Mr. Morris, an' Hightower come to me house, an' den we went to Mr. Morris, an' den we hear de shootin' at nuddah place. De tracks next mornin' roun' Mr. Moore's house looked as ef dah had been a right smart of 'em a shootin'. When we got whah de shootin' was de pahties hab leabe, an' we saw no sight ob 'em."

Mrs. Keene and Mrs. Waldron were next examined. When Mrs. Keene was asked if she would give her testimony in public she said, "You lords of creation ought to know whether it would be better for me to testify in public or private." Her testimony did not differ from the statement made to your correspondent. When asked whether the parties who made the assault were white or colored, she said that she knew no man among them but believed them to be white men. Describing the shooting, she said, "They shot into my lamp, they shot into my Bible, and they shot into my old man's fiddle-box." She would prefer not to tell who she thought was the man who stood at the fence. Had much rather shoot the man than swear to him. During lulls in the shooting heard the voices of those who were firing into the house, and heard them laughing as though they were having a good time.

Mrs. Waldron's testimony did not differ from that already given. She said that Bush had said that Bathay was down on her husband because he took a colored man's evidence in a murder case up in Georgia.

One of the committee then rose and said that this was all a farce. He had business to attend to, and he didn't want another meeting of the committee until somebody would come up and identify some of the parties concerned. He thought it all ought to be left to the Grand Jury. The committee then adjourned subject to the call of the Chair. It is well to remark here that the Grand Jury is drawn by the Clerk, the Sheriff and the County Judge.

After the committee separated I visited James Hightower, the colored blacksmith. He was at his forge, surrounded by half a dozen colored friends. Threats had already been made against his life because he was thought to know too much. It was certain that he was not to be shot down without a struggle.

Sun Correspondent—Mr. Hightower, I am a newspaper correspondent from New York. Have you any objection to telling me what you know about this shooting?

Mr. Hightower—No, sir.

Correspondent—Did you see the shooting?

Mr. Hightower—I saw twelve men firing into Mr. Moore's bedroom window.

Correspondent—Did you count them?

Mr. Hightower—Yes, sir.

Correspondent—Did you recognize any of them.

Mr. Hightower—Yes. I recognized two of them.

Correspondent—Will you give me their names?

Mr. Hightower—I will, provided you will not use them while you are in Lake City.

Correspondent—I promise that I will not.

Mr. Hightower—I recognized Sheriff Bush and Mr. Frank Selph.[29]

Correspondent—Are you not mistaken?

Mr. Hightower—No, sir. I saw them repeatedly firing into the windows. I know them very well, and recognized them by the flash of the pistols.

Mr. Hightower's house is only about 100 yards from Mr. Moore's residence. When the firing began he ran down by the side of a fence, which concealed him from the parties firing, and afterward, hid behind a clump of bushes to the right of Moore's house.

Correspondent—Did the parties see you?

Mr. Hightower—No, sir.

Correspondent—What would have been the result if they had seen you?

Mr. Hightower—They would have shot me dead.

Correspondent—What do the colored men here think of the outrage?

Mr. Hightower—The colored men are dead down on such doings.

Correspondent—Why do you not appear before the citizens' committee?

Mr. Hightower—Because the committee want to know what I know so as to give them a chance to screen the men who did the shooting.

When I left Lake City the town was much excited. Every man, both black and white, was armed, and the air was blue with threats. Napier, the colored cadet who left West Point on account of his failure in mathematics, was drilling about forty colored men who had been enrolled in the State service. Armed men were discovered crawling on their bellies near Mrs. Keene's house, but they had fled when Mrs. Keene attempted to approach them. Colored guards were stationed in the houses of refugees, and everything portended bloodshed. Ellisville was reported to be pouring out her ruffians, and a collision was feared before morning. Nevertheless, the last words I heard as I stepped on the cars were words eulogizing the nice society of the town, and assuring me that it was just the place for a gentleman of refinement and leisure to spend his winter months.

5

THE TROUBLE IN FLORIDA

A TALK WITH EX-GOV. DAY AND SENATOR JOHNSON.

Both Parties Accusing Each Other of Murder and Thief—How the Friends of Grant Govern Florida—The People Overawed By Assassins—Startling Developments.

JACKSONVILLE, MARCH 13. The excitement in Lake City continues. Gen. Varnum, the Adjutant-General of the State, still remains, but he has taken the precaution to send forty stand of arms back to Tallahassee to save them from falling into the hands of the desperadoes. I had a talk with the General last evening. He says the situation is very grave. The Bush Republicans are determined to force the Day faction to leave the county offices in their hands, or quit the place. Colored guards are still stationed in the houses of the five refugees, as threats to assassinate their families have been made. Gen. Varnum informs me that several well-known desperadoes from Ellaville are lurking about the outskirts of the town with rifles and shot-guns, bent upon assassinating different parties. The General has enrolled about forty colored men, and armed them. The barracks is an old unpainted house back of Mayor Baya's store. Twenty people might be crowded into it on a pinch, but no more than that number.

WHAT GEN. VARNUM SAYS.

The General blames Gov. Hart for not giving him written and implicit instructions. He thinks troops ought to be thrown into the county from Jacksonville, and martial law promptly declared. He says the law of the State makes the Adjutant-General responsible for the arms, and he dare not trust them in the hands of irresponsible parties. "Why," said he, "if I did this, after the trouble was over I would have a nice job looking for the State rifles. The darkies would be traveling over the country shooting crows and squirrels. It would be impossible to recover the guns. The Legislature would point to the law and hold me responsible, and not the Governor."

The General further said that it looked to him as though the Governor had purposely placed him in a position where he (Varnum) would be held responsible for anything that might occur. In plain words, he accused the Governor of lack of backbone, and declared that Hart intended to make him his scapegoat. So disgusted was the General at not receiving explicit instructions from the Governor, that he threatened to withdraw the six colored troopers which he had brought from Tallahassee, and leave Lake City in the hands of the Bush faction. Such action would be fatal to the poor negroes of Lake City who had been mustered in as State militia. They would probably be assassinated one after another by the desperadoes.

THE ACTION OF THE GOVERNOR.

The General had a conference with Gov. Hart in Jacksonville on Tuesday, but returned to Lake City that night more dissatisfied than ever. Your correspondent asked the General if he thought Gov. Hart had the power to remove the county officers in direct violation of the provisions of the State Constitution, which say that they shall hold office for four years after they have been appointed and confirmed by the Senate. The General replied that he was of the opinion that Bush's office as Sheriff became vacant when he accepted the position of Assemblyman. He said that he thought it would be ridiculous for Bush the Assemblyman to vote on bills which, if passed, would put money into the pockets of Bush the Sheriff. He thought there was some provision in the Constitution which would prevent such action, but he could not quote it without a copy of the Constitution before him. Your correspondent thought that the trouble with the State Constitution was its loose construction. It was adopted a few years ago solely with the purpose of advancing the interests of the Grant party or the interests of the clique of thieving rascals who rule that party in Florida.

THE SUN'S CORRESPONDENT WARNED.

The town itself seemed paralyzed. The most respectable citizens were cowed by the threats of the ruffians who had fired upon the defenceless women and children. The men engaged in the attempt at assassination were easily discovered. They sat upon the stoops in front of the stores, cleaning their nails with knives and muttering in low tones to each other. It was evident to me, notwithstanding all the assurances I had had to the contrary, that both sides—Bush and Day—were appealing to dormant rebel sympathies. As I was entering Dr. Hunter's drug store[1] I overhead the remark, "He's a ____ Yankee ____ __ __ _____ who came down here to make a report for THE NEW YORK

SUN. You oughter seen him, how eager he took down the evidence before the committee."

Toward night I was informed that it was believed that I was really a United States detective under the cover of a SUN reporter. Some of the most respectable citizens were evidently misled by this report, for they expressed to me their gratification at the interference of the United States authorities. They said that if the United States authorities took the case in hand the United States would foot the bills; whereas if the State troops were quartered upon them the citizens of the county would be compelled to pay for their services.

About dark I was warned not to remain in the town that night, and particularly not to cross the sidewalk in front of an old deserted store above the hotel where I was stopping. My informant, who belonged to a well known secret society, told me that certain persons were satisfied that I was not what I represented myself to be, and even if I was that it made no difference. Parties were hidden behind the doors and windows of the deserted store who had determined to shoot me or Detective Newcomb of the United States Secret service, if we passed that way. This was enough for me. After that I avoided the society of Detective Newcomb. I said that if the desperadoes thought proper to kill anybody I would stay all night, but as affairs stood, I thought I could gain more information in Jacksonville than in Lake City. Senator Johnson[2] and a relative of Sheriff Bush, together with a well-known Southern gentleman, had hired a wagon and driven post haste to Jacksonville on the morning after the Sheriff's arrest. I determined to follow them and get an account of the trouble.

WHAT EX-GOV. DAY SAYS.

I arrived in Jacksonville on Monday night. Sheriff Bush and Senator Johnson occupied rooms directly opposite my room in the National Hotel.[3] At midnight your correspondent sent up his card, but was informed that the Sheriff was not in.

On Tuesday morning I met ex-Gov. Day upon the streets of Jacksonville. The Governor looks like a carpenter. He wore a white shirt, had a crumpled collar, and an old black felt hat. Your correspondent said:

"Governor, I would like to get your statement of the cause of the trouble up in Lake City."

The Governor—Yes. You shall have it. I hear you are a New York newspaper man, and I don't believe you have any bias toward either party. The cause of the trouble is this: Dr. Hunter, a well-known citizen and an honest man, was formerly Treasurer of Columbia county. Nobody ever found fault with Dr. Hunter. He was the last man in the world who would steal. After Harrison Reed was elected Governor he appointed a man named Ridgell[4] County Trea-

NATIONAL HOTEL,

JACKSONVILLE.

GEORGE McGINLEY, PROPRIETOR.

The National, recently completed is now open for the reception of guests. Its situation is unrivalled, commanding a magnificent view of the St. John's River, and convenient to the steamer landings and railroad depot.

Visitors will find here every comfort, large, finely furnished, and well-ventilated apartments, and an excellent table.

Bath rooms, billiard room, livery stable, etc., attached to hotel. In fact, every requisite of a first-class house.

GEORGE McGINLEY, Proprietor.

An advertisement for the National Hotel
(from Rambler's *Guide to Florida*, 1875).

surer. He did this at the solicitation of a man named Johnson, who is now Senator from Columbia county. Johnson is a desperado from North Carolina. There are terrible stories afloat of the outrages committed by him upon Union men during the war. Johnson, Bush, and a man named Duval Selph,[5] who is known to have killed five men in cold blood at different times, turned Republicans and gave their influence to Reed.

SELPH.

Selph seconded Johnson's recommendation of Ridgell for County Treasurer. Selph gained his influence with the Governor in a queer way. He told the Governor not to leave Tallahassee on a certain night, because he had information that the train would be thrown from the track at a given point, and that the Governor would be seized by a gang of desperadoes, and hanged to the nearest pine tree. The Governor headed the warning, and remained in Tallahassee. On the very night mentioned the express train from Tallahassee was thrown from the track. The Governor thanked his stars and Duval Selph for the information that he supposed had saved his life. Selph had put up the job himself, and had the train thrown from the track. Gov. Reed was unaware of this fact, and believed that he was indebted to Selph for his personal safety. Of course his recommendation gave Ridgell the County Treasurership. Dr. Hunter turned over to Ridgell about $7,000 in county scrip.

A MODEL APPOINTMENT.

Correspondent—What is county scrip?

Gov. Day—Scrip issued by the county which is received by the county authorities for county taxes. The State has also issued scrip which is received for State taxes. School boards issue scrip which is received for school taxes.

Correspondent—And Dr. Hunter turned over about $7,000 to Ridgell? Who was Ridgell?

Gov. Day—Ridgell was a young man about 19 years old, who was living with Johnson. He acted as County Treasurer for a few days and then left for New York, where he was pursuing a course of studies. He left the County Treasury with Johnson, and he also left a written paper purporting to make Bush a Deputy Collector. When Reed was impeached and suspended, I became the acting Governor of the State. I appointed a man named Easton[6] County Treasurer. Easton discovered that $5,000 worth of scrip was missing. Johnson pretended that he did not know anything about it. There was what Ridgell left, and that was all the county scrip that Johnson had seen. Well, the first thing we knew Bush was appointed Sheriff and Tax Collector by Reed. Johnson was appointed Assessor, and Selph was made a County Commissioner. These fellows have been holding the thing for about two years. They have collected about $40,000 for taxes and haven't made a single return or quarterly statement.

Correspondent—Why won't the Collector make a statement?

Gov. Day—Because he only makes a statement when the County Commissioners call for it. Selph is the Chairman of the Board of County Commissioners, and he has a couple of niggers under him who do just as he says. There never has been a cent laid out on roads, or any other county improvements, except a bridge, and the man who built the bridge can't force a settlement to save his life. Well, last fall, Selph and Johnson pretended to be buying county scrip, and the first thing we knew the Board of County Commissioners passed a resolution calling in all the scrip for a reissue, and Johnson and Selph turned up with about $7,000 worth of it. Then the Commissioners passed another resolution, declaring that only scrip issued between certain dates would be received in payment of taxes. Then, to everybody's astonishment, it was found that Johnson and Selph were the only men who held scrip receivable for taxes. How much these men have stolen is impossible to tell. The State Treasurer tells me that Bush is over $23,000 behind in his State taxes. As Bush is Sheriff and Tax Collector himself and runs the County Commissioners, the desperadoes have the thing all to themselves. It is easy enough to have a man killed in Columbia county. I can pick out fifty men who will kill a man for $25, provided you furnish them a horse with which to escape. If we are not protected by the Governor, we will raise a party who will clean out the Bush party. We have got the friends to do it, and we will fight assassination with assassination if necessary. The amount of the business is, they have stolen so much that they don't want to be forced to make a report.

Correspondent—How much do you think they have stolen?

Gov. Day—I think it will reach over $40,000.

INTERVIEW WITH SENATOR JOHNSON.

Here the Governor was accosted by a friend. Not ten minutes afterward I was introduced to Senator E. G. Johnson. I asked him if he would talk on the subject of the Lake City disturbances. He said he would be glad of an opportunity to tell me all he knew. Senator Johnson is over six feet high, and resembles Whitelaw Reid[7] of the Tribune. We walked into a saloon kept by the renowned Gallagher[8] the prize fighter, and sat down at a table. The Senator dictated the following interview in a deliberate manner:

Correspondent—Senator Johnson, I have been informed that you know something about the origin of the troubles in Columbia county. Have you any objection to giving me your views as to the cause of the present excitement?

Senator Johnson—Certainly not. I was elected as the Republican candidate to the State Senate in 1879. The Senators hold office for four years. From 1868 to 1870 the county was represented by a Conservative. The State administration being Republican, the Conservative Senator did not control the appointments. Dr. Day, being then the most prominent Republican in Columbia county, controlled the appointments. During the two years there was a great deal of political excitement in the county and quite a number of assassinations, arising in part from a dissatisfaction with the officers of the county and the feelings engendered by the result of the war. Since my election as State Senator, and my assumption of the control of the county offices, there has not been so far as my knowledge extends, a single political murder or assassination in the county. This favorable political change has resulted from the appointment of W. S. Bush and other representative men to all the county offices. For the last two years Dr. Day has been waging a cruel political war against me and the county officers appointed by me with the view to obtain the control of the offices. He failed to do so until certain differences arose between myself and the newly elected Governor, which resulted in the county appointments being left to Day's discretion. All the officers that did not require confirmation by the Senate were then removed, and since the adjournment of the Legislature the positions of those that were confirmed by the Senate have been declared vacant and others appointed in their places by the most unwarrantable assumption of power by the Governor, as the Constitution requires that the Sheriff, County Judge, Tax Collector, and Assessor, and Clerk of the Circuit Court shall be appointed by the advice and with the consent of the Senate. In violation of the Constitution Gov. Hart withheld the appointment of at least one-half the county officers of the State where vacancies existed while the Senate was in session.

Correspondent—Why did he withhold them?

Senator—Because he believed that the appointments would be rejected by the Senate.

Correspondent—But in this case no vacancy existed.

Senator—There were no vacancies.

Correspondent—Has the Governor the power to remove county officers as well as to appoint them?

THE CONSTITUTION.

Here the Senator produced a copy of the State Constitution and read the following:

Article V., section 139—The Governor shall appoint, by and with the consent of the Senate, in each county an assessor and collector of revenue, whose duties shall be prescribed by law, and who shall hold their offices for two years, and be subject to removal upon the recommendation of the Governor and consent of the Senate. Provided, No officer shall be removed except for wilful neglect of duty or a violation of the criminal laws of the State, or for incompetency.

Correspondent—But about the Sheriff?

Senator (reading)—Article VI., sec. 199—The Governor, by and with the advice and consent of the Senate, shall appoint in each county a sheriff and clerk of the Circuit Court, each of whom shall hold his office for four years.

Correspondent—Has Sheriff Bush held his office four years?

Senator—He has not. He was appointed and confirmed in January, 1872.

Before this he had been acting as Sheriff under an *ad interim* appointment by Gov. Reed for nearly a year.

Correspondent—Has Sheriff Bush received any notice or intimation from Gov. Hart of his removal?

Senator—None whatever. In fact, the Constitution gives Gov. Hart no power to remove him.

Correspondent—A little while ago you alluded to certain differences between yourself and Gov. Hart. Were they personal or political?

Senator—Political, or such as referred to my official duty as a Senator.

Correspondent—Is it not customary in this State to give the county patronage to the Senator and representatives of the county?

Senator—It is, provided the Senator and representatives are of the same political faith as the Governor.

Correspondent—Did you see Gov. Hart in relation to the appointments in Columbia county when you entered upon your Senatorial duties?

Senator—Pending the confirmation of his Cabinet officers, I called to see Gov. Hart in relation to my county offices. In the Senate I had opposed the confirmation of McLinn,[9] the present Secretary of State. It was known that my vote would defeat his confirmation. Of course, Gov. Hart asked me to withdraw my objections to McLinn's confirmation. I had understood that Gov. Hart intended to give the official patronage of Columbia county to Dr. Day. The Governor assured me that he intended to be governed by the majority of the delegation from my county, and he told me that if I would withdraw my objections to McLinn's nomination, I need entertain no fears as to my controlling the appointments in my county. I agreed to withdraw the objections to McLinn upon the Governor's assurance. McLinn was confirmed by my vote, and you can see the position in which the Governor has placed himself. The wishes of the majority of the delegation from Columbia county have never been consulted. The Governor has made his appointments at Day's dictation.

Correspondent—I saw ex-Gov. Day this morning. He says that you control a Ring which has absorbed all the tax collections in Columbia county for two years past without rendering an account to the taxpayers. Is his statement true?

Senator—It is not true. I have heard no complaints from the Comptroller of the State, or from the Board of County Commissioners relative to such a charge, except as to the school fund, which has been in a very bad condition for two years past, and has been directly under the control of Dr. Day, as he is President and Treasurer of the County School Board. He has issued and placed in circulation a large quantity of school scrip without any authority, so that the county is flooded with school scrip, and it is going begging at fifty cents on the dollar. He has used the school funds to pay his private debts, speculated in it; in fact in Lake City, where the larger part of the colored people live, there has not been a school in twelve months owing to Day's mismanagement of the school funds.

Correspondent—Have the local authorities known this, and have they not made some effort to correct it?

Senator—I saw Gov. Reed, and told him that the school funds of Columbia county were being used for private purposes by Dr. Day, and asked his removal, together with the entire school board. He referred the matter to the State Superintendent of Schools and to the State School Board. They refused to make the removal. I next asked the State Superintendent of Schools to go in person to Columbia county and make an investigation of the condition of the schools. This he declined or failed to do. I then went before the Board of County Commissioners, and asked them to appoint a committee of five tax-payers of the county to investigate the school fund, with power to send for persons and papers, and to take testimony under oath. This they did. The committee organized, and called on Dr. Day for a statement and a showing of his books and accounts. He refused to make a statement, or show his books. A second committee of seven men was appointed, at my solicitation, by the County Board with similar results. I tell you, sir, all good citizens of Columbia county, acquainted with the facts, know that Day has been stealing the school money for the last two years and living on it, but they can't force him to make a showing. Even he himself has acknowledged that the school matter would not bear an investigation, and gives that as a reason for not showing his books. His object has been to secure the appointments of the county officers so as to prevent his peculations and defalcations from being made public.

Correspondent—But Dr. Day accuses the Sheriff and Tax Collector of making no return of the county funds or collections.

Senator—One word. In this State no quarterly statements are required. The Sheriff has repeatedly told me that he is ready at any time to make a statement whenever the Commissioners call upon him to do so. He has asked the Commissioners time and again to meet and adjust his accounts, but thus far it has not been done.

Correspondent—How do the people of the county generally regard Gov. Hart's or Gov. Day's appointments?

Senator—They regard them as ill-timed, and many of them incompetent. Certain parties were promised office by us in return for their support of Sheriff Bush for the Assembly. The trouble in Columbia county arises from their

dissatisfaction. If the Governor will give the people a good set of county officers that they have confidence in the trouble will be ended. The people are
tired of paying taxes without knowing what becomes of the money.

Correspondent—It is reported that you and Sheriff Bush and Duval Selph
were among the parties who fired into the houses last Wednesday night. Is
there any foundation for that report?

Senator—I have no idea who was concerned in that attack, but I have an
idea that the feeling of disappointment on the part of men who were promised
the offices may have had something to do with it. In fact, I ain't sure that
Moore and King and Waldron and Holt fired into their own houses, so as to
kick up a public sympathy for themselves. A good many people think that
they did. Men are often accused of just such things down in Columbia county.

Correspondent—I have heard that Gov. Day belonged to the original Ku-
Klux organization. Do you know if that is true?

Senator—I do know it to be true. It is well known throughout the county.
Day belonged to a similar organization which flourished before the war. Since
the war he was present at the lynching of a colored man, whose name was
Dick Ogden.

Correspondent—Did Sheriff Bush ever belong to a Ku-Klux organization?

Senator—I don't know.

Correspondent—How many men have you killed in your life?

Senator (smiling)—I never counted them, probably because no bills were
sent to me for their funeral expenses.

THE GREAT DESPERADO.

Here Sheriff Bush entered the room and was introduced to THE SUN'S correspondent. He was a small man, and was a perfect picture of Maj.-Gen. John
Newton,[10] as he appeared in 1863. He was very affable, and looked like anything else than a ruffian. As he was in a hurry he declined to talk, but said that
Senator Johnson would give me more information than he could.

Meanwhile, the United States authorities heard that your correspondent
had gleaned important information from Mr. Hightower, the colored blacksmith. The examination of Sheriff Bush, which had been set for 3 o'clock that
afternoon, was postponed until the next day, so as to secure the attendance of
Hightower. At 3 P.M., Wednesday, the Sheriff was taken before the United
States Commissioner. His counsel discovered that the Sheriff was charged
with conspiracy, and as the complaint did not specify any other party to the
conspiracy the Court held that the Sheriff could not conspire alone, and
therefore discharged him from custody. Other and corrected complaints were

immediately made, and warrants are now out for the arrest of Sheriff Bush, Duval Selph, and a desperado named Connors[11] living nine miles south of Lake City. The people here sympathize deeply with United States Marshall McMurry,[12] who says he is going after Connors to-morrow morning.

The investigation will probably prove a farce. Both parties are Grant Republicans, and know too much of the operations of Grant's Florida Ring to be punished. If a Democrat had been concerned in the outrage, the whole country would have rung with reports of the most dastardly Ku-Klux outrage on record; but as it is the whole matter will be hushed up.

6

THE TROUBLE IN FLORIDA

THE REFUGEES RETURNING TO LAKE CITY WELL ARMED.

More Attempts at Assassination Expected—Postmaster Moore Accuses Three County Officers of Robbery—Grantism Run Wild in the State—The Instructive Story of Ex-Lieutenant-Governor Gleason.

JACKSONVILLE, FLA., MARCH 14.—Yesterday Mr. Waldron, the newly appointed Clerk of Columbia county, who escaped assassination a week ago, returned to Lake City. He declares that his family has been threatened long enough, and that he is now going to protect his wife and child. He entered Lake City in the day time, and thus escaped assassination. Last night he remained in his house with six colored militia, who were detailed to repel any attack that might be made upon him. Ex-Gov. Day and Postmaster Moore are still here, but tell me that they shall go to Lake City within a day or two, determined to fight the desperadoes with their own weapons. Keene's wife appears to be able to take care of her homestead without her husband's assistance. It is known that men are prepared to assassinate the refugees at the first opportunity.

It is a singular fact that Sheriff Bush occupies Postmaster Moore's house as his office, and that Moore lives in a house owned by Senator Johnson. It seems that the Constitution gives the Governor power to appoint the County Commissioners without the advice and consent of the Senate. The immediate cause of hostilities now appears to be that the new Board of Commissioners showed a disposition to force Bush to make a statement of his accounts.

WHAT POSTMASTER MOORE SAYS.

To-day I met Postmaster Moore. He requested me to write the following statement as his explanation of the cause of the trouble:

"I was Tax Collector in 1870. I resigned the position on account of my business and because I was sick of the trouble of collecting the taxes. Bush was appointed Tax Collector in my place. My accounts were settled up. The State Comptroller discovered that I had paid $40 too much into the State

Treasury. He gave me a drawback for $40 on Bush. Bush has steadily refused to pay me back this money. About the time that I resigned Duval Selph was driven out of Hamilton county. He had been Sheriff of that county, but he had murdered so many men and had become such a terror to the community that the people arose in a body and drove him from the county. Selph then came to Columbia county and immediately turned out to be an active Republican and an ardent supporter of Senator Johnson. Bush, Johnson, and Selph then apparently formed a Ring for the purpose of robbing the people of the county. The first move was the removal of Dr. Hunter, County Treasurer, and the appointment of Ridgell. Ridgell cleared out and has never been seen since. He left the county assets with Johnson.

THE MISSING SCRIP.

When I resigned as Tax Collector I turned over to Ridgell $3,500 in scrip cash orders. Of course they fell into Johnson's hands, and that was the last of them. They have never been paid back. Meanwhile Gov. Reed appointed me County Commissioner. I was elected President of the Board. It was my duty to look into the accounts of the Treasurer, Tax Collector, and Sheriff. I suspected something wrong, because I could get no statements from them. My first object was to discover what had become of the $3,500 in scrip which I had turned over to Ridgell. The only way to do this was to ascertain how much county scrip there was out. The County Commissioners therefore issued notices to the people to register their scrip so that it might be cancelled and new scrip issued in its place. Well, the people registered, and only between $600 and $700 was found to be afloat. Johnson and Selph were afraid to register the $3,500 in scrip which they had stolen, because they thought that as I had turned the scrip over to Ridgell I might recognize it if they offered it for registration. Their next move was upon Gov. Reed. It was a successful one. I was thrown out of the office of County Commissioner, and Duval Selph was appointed in my stead. During this time Johnson and Selph were making great pretensions of buying in scrip so as to cover themselves.

THE SCRIP TURNS UP.

After I was removed from office, Selph and Johnson turned up before the County Commissioners loaded with scrip, which they registered and had exchanged for the new issue. All the scrip that was cancelled while I was Commissioner was filed away where it could be seen at any time. As soon as Selph was made Commissioner, and his and Johnson's scrip was changed, the cancelled scrip was burned. They issued as much new scrip as they pleased in lieu of the burned scrip. It is impossible to ascertain how much scrip they really set afloat, but it is certain that they not only ran in the $3,500 that I turned over to Ridgell, but that they issued about $6,000 more scrip to themselves, than they had actually turned in. Selph made the next move. As President of the County Board he had the County Commissioners under his thumb. Last fall the Commissioners passed a law that only a certain kind of scrip should be received for county taxes. It turned out that there was about $10,000 of this certain kind of scrip in existence, and that it was all owned by Selph and Johnson.

LOOKING INTO THE MATTER.

The new County Commissioners have taken steps to investigate the matter, and that is one cause of the shooting in Lake City. As I have been appointed Tax Collector by Gov. Hart, Bush will be compelled to turn his accounts over to me, when it will be discovered what has become of all the money he has collected for two years past. Of course he (Selph) and Johnson are in desperate straits at the prospect of an exposure. Only a day or two before the shooting Bush told me that his friends didn't want him to give up the office and that he wouldn't give it up. He endeavored to intimidate me by saying that Selph had promised to back him with money and pistols. There is only one way for them to keep the money they have stolen and get out of the trouble they are in. That way is for them to secure a Board of County Commissioners who will certify to any deficiency in their accounts and accept county scrip in payment of any defalcation.[1] As they have stolen and manufactured the scrip, this would bring them out of the trouble and leave them in possession of the swag."

Correspondent—Do you know, Mr. Moore, that Sheriff Bush is a defaulter?

Postmaster Moore—All I know is that I am one of Bush's sureties, and that the State Comptroller has informed me that he has begun a suit against Bush for twelve or thirteen thousand dollars, State taxes, which Bush has collected, but has not turned over.

ANOTHER TALK WITH GOV. DAY.

While Mr. Moore was making this statement ex-Gov. Day entered. He said that he had heard that I had been talking with Senator Johnson, and that Johnson had told me that he (Day) was a defaulter in his accounts as Treasurer of the County School Board. Gov. Day said that the Johnson Ring wanted to get control of the School Board. Their first move was to accuse him (Gov. Day) of being a thief. The Governor continued:

"Selph put a resolution through the Board of County Commissioners to appoint a committee to examine my books. Being President of the board,

Selph appointed the committee. Of course the committee was made up of my personal enemies. I wouldn't show them my books. I knew what would happen if I did. They would go to work and alter the entries, and then declare that they had discovered a defalcation. Thereupon I would have been kicked out and a murderer or thief would have been appointed Treasurer of the County School Board in my stead. Johnson told you that I had refused to show my books. Johnson lies. After I had refused to allow Selph's county committee to look at my books, I sent over to the Grand Jury, which was then in session, and asked them to come over and look at the books. They came, examined the books, and reported everything correct. Now to show you that what Bush has been at. At the very time that the Grand Jury examined my books I had vouchers showing that Bush had collected $3,277, school tax, but had only paid over to me $2,900. I never could get another cent out of him, though he kept promising to make it all right. This is not the first time that my vouchers and Bush's payments were at variance. Take the tax of 1872. I had vouchers for $2,200, and Bush never paid over but $1,900."

A SUMMING UP.

Such is the history of the troubles in Lake City from the lips of the men concerned. It shows that Florida has a Constitution which gives its Governor complete control of every county in the State. It shows that the Governor uses this power without regard to the welfare of the taxpayers in the different counties, and solely with a view to advance his personal and political interests. In Columbia county it seems that the Governor has deliberately placed the interests of the taxpayers in the hands of noted desperadoes, and they in return have unscrupulously advanced the Governor's schemes in the Legislature. All this is shown by their own admissions. They virtually acknowledge that the Governor gives them permission to rob the people in return for their influence in political conventions and elsewhere.

MODEL REPUBLICANS.

Columbia and Jackson counties have the reputation of being the most lawless counties in the State. Assassination is common in both counties. The more respectable citizens shrug their shoulders and say that it is none of their business. The man who has killed the greatest number of men is looked up to as a hero by the young men who lounge about the stores and hotels, and many of these young men only await an opportunity to emulate his example. In Mariana, Jackson county, last year, a stranger was shot down in the public streets by a young man, solely because he was a stranger and had no friends there. The young man who committed the murder was not even arrested, and has swaggered about the county ever since, glorying in the reputation he has achieved. In Ellaville, a small town in Columbia county, it is unsafe for a stranger to appear. Men have been known to partake of a stranger's hospitality and to blow out his brains from pure love of blood-shed while shaking hands at parting. All this lawless element is used by the Republican politicians. So long as the murderers support certain men for the Legislature and for State offices, so long they are secure. The Governor appoints the men who select the Grand Jury, and the Senator or Representative who does the will of the Governor, or the will of the Ring that controls the Governor, has it in his power to protect any man, no matter with what crime he is charged.

WEAK-KNEED DEMOCRATS.

Nor are the Democrats entirely free from blame. When the controlling Ring in the Republican party need their services they always find enough weak-kneed Democrats to pull them through. The election of Conover[2] to the United States Senate proves this. In making up the Committee on Contested Seats, Conover managed to pack it with men who were subservient to his interest. The seats of many conservatives were contested by men who had not the shadow of a right to them. It was well known in the Legislature that no man whose seat was contested was secure unless he cast a vote for Conover. I was informed by a Democratic member of the Legislature that several Democrats cowed under the crack of Conover's whip, and saved their seats by casting their votes for him.

OPERATIONS OF A LEADING GRANTITE.

William H. Gleason,[3] one Lieutenant-Governor of the State, is another fair example of a Florida politician. A Democratic member of the Legislature informed me that Gleason spends the most of his time in New York city. Some years ago he managed to rake a land grant out of the Legislature. This grant is situated along the Miami river, bordering the Everglades, on the southeast coast of Florida. It lies in Dade county. Eight or ten persons live upon Gleason's grant. Of course Dade county sends a representative to the Legislature. Three years ago, while Gleason was in New York, a State election was held. As Gleason himself held one half of the offices in Dade county, and the other half were held by men in his interest, but of less than average intelligence, no notice of an election was given in that county, and consequently nobody was elected to the Legislature. Accidentally hearing of this, Gleason put for the Miami settlement, and about a month afterward held an election on his own account, walked in the Assembly at the proper time and claimed the seat for Dade county. He held it two years. Last year he was defeated by two votes.

THE REFUGEES RETURNING TO LAKE CITY WELL ARMED

Portrait of Governor William H. Gleason.
Courtesy of Florida State Archives.

This would never do. He was County Judge, County Clerk, County Commissioner, and one of the Board of Canvassers, and as might be expected he was counted in to the Assembly. When he appeared at Tallahassee during the late session, he astonished the natives by claiming mileage from New York city. Through some miracle his claim was disallowed. It may interest some people to know that the taxes collected from Dade county are not sufficient to pay the mileage of her Assemblyman.

HOW TO ELECT A GRANT SENATOR.

But this is not all. Brevard and Dade counties send a Senator to Tallahassee. The Conservative candidate last year was a gentleman named Stewart,[4] who owns property and has lived in Brevard county for over thirty years. The Grant-Gleason candidate was one Sturdevant,[5] a chum of Gleason's, living in Dade county. Stewart carried both counties—Brevard by a unanimous vote and Dade by two majority. Through some hocus-pocus the returns from Brevard were held back, and finally thrown out altogether. Sturdevant and Gleason, being on the Board of Canvassers from Dade county, threw out three Stewart ballots, on the ground that they were cast by foreigners who were not qualified to vote. The Board of County Canvassers then gave Gleason and

Portrait of Governor William D. Bloxham.
Courtesy of Florida State Archives.

Sturdevant their certificates of election as Assemblyman and Senator respectively. They appeared at Tallahassee and obtained seats in the Legislature, notwithstanding the fact that the three foreigners whose votes were thrown out in Dade county went to the Capitol and exhibited their naturalization papers. Thus Sturdevant, though receiving not a single vote in Brevard and only a half dozen in Dade, holds the Senator's seat for the next four years. Gleason is now Assemblyman, Collector, and Assessor of Dade county, while Sturdevant is County Judge, County Clerk, and Senator from the same, while there are not twenty voters in the county. It is also asserted that both gentlemen hold Federal offices.

From this statement it is easily seen where the Grant party in Florida obtain their five majority on joint ballot. There is no doubt but what the Conservatives carried the State. If the will of the people had been carried out, Bloxham[6] would now be Governor, and an honest man would be sitting in Conover's seat in the United States Senate. There is but little hope for Florida in the future. The negroes and carpet-baggers in Georgia, having discovered that there is no hope for them in that State, are flocking to the land of flowers by hundreds. They will cast a solid vote against honest government, and the trouble at Lake City is only an outcropping of what may be expected in years to come.

THE REFUGEES RETURNING TO LAKE CITY WELL ARMED

An Unsettling Epilogue to "The Trouble in Florida" Articles

As noted in my introduction to Amos Cummings's three articles about the conflicts in Lake City in March 1873, the *New York Sun* published a fourth article on March 20. It is datelined "Jacksonville, March 15." I believe it was written by someone other than Cummings.

The article is entitled "The Lake City Outrage," with the subheading *"THREE GRANT REPUBLICANS BEFORE THE U.S. COURTS,"* followed by the readout: "Testimony of the Refugees—The Sheriff, County Commissioners, and Another Prominent Republican Recognized while Firing into Private Homes—James Hightower on the Stand—Tussy Berthay, the Desperado."

On March 13, the article reports, the Columbia County sheriff, Warren Bush, was brought before a judge in Jacksonville and charged, but the prosecuting attorney, A. A. Knight, asked the judge to dismiss the case because of irregularities with the paperwork. Bush was released. Immediately, however, a United States marshal issued new warrants for Bush and for the brothers Duval and Frank Selph and for William P. Roberts (Roberts is not mentioned in Cummings's articles). As reported by Cummings, U.S. Marshal Thomas McMurray then went to Lake City, apprehended the men, and brought them back to Jacksonville.

At a hearing the next day, the defendants' attorneys tried to have the charges thrown out. The prosecutor prevailed, however, and a new hearing about the charges began on Saturday, March 15. Prosecution testimony was taken from the Lake City postmaster, W. W. Moore, whom Cummings wrote about, and James Hightower, the blacksmith, whom Cummings also wrote about. Next to testify was George Keene, the acting sheriff whose house had been shot up, followed by T. F. Harris, who had lived in Lake City for only two years and worked as a store clerk. Finally, testimony was collected from Edward Hall, identified in the 1870 federal census as an African-American laborer.

Following that day's testimony, which consisted of several depositions that seem to have been quite damning, the hearing adjourned until Tuesday of the next week, which would have been March 18.

For the rest of the story, I turned to Jacksonville's *Tri-Weekly Florida Union*. The paper noted that on the morning of Tuesday, March 18, when the hearing was to restart it was postponed until 3 o'clock in the afternoon. The postponement was necessary because the train from Lake City bringing some of the principals to court had not arrived yet.

The train did roll into Jacksonville later in the day, and the hearing reconvened. The attorney for the four arrested men stood up and said he would like to dispense with the hearing and go straight to trial. Upon the recommendation of the pros-ecuting attorney, the charges against Duval Selph were dropped; the prosecutor stated that he was satisfied that those charges were filed in error. Bond was set at $5,000 for Bush and $1,000 for both Frank Selph and Roberts. Then everyone went home.

Over the next two weeks, the *Union* carried a series of follow-up stories, some critical of the *Tallahassee Sentinel*'s coverage of the outrage and urging state and federal officials to do their jobs and prosecute the case. Also reported was a trip by Governor Ossian Hart and a handful of his cabinet members to Lake City, where the governor gave a speech and a town meeting was held on March 29. Several resolutions pledging an effort to seek justice were passed.

But, as the *Union* would write on April 8, 1873, the governor's "labor . . . produced [only] barren results." Indeed, that same issue of the paper carried a story about the Lake City trial of the three defendants on April 4. The three ap-peared before a local justice of the peace and in short order produced alibis. All three were discharged.

Sheriff Bush then appointed Roberts, his former codefendant, as a deputy, who promptly arrested James Hightower, the African-American blacksmith who had testified in the Jacksonville hearing against the men. The charge? Perjury.

Bond for Hightower initially was refused. A large crowd of African-Americans soon collected and protested. A "desperate riot" seemed about to ensue. To avoid it, Hightower was finally released on bond. The Lake City citizens who had stood up to Bush, Selph, and Roberts gave up hope that law and order might prevail. Moore put his house up for sale and prepared to leave town. Racism had won in Lake City.

Why didn't the *Sun* carry any follow-up stories on the case? It may be that the fourth *Sun* article was indeed written by Amos Cummings, and that he simply left town. Or perhaps he arranged for a local journalist to submit the story, but when no paycheck appeared promptly, the stand-in journalist instead went fishing that next Tuesday.

Wilderness No More

As high school students in Orlando in the 1960s, my friends and I hung out at New Smyrna Beach. It was the stretch of beach closest to Central Florida. At one time I probably could have made the drive from Orlando over and back with my eyes closed. Sanford and Samsula, places Amos Cummings writes about, were stops along the way, at the former to look at the zoo and at the latter to buy oranges or juice.

Ninety years after Amos Cummings visited Smyrna, that town and the land to the west toward the St. Johns River looked nothing like the wilderness Cummings saw in 1873. When he was there, there was not a single beach bar or motel built atop the former dunes. New Smyrna was the sticks, a place about which hardship stories were told by the hotel and boardinghouse proprietors in the "civilized" towns of Palatka, Mellonville, and Enterprise.

While doing research for this book, I ran across an interesting photograph in the State of Florida Archives (image number RC 12083). It is dated 1908 and is entitled "9 Beached Whales: New Smyrna Beach, Florida." The text with the photographs reads "9 whales, 35–43 feet long, washed ashore near the lighthouse. Frank Sams, Albert Moeller, Elmer Oliver and Jerome Naley formed a company with John Pettigrew and Captain S. Bennett (a one time New England whaler) of Daytona Beach for the purpose of extracting whale oil. Using giant kettles from the historic Sugar Mill and any other iron cauldron available, they set about boiling the whale blubber but something went wrong. The final result was minimal and valueless. What they did accomplish was creating a whale of a mess and a city wide stench. Smaller pieces of whale were hauled out to the inlet, but dynamite was used on the remaining carcasses before disposal. June 13, 1908." Frank Sams is certainly the same man mentioned in this and several other of Cummings's articles from 1873, thirty-five years earlier.

The photo not only documents Frank Sams as still being around, it also would seem to dispel the blame that some members of the public place on underwater communications or other modern technology associated with submarines or ships as the cause of sea mammal beachings. As this photograph attests, there is much more to the story.

Nine beached whales on New Smyrna Beach in 1908. Courtesy of Florida State Archives.

Forty years have now elapsed since my New Smyrna Beach visits and changes continue to sculpt the town. Other than the beach itself, there is little in New Smyrna Beach I recognize from four decades ago. Certainly Amos Cummings would never identify the town. The bears, whooping cranes, and panthers he mentions are, of course, long gone. Only the sand flies still remain.

This article was in the April 14, 1873, *New York Sun,* and it appeared four days later, April 18, in the *Semi-Weekly Sun.*

7

A TROPICAL WILDERNESS

A WINTER'S SPORT ON THE EASTERN COAST OF FLORIDA.

Where Uncle Sam Gets his Live Oak—The Hunter's Paradise—The Garden of Florida—A Day in the Pines—A Kentucky Hunter and a New York Fisherman—Acres of Fish in a Fight—The Midnight Drumfish.

New Smyrna, Fla., March 15.—This place is a paradise for hunters and fishermen. It is on the Hillsborough river,[1] about eighty miles south of St. Augustine. Hillsborough river is simply an arm of the sea, like Barnegat bay.[2] The connecting inlet is opposite Smyrna. The bar is ever shifting, but vessels drawing eight or nine feet can pass at high water. Smyrna is about a mile from the ocean. The roar of the surf is borne over the small mangroves skirting the river—now from the south and anon from the north, according to the shifting of the wind. The town consists of nearly a dozen houses scattered over an area of ten or fifteen miles. At one point three houses can be seen at once. The dwellings seem to have been dropped in a tropical wilderness by the action of a whirlwind. They are generally old, black, weather-beaten structures, some of them being built of unplaned boards, and one or two having a thatched palmetto roof. I saw one that was not over ten feet square. There were four in the family, and as house-room was plenty the proprietor economized a little by taking in boarders.

A WINTER DINNER-TABLE.

A good hotel[3] stands on a small strait leading to the Hillsborough river at either end. The accommodations are not luxurious, but substantial and comfortable, and the table excels anything that I have seen in Florida. In the middle of January we have had green peas, new lettuce, new potatoes, new tomatoes, fresh cabbage, cauliflower, string beans, boiled sheep's head and bass, roast venison, bear's paws, wild turkey, and roast Mallard duck for dinner. The cooking in Florida is generally execrable, but here I have found it unsurpassed. Fig trees, oleanders, and orange trees loaded with fruit dot the

A steamship at a New Smyrna Beach dock on the Indian River in the 1880s. Courtesy of Florida State Archives.

yard fronting the hotel, and there is a beautiful water view from the piazza. The house is partly embowered in palmettos, and is situated on the edge of the most picturesque palmetto hammock in the State.

THE GREAT TURNBULL SWAMP.

Back of this hammock is the great Turnbull swamp, which stretches from the Halifax river on the north past the head of the Indian river on the south, over thirty miles in length. It is this swamp which is supplying the United States navy with live oak. This timber is now very scarce, and when Turnbull swamp gives out, live oak will only be procured in small quantities, and far away from navigation. In fact, it is now worth almost its weight in silver. It is nearly as heavy as lignumvitae, and will not float. A small schooner will sometimes carry away over $50,000 worth of it.

Beyond Turnbull swamp stretches clear to the St. John's a vast expanse of pines, carpeted with palmetto scrub and small sand heaps thrown up by a little red rat called a salamander, and intersected with long savannas and swamps. This stretch of pines runs past St. Augustine to Jacksonville on the north, and is lost in the Everglades on the south. It must be at least four hundred miles in length, and from three to forty miles in width. Perhaps fifty families live in this vast pine section, but certainly not more than fifty. I don't believe there are five miles of fences in the whole tract. This wild region is alive with deer, black bears, wild-cats, panthers (called tigers by the Floridians), coons, opossums, wild turkeys, ducks, and game of all kinds. The tigers, wildcats, and bears flock to the hammocks skirting the seashore, picking up a hog or a pig now and then, and falling back on the oysters, which fringe the shores of the rivers in bunches as large as waterpails, for dessert. It is no uncommon thing to kill bears, deer, wildcats, or even tigers in the thick hammock within gunshot of the hotel. All of these animals, however, excepting the tiger, will flee in terror at the sight of a human being. But few bears and tigers are seen during the winter. I am told that the tigers only attack a man at night, and never then unless the animal is suffering from extreme hunger.

HOW STRANGERS ARE FRIGHTENED.

I have been particular in describing Smyrna, because, while its climate, hunting, and fishing are superior to those of any other place supporting a hotel in Florida, it is really known to but one in fifteen hundred of those who visit the State for health or recreation. Jacksonville and vicinity catch one-third of the winter visitors, and hold them. They are told of the discomforts attending a journey to St. Augustine, and are assured that the climate of Jacksonville is far superior to that of the Upper St. Johns, which is declared to be very unhealthy on account of the swamp fogs. Probably 5,000 people believe this, and settle down on the threshold of Florida for the winter. A majority of visitors drift to St. Augustine, which is far superior to Jacksonville. They are assured by the disinterested boarding-house keepers and hotel proprietors of St. Augustine that the Upper St. Johns is alarmingly unhealthy and that the steamers bring down a dozen corpses of invalids each day. One-third of the strangers take this down unsalted, and anchor in St. Augustine for the winter. The others float up the St. Johns to Palatka, Mellonville, and Enterprise. They then imagine they have reached the jumping off place. After they have been housed for a few weeks, they possibly hear that there are such places as Smyrna and Titusville, and that they are supplied with hotels. Instantly every native is on the alert. Horrible stories about mosquitoes, bad roads, rotten steamboats, and so on, are dinned in the ears of the visitors. Their wives are frightened, and they themselves settle down where they are, and shell out their money, thanking the liars for their kindness. Up to the 10th of March just four strangers, including myself, had succeeded in reaching Smyrna.

THROUGH THE PINES.

I came thirty-two miles through the pines from Enterprise, hiring a team of mules and a rusty but staunch rockaway wagon for $6. The natives of Enterprise sarcastically advised me to take a boat along, declaring that before I reached Smyrna I would find it more useful than the wagon. Though the season was dry, I found four miles of the road a canal, containing about a foot of water. The bottom, however, was sandy and hard, and as the mules never struck into a trot, there was no delay. We forded Spruce Creek, but the water did not reach the wagon body. On this stretch of thirty-two miles I saw but three houses, and met but two men. One was the mail carrier and the other a naturalized Vermonter named Wickwire,[4] who was toting a load of wild orange bushes to Enterprise. The mail is carried on horseback. The carrier had tethered his horse in the scrub at the side of the road, built a fire, cooked his breakfast, and was fast asleep in the shade of the saw palmettos with his mail bag for a pillow. He makes a trip once a week. Not a fence was to be seen for thirty-two miles. One of the three houses was surrounded by a flock of sand hill cranes, who had been tamed, and who walked to the roadside as we passed, looked at us sideways, and commented upon our appearance with cracked voices. At 2 P.M. we stopped the mules, built a fire of pine cones, cooked coffee, and took dinner. As we drove off, the fire had lapped up the rotten pine branches near it, and was jumping up the trees with a vigor that indicated a fair forest conflagration. Everybody seems to delight in firing the Florida woods. Where there have been large "burns" the hunting is the best, as the deer turn out to eat the tender grasses that spring up in the burnt district. The soil was white sand, occasionally tinged with a red color. Where the trees were high the road was good, as it was covered with pine siftings and rotten cones, which made it hard and smooth. There was not a hill nor even a rise of ground to be seen. At one time a group of deer dashed across our track, but not within rifle range. We passed several marshy lakes filled with ducks and alligators. It was dusk when we reached the tropical hammock near Smyrna. For almost a mile we drove through a natural tunnel formed by the green waxy foliage of the cabbage palmettos, and lighted by millions of fire flies, and then emerged upon the sward fronting the hotel.

WEALTHY SPORTSMEN.

A few wealthy gentlemen have discovered the advantages of New Smyrna, and are annual visitors. They love hunting and fishing, and keep their own sail boats, engaging their favorite guides every year. Among these gentlemen are Mr. Lawrence, an uncle of the Hon. Abraham H. Lawrence of New York city; Mr. Benson, President of the Brooklyn Gas Company; Mr. A. J. Alexander, the famous breeder of thoroughbred stock, of Woodburn Farm, Ky.; and Mr. S. T. Brown of the Mechanics' and Traders' Bank, New York. Messrs. Alexander, Lawrence, and Benson have been here this winter. Mr. Alexander spent seven weeks in hunting deer and wild cats. His guide was Capt. Frank Sams,[5] one of the most noted hunters on the eastern shore of Florida. They brought in twenty-nine deer and much smaller game, but no wild cats. Every day, except Sundays and rainy or cloudy days, was spent in hunting. At no time did they go over seven miles from the hotel. They hunted on small marsh ponies, and made a novel show as they rode off under the palmettoes, with their rifles balanced on the pommels of their saddles and their hound dogs under their arms. The contrast was laughable. Mr. Alexander's legs were very long and almost dragged upon the ground, while Sams's were very short, hardly clearing his saddle. Mr. Alexander wore high-topped boots, with silver spurs, both carefully polished every morning by Ben, his negro servant, while Sams wore low-cut shoes and a solitary iron spur as big as a small-sized cart-wheel. The Kentuckian wore a stiff black felt hat and a leather belt strapped about his waist filled with metallic cartridges, while Sams dashed off with an old slouched hat and an old-fashioned hunting rig, as if to the manor born. They carried their dogs on horseback until they got beyond the cockspur boundary. The cockspur is a burr or spur which works into the feet of the dogs, and renders them useless until the spur is removed. Deer are hunted in the scrub beneath the pines, and the savannas running parallel with them, though they are frequently found in the hammocks. The savannas are from 50 to 200 yards in width, and frequently many miles in length. They are covered with wire and saw grass, and in many places are wet and swampy.

DEER HUNTING IN FLORIDA.

Dogs are fairly trained and strangely named. Sams's best dog is a small hound, which he calls Scavenger. When she strikes the trail of a deer, she makes her way through the scrub, so slowly that she is easily followed. As the track freshens and she nears the game, she gently whimpers. This is a warning to the hunter to be on the alert. When the deer breaks cover in the palmetto scrub, it is like the starting of a rabbit in the furze. The hunter must be as cool as the heart of a cucumber, and as quick as lightning, or he will lose his game. There will be a bound or two over the stunted palmettos, the flash of a white tail, and the deer is gone. Frequently, the hunter will be compelled to turn half-way round in his saddle to take aim, and this must be done in a second. If he shoots and misses or wounds the deer, away go the dogs and marsh ponies leaping the scrub like mad, and endeavoring to head off the game. When seeking or following a trail at a distance from the hunters, the dogs are encouraged by shouts of "Hoo-ya-a-a," "Sick-'em-fellow," and so on. This sets the dogs baying, and the hunter easily finds and follows them. Only the best dogs are useful in deer-hunting, but when a sportsman is after bears or wild-cats all the curs in creation can be placed to good advantage.

A Florida deer hunters' camp, 1880s. Courtesy of Florida State Archives.

RETURN OF THE DEER HUNTERS.

The hunters looked odd when they left the hotel in the morning, but they appeared grotesque on their return at sundown. Mr. Alexander came in one day with a buck thrown across the pommel of his saddle, and a wild turkey, two whooping cranes, and a coon stringing down the side of his horse. He looked like a travelling butcher's shop. Sams was even more heavily freighted. His horse carried a heavy doe, three coons, two wild turkeys, and about a dozen black ducks. He had borne the doe on his shoulders nearly two hundred yards before he had strapped it on his horse. She was so fat that Sams declared that he greased his gun for three weeks afterward by simply drawing it under his arms.

Mrs. Alexander occasionally accompanied the hunters. She is a remarkable horsewoman, and dashed over the scrub in the chase like a swallow on the wing.

A LEAF FROM HISTORY.

While Mr. Alexander passed his hours in hunting, Mr. Lawrence spent his time in fishing. His guide, or "nephew" as the natives term it, was Bartolo C. Pacetti,[6] a descendant of the Minorcans brought to Florida a hundred years ago by Turnbull. Turnbull was an Englishman who owned a land grant at Smyrna. He had an idea that vast sums of money could be made by cultivating indigo in Florida. He induced several hundred Minorcans and Greeks to emigrate and furnished them transportation, promising them so many acres of land a piece after they had worked for him a given number of years. The poor foreigners found themselves but little better than slaves. Pacetti tells me that he has heard his grandfather say that they were worked without intermission from dawn until dark, and then dismissed with the coarsest kind of food. They were confined and even whipped on the slightest provocation. This lasted three or four years, when the colony filtered away to St. Augustine, and complained to the Spanish authorities. Turnbull was arrested and sent to Spain in irons. He afterward died in prison. But he made the tropical wilderness blossom in doubloons. His indigo scheme was a success, and if he had only conciliated his laborers he would probably have become one of the richest men in the world. He has left his mark behind him. Wild indigo is scattered throughout the country. It is not cultivated because Yankee blueing has superseded it, and it would not pay to raise it. Two canals cut through the soft coquina rock for the purpose of draining Turnbull swamp still remain almost hidden in tropical undergrowth. A shattered stone pier, once hundreds of feet in length, can be seen half a mile below the hotel. Stone wells and ruins of stone houses are found in dense thickets, and appearances indicate that a large part of Turnbull swamp has been under cultivation, either by the Spaniards centuries ago or by Turnbull himself.

THE CURSE OF FLORIDA FISHERMEN.

Mr. Lawrence went fishing every favorable day in a cat-rigged sail boat, called the Amanda, and invariably returned with a boat load of sheepshead, drums, groupers, snappers, and kingfish. Occasionally you would see the genial old gentleman spinning along against wind and tide with a lily-iron fast in the back of an enormous shark. He was the most inveterate fisherman that I ever saw. The best fishing is in the channels skirting the mangrove swamps. When there is a fair breeze it is glorious sport, but when there is no wind one of Pharoah's [sic] plagues is poured upon the fishermen. Quintillions of sand-flies or midges boil out of the mangroves, and gather about the luckless sportsman. The fish may bite every minute, but the sandflies will bite every thousandth part of a second. And such bites! The insects cover your hands, your wrists, your face, and the back of your neck. They go down to the roots of your beard and hair, and revel in your blood. An attack from musquitoes is a luxury after a sandfly on-slaught. You can smoke until you are blind, and a sandfly will laugh at you. The bites will itch for two weeks, and itch continually. A man's skin will resemble a nutmeg grater for days, and his face will look as though he had a clear case of small-pox. I have fished probably twelve days in Smyrna, and during this time have thrice fallen into the clutches of the sandflies.

ACRES OF FISH IN CONFLICT.

But the fishing surpasses comprehension. Mr. S. T. Brown, of the Mechanics' and Traders' Bank of your city, and two companions have caught over one thousand pounds of sheepshead in one afternoon with hook and line, and got in before sundown at that. The little strait in front of the hotel is frequently so packed with channel bass, sheepshead, and other fish, that it is impossible to get a boat through. The narrow channels in the river are occasionally fairly choked with the choicest kind of fish. At such times sharks and porpoises descend upon the multitude and slaughter them without mercy. In September and October channel bass throng the inlets like buffaloes on the prairie. There are acres upon acres of them. Frequently the water is black with them as far as the eye can reach. The mullet season is then at its height. They are more numerous even than the bass. They are the legitimate prey of the bass. When five acres of bass in layers four feet thick strike ten acres of mullet there is a slight commotion in the water. The bass slaughter the mullet most unmercifully, and occasionally a school of sharks interfere and attack both mullet and bass indiscriminately. At such times the air is darkened with thousands of screaming gulls, which hover over the battle field and joyfully pounce upon the dead fish that reach the surface of the water. At this season of the year thousands of mullet are continually leaping from the water, and at night when the tide is high the air is filled with the music of the drumfish crushing the coon oysters ashore at low tide. The drumfish is a remarkable fish. His throat is paved with teeth on the Belgian pavement plan. He sucks the oyster in his throat, cracks the shell, and swallows the dainty. He is a game fish, is striped like a sheepshead, though built more like a yellow perch, and has not the sheep lip and teeth which give the sheepshead his name. Some of them weigh as much as a hundred pounds.

Monuments of the First Floridians

Turtle Mound, believed to be the largest shell mound in the United States, is no longer "a day's ride from civilization," as it was when Amos Cummings visited the site. Today this archaeological site, which is more than 600 feet long and 35 feet high—Cummings estimated its height at 80 feet!—lies within the Canaveral National Seashore. It is listed in the National Register of Historic Places and is recorded in the State of Florida Archaeological Site File as site 8Vo109 (8 for Florida; Vo for Volusia County, and 109 for the 109th site recorded in that county).

The mound is immense. The National Park Service estimates it contains 1.5 million bushels of oyster shells, the remains of thousands of pre-Columbian meals that were deliberately stacked up by local Indians to make the mound. In his book *Space and Time Perspectives in Northern St. Johns Archeology, Florida,* University of Florida archaeologist John M. Goggin dates the mound to ca. A.D. 750–1565. It would not be at all surprising if much earlier shell deposits were within and under the mound.

Coastal heights are a rare sight indeed in Florida, and Turtle Mound stood out. It is marked on early maps and was used as a navigational point for ships. It drew the attention of colonial-period Spaniards, who recorded that it was called "Surruque" by the local Indians, who may have spoken a dialect of the Timucuan language. The modern name of the mound comes from its shape, that of a huge turtle.

In this article (from the April 17, 1893, *New York Sun* and the April 23 *Weekly Sun*), Cummings mentions Sir Francis William Sykes. I delved a bit into historical records to try to find out about him and to try to determine what happened to the archaeological collections he purportedly took back to England. Sir Francis, a baronet, was a career military officer who was born June 10, 1822, and died January 1, 1866 (*Modern English Biography,* London, 1921, 6:654). But Sir Francis probably was never in Florida. In *Brevard County* (45), John Eriksen says it was Sir Tatton Sykes who had a hunting camp near New Found Harbor at the south end of Merritt Island in 1857. Sir Tatton, fifth baronet, was born March 13, 1826, and died May 4, 1913 (*Who Was Who 1897–1915,* London, 1935, reprint of the 1916 edition, 510). It is likely that he was the person Cummings meant (Sir Tatton's father, also Sir Tatton, would have been eighty-five years old in 1857, and it is very doubtful that he was the person responsible for sending "one hundred and sixty eight perfect roseate spoonbills" back to England, after shooting "over five hundred to secure this number," as reported in Rambler, *Guide to Florida*, 137).

Cummings mentions several archaeological sites in the article. Old Cone's "favorite resort" is most likely the Orange Mound (8Or1) noted by Le Baron on his 1885 *Map of Brevard County*, well south of Lake Harney near the mouth of Salt Creek on the west side of the St. Johns River in Orange County (see Rouse, *A Survey of Indian River Archeology*, 127–29), and dating to ca. 2000–500 B.C. Philadelphia archaeologist Clarence B. Moore dug in the site in the early 1890s, as reported in his 1893 article "Certain Shell Heaps of the St. John's River, Florida, hitherto Unexplored (Third Paper)."

I love Amos Cummings's description of the view from Turtle Mound. Today you can enjoy that same view without leaving your desk. Log on to http://virtual volusia.com/Canaveral3.html and http://virtualvolusia.com/Canaveral4.html; two Web cams on the mound provide panoramic vistas. Take a look.

8

FLORIDA'S INDIAN MOUNDS

THE MYSTERIOUS MONUMENTS OF AN EXTINCT RACE.

A Visit to the Great Turtle Mound—A Lost Pillar of Hercules—The Disappointed Eagles and the Wet Vultures—Sir Francis Sykes's Skeletons—Ancient Pottery— Were the Mound Builders Freemasons?—Startling Discovery of an Old Alligator Hunter.

DE SOTO GROVES, FLORIDA,[1] MARCH 20.—I visited Turtle Mound in a cat-rigged sail boat. With a fair wind it is a day's ride from civilization. The mound is on the beach side of Musquito Lagoon, nearly a hundred miles south of St. Augustine. About eighty feet in height, it covers nearly an acre of ground, and can be seen at a great distance looming up on the eastern horizon far above the palmetto scrub fringing the ocean. It is shaped like an immense turtle. This shape gives it its name. It is the highest point of land on the eastern coast of Florida, and stands within three hundred yards of the roaring ocean surf. From the deck of a vessel ten miles at sea it resembles a ruined fortification upon a hill.

THE MOUND.

Turtle Mound is a great heap of very large oyster shells covered with from one to two feet of dirt. On the northwest corner the rain has washed away the dirt, leaving a perpendicular bank of shells, eighty feet high. The builders of the work evidently raised it with the greatest care. Every shell was placed in a given position. Where the slide has occurred the oyster shells rest in plumbed layers, with the smooth surface facing the sky. A stone wall could not have been erected with more precision. The mound is alive with tropical shrubbery. Wild orange trees loaded with fruit wave on its summit above an almost impenetrable thicket. A hollow covered with rank vegetation has been scooped out of the top of the hill. It has an easy slope and is probably twelve feet in depth. It looks as though the bones of some huge animal had been dug out of it in ages past. Mosquito Lagoon washes the western base of the mound.

Turtle Mound as it appeared in 1915. This photo was taken by E. H. Sellards of the Florida Geological Survey. Courtesy of Florida State Archives.

FROM THE TOP OF TURTLE MOUND.

I found a small deer path which led from a little sandspit up the side of the hill. The path, however, was soon lost in the thicket, and it was with the greatest difficulty that I finally succeeded in forcing my way through the thorny undergrowth and sharp-pointed Spanish bayonets to the top of the mound. Even then the shrubbery was higher than my head, and the wild oranges were higher than the shrubbery. I spent half an hour in forcing myself to a point of observation.

The view was magnificent. I stood upon the verge of a precipice of oyster shells. There was a stiff east wind. Away to the north I could distinctly see the white-capped breakers dashing over the bar at Smyrna. With a good glass the lighthouse at Cape Canaveral, forty miles to the southward, could be seen. The ocean view was unsurpassed. Triple lines of foam were breaking upon the beach, a hundred porpoises were rolling outside, and an immense school of large fish were skipping from wave to wave, nearly a mile from shore. Two miles north a bear was loping along the ocean beach, apparently hunting for turtle eggs. There was no sail in sight, but the dangerous nature of the coast was shown in the old wrecks that dotted the southern sands. The Hillsborough river,[2] with its green mangrove island, stretched away toward St. Augustine, and Mosquito lagoon bore away toward Dummitt's Grove.[3] A thin line of sand, covered with the inevitable saw palmetto, ran north and south as far as

View from Turtle Mound in 1929. This photo also was taken by E. H. Sellards. Courtesy of Florida State Archives.

the eye could reach, shutting off the river and lagoon from the ocean. On the west was Shipyard Island, fringed with white cranes and herons, and beyond that marshes loaded with ducks, while beyond all lay the great pine woods lapping the St. John's river and losing themselves in the everglades of the South.

THE WET VULTURES.

Five hundred feet above me were a dozen bald eagles sweeping through the air in great circles, with piercing cries, and watching a half dozen ospreys that had been fishing near the mound. Near by was an island covered with dead mangroves. A hundred vultures sat upon the limbs of these leafless trees, with their wings spread out as if pasted to the wood. It had been raining, and the wet vultures were drying their feathers in the sun. The mangroves had been killed by the frost over forty years ago; yet none of them showed any signs of decay. The mangrove is a tough tree, for it draws its sustenance from the salt water, and the salt is drawn up into the fibres of the wood, preserving it for centuries. Northern settlers have been known to use mangrove for stove wood, but not long, for while it makes a hot fire, the salt in the wood destroys a stove within two weeks.

WHO BUILT TURTLE MOUND.

No mountains nor hills could be seen from the mound; nothing but one vast flat surface veined with lagoons and rivers and covered with great splots of wax-like vegetation. The builders of Turtle Mound are unknown. They were undoubtedly a race of Indians who were wiped out of existence centuries ago. The Seminoles and other Florida tribes declare that they have no traditions that explain the mystery. They look upon the mounds with nearly the same awe as the whites. What is singular with regard to Turtle Mound is the fact that there are no oysters excepting the small coon oyster, within thirty miles. It would be interesting to know why these shells were brought from an oyster region far away, and so carefully deposited at this spot. Some think that the mound builders of Florida were contemporary with the mound builders of the West. They believe that the whole State was once under their control, and that thousands of years ago they were accustomed to visit Turtle Mound once a year to fill themselves with fat oysters which might at that time have been found in the vicinity, and pile the shells in layers as they now appear in the mound. This may have been a religious observance with the Indians. But the whole thing is speculation. Nobody knows anything about it, and there is no probability that any one will ever discover the secret.

DR. WALLACE'S DISCOVERIES.[4]

Indian mounds are scattered throughout the state, but Turtle Mound is the only one made of oyster shells. Three miles below it are two mounds, side by side, about sixty-feet in height.[5] Dr. Wallace, formerly of Savannah, and a well-known Confederate machinist during the rebellion, has made a residence on the summit of one of these mounds; on the other he has a blacksmith's shop. There is nothing fancy about the house, but it is comfortable, and the Doctor spends his time in hunting and fishing and doing odd jobs of iron work for men living from fifty to a hundred miles away. The mounds are covered with bananas and bird peppers. The bananas are of a delicious flavor, and far ahead of those raised on the St. John's. Beads and arrowheads of red flint have been exhumed from the mounds, and they seem to be filled with human bones. The Doctor, however, has made no excavations, and takes more interest in his bananas, guavas and red peppers than he does in his mounds. The mounds are squatted upon the borders of a rich hammock, and the Doctor is doing his best to make it productive. With salt water on either side of him, he claims to be out of the line of frost, and declares that he can raise all kinds of tropical fruits.

SIR FRANCIS SYKES'S SKELETONS.

One of the most interesting mounds in the state is that at Burnham's Grove, five miles west of Cape Canaveral. Situated in the centre of Capt. Burnham's celebrated orange grove,[6] it is now but a heap of dirt.[7] Some years ago Sir

Francis Sykes, a British nobleman, visited Cape Canaveral. By Capt. Burnham's permissions he excavated the mound, and took out twenty-seven complete skeletons, which he forwarded to England. The skeletons were found lying side by side in a circle, with their heads toward the centre of the mound. The bones showed that their owners were men of powerful physique. They must have averaged six feet in height. Their shoulders were broad, and the jaw bones particularly of remarkable length and strength. The skulls were very thick, and the thigh bones long and solid.

Sir Francis Sykes also took out of the mound several complete pieces of pottery in the form of vases. These were sent to England. To-day the mound is strewn with bones and fragments of ancient pottery. The vases were primitive in their design. They appear to have been made of clay, and baked. The broken pieces are creased in diamond-shaped squares, as if an effort at ornamentation had been made.[8] It is probable, however, that this was caused through backing the clay against a wicker palmetto basket, as this would hold it in place until it was thoroughly baked. The inside of the vases was blackened by fire. The clay may have been pasted inside the basket, and then hardened by a fat-pine fire built within the vase. This is the only pottery known to have been taken from an Indian mound in Florida. It would look better in the Smithsonian Institute than in a British museum.

DR. WHITFELDT'S DISCOVERY.[9]

I found a remarkable mound on Merritt's Island, at the mouth of New-Found Harbor. It was near the house of Dr. Whitfeldt, a German from Philadelphia, who is the only man that has preempted a homestead on one of the richest islands on the Southern coast. The mound was on a little ridge that forms the backbone of the island.[10] It commanded a view of the Indian river on the west, and Banana river and the ocean on the east. This mound has never been explored, though it promises strange developments. Dr. Whitfeldt told me that he once spent two hours in digging into it, with good success. Of course there were the usual number of skeletons, but in addition to these he unearthed a dozen arrowheads and a half dozen plumbs.[11] Five of these plumbs were rough, made out of fish bones and coquina rock. The sixth is a kind of dark flint, beautifully polished, and as true as if it had been turned by the most accurate machinery. There is no stone resembling it in Florida. Red flint, out of which the arrow heads are made, is unknown in the state.[12] This flint is so pure in color that it resembles agate. In no other mound have plumbs of any kind been discovered. It is evident that the mound builders understood the use of the plumb. If so, they are probably the only race of savages that used the instrument. Whitfeldt suggested that the Indians were Free Masons, and that the plumb was a masonic emblem, which they had buried with the dead. He afterward presented me with the plumb as a token for the first newspaper man that had visited the Indian river country.

OTHER INDIAN MOUNDS.

Between Titusville and Sand Lake[13] a beautiful Indian mound raises itself among the pines north of the road. It is covered with circular rows of trees, but is entirely free from undergrowth. This mound has never been explored. It is one of the largest in that part of Florida, and seemed to be perfect in its cone-like formation.

A mile above Enterprise stands what is called the Shell Mound.[14] It is composed of thin white shells resembling snail shells. The country thereabouts is covered with these shells. This mound has been partly overhauled. A few beads and the usual quantity of bones were brought to light. An immense sulphur spring stands within one hundred and fifty yards of this mound.[15] The spring is over a hundred feet deep and a hundred yards in circumference. The water is a delicate green in color—"a lovely color for a silk dress," a lady remarked when she first saw it. About a thousand gallons a minute pour from this spring. Its depths reveal schools of tiny fish, which sport about the water coated with sulphur. The spring is in the woods surrounded by cabbage palmettos and half filled with sulphur-varnished logs.

OLD CONE'S STARTLING THEORY.[16]

An Indian mound, known as the Orange Mound, stands on the banks of the St. John's, a few miles above Lake Harney. It is fairly smothered in orange trees, and it is a favorite resort for Cone, the alligator hunter. Says Cone:

"I've ketched the biggest 'gators roun' that thar Orange Mound uv any place on the St. John's. But I want you to remember one thing. These here fellers what pretends to know everything about these here Indian mounds don't know nuthin' about 'em. Now, they're always sayin' that these here Indians buried their dead Indians in these here mounds. What I want to know is if them thar Indians had rifles, because if they had rifles old Cone is wrong and them thar fellers is right."

"No," I said; "the mound builders were all dead before gunpowder was invented."

"Then," replied the alligator hunter, "them thar fellers is wrong an' old Cone is right, an' you can't git shut uv it. I'll tell you why. Because two weeks ago I dug up a skull, an' it had a bullit hole in it, and when I picked it up the bullet was there, too, a rattlin' around in the skull. I tell you them was white men buried thar, an' you can't git shut of it."

There was no doubt of the truth of Cone's story, for he dropped into his skiff, which was towing astern the steamboat, and produced the skull. It may have been the head of an old Spanish soldier, the skull of a murdered man, or the cranium of some poor victim of the Seminole war, but there is no doubt the owner was killed by a bullet, and that Cone dug up the bones at the Orange Mound.

There are two Indian mounds on the right bank of the St. John's, just above Lake Monroe.[17] Capt. Tom Reeves of New York, who has spent eighteen winters in Florida to avoid suffering from asthma, has dug over these mounds for hours. Arrow heads and beads he has found in profusion, but nothing else except bones.

Such are the Florida mounds. It is estimated that there are over five hundred of them scattered throughout the State. They are even found upon the hammocks of the Everglades. All but one have been used as burial places. Turtle Mound stands alone with its oyster shells. No bones have been discovered beneath its surface. It looms up on the eastern shore of Florida like a stray pillar of Hercules, silent and alone; but if it could speak, it might tell a story as old as the siege of Troy, if not as interesting.

"Hopelessly Doomed"

Amos Cummings was not very optimistic about the future of Florida farmers. He was even less optimistic about the ability of the state's politicians to provide informed and fair leadership for Florida's residents. Poor soil, mosquitoes, fleas, sand flies, cockroaches, horse flies, and ignorant and corrupt politicians left him with "no hope for Florida." Things were so bad, so despairing, that Cummings was forced to compare the Florida of 1873 to her southern sister state South Carolina, which in his mind was truly a lost cause. The Civil War had devastated much of the South, and Reconstruction reforms held little prospect.

Cummings, of course, was wrong. As he would write in 1893 in his article "The New Sugar Kingdom," a "once dead state" would find new life, stimulated in part by the draining of thousands of acres in South Florida and turning it into rich farmland.

Agricultural growth and Florida's development, however, have come at a price: the destruction of many of the state's natural areas. In 1873, it was Florida's unique wildness that drew visitors like Amos Cummings. Today the things he saw no longer exist. The land and its resources have been abused, perhaps beyond repair. Would Cummings ever have believed that a century and a third after he visited Fort Capron at the southern frontier of the still-expanding United States, even Florida's freshwater supply would be under attack?

If we draw a line from William Bartram to Amos Cummings to the present, charting natural Florida, it does not take much brain power to see where that line is headed. Florida's future looks grim.

Cummings dated this article April 1, 1873. It was not published in the *New York Sun* until two months later, on May 28, and it appeared in the *Weekly Sun* still later, on May 30.

I keep wondering how Amos Cummings got his articles to his editors back in New York. Did he write them longhand on legal-size pads of paper and then send them through the U.S. mail? Were the articles sent by telegraph? Or did he actually carry them back with him? One thing is certain: whatever method he used worked.

9

THE FARMING IN FLORIDA

THE MUSIC-LOVING COWS OF THE INDIAN RIVER.

What Northern Farmers Can do in the Land of Flowers, and What They Can't do—Land Sharks—Big Sugar Cane and Big Potatoes—Mosquitoes, Fleas, Sand Flies, Cockroaches, and Biting Horse Flies—Price of Land—Troubles of Northern Farmers.

Fort Capron, Fla., April 1.—About three years ago a farmer named Sawyer[1] came to New Smyrna from New Hampshire. He found a fine hammock ridge three miles south of the hotel and preempted it. It was situated on the edge of the Hillsborough river, and covered with beautiful cabbage palmettos. The great Turnbull swamp margined it on the west. Sawyer went to work with the indomitable energy of the true Yankee farmer. He built a log shanty, eight feet square, and thatched it with palmetto leaves. He was alone, having neither wife nor children. Up at daylight in the morning, he worked until dark, cutting out the thick tropical undergrowth, and burning out the sinewy trees. The hot summer days came, but the New Hampshire farmer took no rest. Morning, noon, and night he labored the same as he would have worked upon a farm among the Granite hills. The climate failed to make him lazy. His nearest neighbor was three miles away. Occasionally he paid him a visit, but always after dark. His furniture was of the primitive order, and he slept upon a bed of Southern moss which he gathered from the cypress trees in Turnbull swamp. Winter was the same to him as summer. It did not lighten his labor, except that the days were shorter. There was neither snow, ice, nor frost. In fact he could raise more in January and February than he could in August or September.

MAKING A HOME.

Within a few months Sawyer cleared up two acres of ground. He planted it with corn, beans, and potatoes, occasionally setting out a bitter sweet orange tree. The potatoes and beans turned out well, but the corn did not amount to much. The orange trees, however, thrived wonderfully. Sawyer lived upon the fish and oysters that filled the river and upon the vegetables that he had cultivated. The woods were full of game, and he never suffered unless through want of a rasher of bacon. In the spring of the year the beach was lined with turtles' eggs, and these were always easy to get. Wild plums and grapes as sweet as honey flourished in the forests, while oranges and lemons could be picked by the bushel in nearly every thicket.

Once in a while a neighbor called upon Sawyer. The latter treated his visitor courteously, but never stopped work to talk with him. The New England man was cautioned against excessive labor, but he insisted that it would never hurt a man to work, and paid no attention to the warning. The second summer was unusually hot. One day a native discovered the Yankee farmer hoeing corn in the burning sun without hat or shirt. His skin was blistered by the heat, and his face was dripping with sweat. Sawyer declared that the spirits had visited him during the night, and told him that Adam had worked in the Garden of Eden without shirt or hat, and that he would find it more comfortable to follow Adam's example. He declared that the spirits came to him every night, and dictated to him long reams of manuscript. The neighbor was invited to come at night, and hear what the spirits had said.

THE RESULT OF OVERWORK.

It was evident that Sawyer was becoming crazy. One day he disappeared. He was gone for a week. When he returned he roamed the woods at night beating a tambourine. He said the spirits had sent him the instrument. But there was no let-up to his work. He hardly stopped for dinner. Day after day he toiled in the broiling sun until his white skin turned as brown as the hide of an Indian and his blue eyes faded through want of rest. By this time he had about eight acres under cultivation, but he planted as he had planted in New Hampshire, and the result was not encouraging.

As the summer advanced Sawyer discarded all his clothing, and went to his work stark naked. One day he appeared at Lowd's hotel,[2] Smyrna. Meeting the proprietor he stooped and kissed his feet before Mr. Lowd was aware of what he was at. From this time on he paid but little attention to his clearing. Whenever he saw a neighbor he would cautiously creep up behind him, throw his arms around his neck and kiss him. At one time a colored man stood in front of the hotel tinkering a sailboat. Sawyer saw him and carefully approached him. He had not seen the negro's face. Suddenly he threw his arms about him and turned his head to salute him. As the black face was revealed, the insane man stared at it for a full minute, and then ran as if his life depended upon his speed. The natives say that this was the first spark of sense that Sawyer had shown for months.

THE MUSIC-LOVING COWS OF THE INDIAN RIVER

THE WORK OF THE SPIRITS.

A week afterward he came into Smyrna dressed in white muslin and beating his tambourine. The spirits again appeared to him. They told him that his brother was waiting for him in Savannah, and they promised to meet him in the hammock back of the hotel, and carry him to that city. He said he was going to sail through the air over the tops of the palmettos on a broomstick, and that he would reach Savannah that night. He was seen no more at Smyrna, but was found a week afterward nearly starved, wandering in the great pine woods near Enterprise. Capt. Brook[3] passed him down the river, and he reached his home in New Hampshire within a month through the generosity of steamboat and railroad men, who gave him free passage. He recovered his senses after spending some time in an asylum, and his neighbors say that they have received letters from him announcing his intention of returning to Smyrna as soon as he can raise money enough to pay his fare. As he has not lived upon his homestead for nine months, the land, with all its improvements, is open to the first man mean enough to squat upon it. Such a person, however, would merit and receive rough treatment from poor Sawyer's neighbors.

LAND IN FLORIDA.

This is the story of a Northern farmer in Florida. The truth is that no farmer in the enjoyment of good health has any business in the Land of Flowers. A farmer in poor health can barely earn a living here, and that is all. Half of the land is composed of shells and sand. Sometimes you will strike what seems to be a rich black muck, but give it a kick with the toe of your boot, and the inevitable sand will appear. The hammocks which dot the immense sandy scrubs like oases in a desert are unusually rich, but neither grain nor hay can be raised upon them. Much of this land is open to preemption, but the carpetbaggers are scooping it in through legislative land grants, and a preemptor is generally sure of a lawsuit as soon as he improves his homestead. Good hammock land can be had for from ten shillings to five dollars an acre. Land sharks roam the State looking for Northern victims. They can be found upon every steamboat and in every hotel, and can take the eye-teeth out of a Northern farmer quicker than a pocketbook dropper can do it in New York. It is due to the Floridians to say that nine-tenths of these sharks are Northern men. I have seen a dozen farmers from Wisconsin, Iowa, and Michigan here this winter, but I have not seen one who has located a farm. The first look at the soil frightens them.

"Hopelessly Doomed"

THE RICHEST HAMMOCKS.

A Northern horse, or cow, or dog cannot live in Florida. There is neither sweet grass, clover, nor timothy. They will not grow. Neither will wheat, rye, oats, barley, or corn. Both Irish and sweet potatoes thrive well in winter, but it would cost a fortune to get them to New York. Peas, beans, cauliflowers, asparagus, turnips, beets, radishes, cabbages, strawberries, and innumerable other vegetables ripen along the Indian river in December, January, and February, but they might as well ripen in the moon so far as a market is concerned.

I believe that the Indian river hammocks contain the richest land in the United States. Capt. M. O. Burnham,[4] of Cape Canaveral, has raised sugar cane that will average over two quarts of juice to the stalk. One cane alone produced a gallon, a quart, and a pint of raw syrup. I saw a stalk that had fifty-two joints, averaging four inches to the joint. So rank does the cane grow that many of the stalks tassel like corn. Burnham planted this hammock with cane many years ago. It produced immense crops for seven years, without manuring or putting a hoe to the ground. But the Captain's nearest neighbor is twelve miles distant, and there is neither doctor, school house, post-office, or church within thirty miles. His only way of reaching them is by a cat-rigged sail boat, and he is entirely dependent upon the caprice of the wind. All his children and grandchildren were born far away from any physician or schoolmaster. I went to his house at Cape Canaveral, and his good wife declared that a lady in our party was the only woman who had visited them in four years. The Captain has a wonderful sugar field and a rare orange grove, but there is no way of getting sugar or orange to market.

A GERMAN FARMER'S EXPERIENCE.

Col. Titus[5] raised a sweet potato at Sand Point[6] that weighed eighteen pounds and three-quarters, and Dr. Whitfeldt[7] of Merritt's Island produced one that made thirty pounds kick the beam. The Doctor showed me a sugar cane seventeen feet long, weighing thirteen pounds and a half, and his hammock is not nearly so rich as Burnham's. His cane was bending with saccharine sweetness, but as he was compelled to grind it by hand he did not think it worth his while to cut it. The bears and deer were grinding it for him. The Doctor is a hard worker, and has 160 acres of marvellous richness, but there is no market for his products. He can't even give them away. A year ago he raised a thousand cabbages. They headed in January. One of his neighbors stopped at the Doctor's house in a sailboat. In fact, this is the only way of reaching the house. Whitfeldt pointed to his cabbages, saying, "You are welcome to a boat-load of them if you want them."

THE MUSIC-LOVING COWS OF THE INDIAN RIVER

"Well," replied the Floridian, with characteristic laziness, "I reckon I don't keer a heap about 'em, but ef you'm a mind to heave a few of 'em in the sharpy I'll tote 'em off for you."

The water was so shoal that the boat lay about thirty feet from the shore. The Doctor actually waded out and filled the craft with cabbages, while the Cracker looked on and sucked his pipe.

Dr. Whitfeldt is a German from Philadelphia. He went to Merritt's Island about four years ago with his wife and two little children, and preempted his hammock, paying the State $1.25 an acre. He built a shanty, thatched roof and sides with palmetto, and began to clear up his place. His worthy wife was compelled to cook out doors. Merritt's Island is about thirty-five miles long and from twelve to fifteen wide. Whitfeldt and an old hermit are the only inhabitants. By hard work, the Doctor soon succeeded in getting enough drifted timber from the ocean beach to put up a sort of a house. He began to raise chickens, but the opossums ate more of them than the doctor's family. The bears attacked his sugar cane, and he was compelled to cut lanes through the stalks for the purpose of flanking the robbers. Mosquitos visited him winter and summer. In January and February he could grin and bear it, but in July and August his wife was compelled to sit in the open air surrounded by a triple mosquito bar of fine Swiss muslin while she was doing her sewing. Occasionally the sand flies made a descent upon them. These insects were worse than mosquitos. "But the worst of all," said Mrs. Whitfeldt, "are the big horse flies. I can put up with the sand flies and mosquitos, but the horse flies are utterly unendurable." The flies appear about the middle of May and last until the end of June. The air is filled with them. They buzz night and day. They are as persistent as mosquitos, and bite with savage energy. Touch the butt of a lighted cigar to a man's skin and he will have a fair idea of the bite of a Florida horse fly. After fighting them six week the inhabitants arise some fine morning in June and find the ground strewn with dead flies. In some places they cover the soil to the depth of an inch or more; but they are snuffed out in a single night and do not reappear until the following year. The flea season ends as the horsefly season begins. The earth fairly boils with fleas for six weeks.

DR. WHITFELDT'S GREATEST TROUBLE.

Through all these annoyances the Doctor persevered in clearing up his hammock. On the night of August 17, 1871, the island was swept by a terrible gale. The Doctor's crops were torn to pieces, and his house blown to the ground. His family barely escaped with their lives. They were drenched by the rain, and passed the long night cowering in an outhouse. Everything was ruined, and the Doctor had to begin anew. It took him nearly a year to recover his lost ground, and then a second tempest burst upon him. His house stood the storm, but the garden was again destroyed. Within a few months, however, the indomitable German was once more upon his feet, and his land bore evidence of his thrift. Then he encountered a third danger. A party of Seminoles camped upon the island, and set the woods on fire. The wind was in the north, and swept the flames down upon the Doctor's clearing. His wife and his children turned out, and after hours of work in the excessive heat saved the property.

The doctor has about twelve acres cleared. It is planted with sugar cane, potatoes, and all kinds of vegetables. Orange trees, bananas, West India pawpaws, limes, and similar fruits are scattered over the clearing. Everything bears the mark of industry, but it produces no income. The doctor may get his reward in the increased value of his land, but even this is doubtful, as within the last year the Clinch family of Georgia have claimed the land under cover of a land grant made to the old general during the Indian war in 1836.[8] The doctor raises his own tobacco, and his little children, despite the scarcity of schoolmasters, speak and read both German and English. Whitfeldt stays in Florida on account of his health. With all the drawbacks, the climate is wonderful. Frost is rarely seen, and there are no extremes of heat or cold. The thermometer ranges between 35° and 87° above zero. The doctor makes a little money by boarding transient travellers, but if an invalid should die at his place it would be a hard matter to find a coffin for his body. An invalid who is strong enough to reach Merritt's Island, however, can never die of a pulmonary complaint.

DR. FOX'S EXPERIENCE.

Five years ago Dr. Fox[9] came to the Indian river country from Savannah, Ga. He was in poor health, but the climate strengthened him wonderfully, and he determined to become a permanent resident. So he preempted a lovely palmetto hammock on the border of Mosquito lagoon, a few miles from Dummitt's grove,[10] erected a little cabin, and sent for his wife and children. The party spent a year in fighting the mosquitos, but during the second summer they were compelled to surrender. The insects swept down upon them by myriads, and the doctor tells me that he was forced to take to his sail boat at midnight to escape being eaten alive. He went to Smyrna, where he now resides. He is one of the most careful and trustworthy guides in eastern Florida. His hammock is still unoccupied, and can be preempted by any healthy Northern farmer who thinks he would like to buy it. It is covered with orange trees and is as rich a piece of land as there is in the State.

So much for the most productive land in Florida. Its only mark is that sickness is unknown. But the natives all have a jaundicy look similar to the complexion of the people in Lower Georgia. An invalid who can't live in any other part of the United States can live in Eastern Florida. There is plenty of land to be preempted, some of which has been under cultivation, for many of the natives keep changing around from hammock to hammock endeavoring to better themselves. There is but little demand for labor. Men can be had to clear up and plant land for $1 a day and find themselves.

THE LAND ALONG THE ST. JOHN'S

is the first that attracts a Northern farmer's attention. It is good for garden truck and orange trees, but the oranges lack the flavor of those on the Indian river. The inhabitants and land agents will tell you that it is healthy, and savagely scan any one who asserts the contrary. My inquiries revealed the fact that fever and ague prevail in the summer time, and that malaria fevers are not uncommon. Many of the inhabitants desert their homes during the hot season, and live with the bull drivers in the pine woods, or visit the sea shore. The river is bordered with swamps from its source to its mouth. Cold fogs frequently cover the country winter mornings. Frost and ice appear at times, and the air is damp and chilly. The most of the land along the river is in the hands of speculators. In some places little villages filled with white houses and green blinds have grown up. This is especially the case in Orange county. Sand Point, in Volusia county, resembles a New England town, but its communication with Jacksonville is uncertain. The mails only come in once a week. The land of both Volusia and Orange counties is said to be as good as any away from the sea coast.

COWS THAT LOVE MUSIC.

In going to Florida a Northern farmer must bid farewell to milk and butter. Three thousand quarts of milk a day may be produced in the whole State, but I doubt it. I can never forget the face of a Northerner who became aware of this fact in Jacksonville. He had paid several thousand dollars for the exclusive right of peddling a patent churn in the State. "My God, sir," he said, "what an ass I have been. There are not a hundred pounds of butter made in Florida in a year." And he was right. There is no grass for the cows. Their best pasture land appears to be in the St. John's river. A kind of coarse grass, or lichen, grows beneath the water, for which they have a great liking. I noticed a dozen cows standing belly-deep in the river in front of Mrs. Stowe's place with their heads under water. They were feeding upon water grass. I have found but one place in Eastern Florida where I could procure a glass of fresh milk. That is in the residence of Judge Paine[11] in this place. His cows roam the savannas and pine wilderness, and eat the stiff wire grass that grows upon the borders of the swamps. The cattle are wild, but are susceptible to the charm of music. They are only got to the house by singing to them. Morning and night young Tom Paine,[12] the Judge's son, rides to the woods on a marsh pony, and rolls out over the wet prairie the notes of some mournful song like *Way down the Mississippi floating.*

The cows listen, and begin to gather about the musician. Tom's voice is sweet and powerful. When the kine are in line he begins to urge them home, but there are no roads nor fences, and he must keep up his singing for the instant he stops the cows break like a New York audience at the close of an opera. The cattle appear to have acquired a taste for music, as it requires a good singer to drive them home from the pasture in lower Florida.

TURPENTINE FARMS

are the feature of Northern Florida. The owners tap the pine trees as the Yankees tap the sugar maple, and boil the sap down into tar and turpentine. The land is excellent for cotton and tobacco, but so far as I could learn is good for nothing else. The climate is bracing and healthy though not so warm as along the St. John's. Land can be bought for from five to ten dollars an acre. The cotton can be teamed to any point along the Tallahassee Railroad, and sold for ready money. Georgia planters succeed well in the northern tier of counties, but it is doubtful whether Wisconsin or Ohio farmers would be satisfied.

THE GREAT DRAWBACK

is the State Legislature. This is filled with ignorant negroes and thieving carpet-baggers. They go to Tallahassee with the avowed purpose of making all they can. They have run the State into debt over $15,000,000, and with county and other indebtedness she now owes $100 a head for every one of her inhabitants. The taxes reach about 2 per cent, but they are very unevenly divided. The settlers are taxed for the full value of their property, while the owners of the enormous land grants escape without paying a cent. Thousands of acres are covered by old Spanish claims, and these were exempted from tax by the terms of the treaty with Spain when the country was ceded to the United States. Thus the small owners are not only compelled to improve the value of the vast tracts owned by carpet-baggers and others, but are actually forced to pay the taxes of the thieves. Then the whole State is flooded with scrip. First there is State scrip, then county scrip and school scrip, and the Lord knows how many other kinds of scrip, averaging in value from twenty-five to seventy-five cents on the dollar. Sometimes it is receivable for taxes, and sometimes it is not just as the thieves who own the Legislature determine.

Nor is the stealing confined to the carpet-baggers. Congressmen from other States appear to be recipients of the plunder. They get their share of the land grants. Ben Butler,[13] I am credibly informed, owns 12,000 acres of land in Florida. But he didn't steal it. He got it legitimately. Gov. Gleason[14] managed to secure 24,000 acres through a manipulation of the Legislature, but got it in such a way that he got into trouble. Butler acted as his lawyer, and took half the land as his fee. The great Key West Railroad steal is said to be backed by Congressmen or Senators who are to share in the plunder.

NO HOPE FOR FLORIDA.

There is no hope of reform. The State seems to be hopelessly doomed. She is treading upon the heels of South Carolina. The Constitution gives the Governor the appointment of all the county officers. Sheriffs, tax assessors and collectors, county judges, county clerks, county commissioners, county treasurers, and county canvassers all hold their places by the will of the Governor. The consequence is that all the counties are left at the mercy of the mercenary scoundrels who control the party primaries. Noted counterfeiters and desperadoes either hold county offices or control them. Each county has its little Ring. If one of the officers is caught stealing, the Ring Sheriff packs a jury and a Ring Judge presides at the trial. In many counties no quarterly reports are made by either collectors or treasurers. Such reports are only made at the request of the County Commissioners, and these are men who belong to the Ring and share in the robbery. A Democratic Assemblyman tells me that fully one-half of the taxes collected in the State are stolen. The last election was undoubtedly carried by the Liberals, but the County Canvassers—all appointed in the interests of the Ring—threw out votes enough to save the Grant ticket. Until the State Constitution is changed, any Governor or Senator has the power through the appointed canvassers to count in any man who is running for Assembly or other State office without reference to the votes cast. The Liberals honestly carried the State last fall, but they have lost strength since then. The success of the Democracy in Georgia has disgusted the carpet-baggers and negroes in that State, and they are now pouring into Florida by hundreds. This turns the scale, and the old Floridians—men who went into the rebellion from honest convictions, and who have as honestly accepted the issues of the war—are relapsing into despair. Their only hope is that the thieves may fall out among themselves, in which case they might redeem their State, and stand upon a level with the proud Empire State of the South. Until that time comes Northern farmers had better keep away from Florida.

"Hopelessly Doomed"

Vulcan's Forge

The main reason I like trains is that they are not airplanes. The main reason I don't like airplanes is that when flying in and out of Gainesville, Florida, one almost always changes planes in Hartsfield-Jackson Atlanta International Airport. Over the years, I have had a lot of bad days in the Atlanta airport while dealing with late arrivals, late departures, and missed connections.

One of the things (the only thing?) I like about that airport is the trains that take you from one concourse to the next. They are fast, clean and air-conditioned, and they almost always work. Only twice in the hundreds of times I have ridden the trains have they not properly taken me to my destination. Once the train simply stopped, and once the whole system was shut down when some really dumb University of Georgia football fan ran down the up escalator, bypassing security and causing the entire airport to be evacuated.

After you read this article, imagine Amos Cummings stepping off the St. Augustine and Tocoi Railroad car into one of the Hartsfield-Jackson Adtranz C-100 people mover cars (capable of moving 128,000 passengers per hour). Wow! It is hard to imagine a mule-driven railroad car as the predecessor of the Adtranz people mover, but it is. We may not have gotten any better at taking care of our natural environment, but we sure can move tourists from one place to another faster and more comfortably.

Amos Cummings was not the only New York journalist to look down his nose at the Yankee-owned St. Augustine and Tocoi Railroad. While researching the annotations for this book, I ran across an article in the March 17, 1873, *New York Times* headlined "Florida" and datelined "St. Augustine, Thursday March 6, 1873." Cummings's fellow journalist had sailed from New York on February 27 in a snowstorm. After a landing in Charleston and then Savannah (where seasick passengers sought succor), the vessel pushed on to Jacksonville, where the journalist boarded a steamboat up the St. Johns River as far as Enterprise and Mellonville before reversing course.

At Tocoi, the traveler took the same train journey to St. Augustine that Cummings enjoyed less than a month later and that he describes in this article. This second New York journalist wrote:

On our return down the river we stopped off at Tocoi, the river station of the railroad to St. Augustine, an important town, consisting of a baggage-room on the wharf, a sitting-room for lady passengers, and an old shed, where Vulcan presides, which I concluded was the machine-shops of this railroad company. A ride on this railroad from Tocoi to St. Augustine, fifteen miles, is enough to satisfy any one of sound mind that railroading in Florida is in its primitive state. The track is of wood, with a flat iron rail laid on the top for a distance of one mile, intended, I should judge, to deceive the people with the idea that they were to ride on an iron-track railroad and glide rapidly on to their journey's end. The track at the St. Augustine terminus had on it the same deceptive rail. The cars are propelled by two horses or mules, driven tandem, and the trip is made (fifteen miles) in from three to four hours, depending upon the liveliness of the negro driver. The only first-class car on this road is similar to any well-worn street-car in New York. The fare is reasonable, being only $2, i.e., the rate of fifty cents per hour, and one gets the full worth of his money. [The article is signed W.D.C.]

The St. Augustine and Tocoi Railroad was one of Florida's earliest. According to Gregg Turner's book *A Short History of Florida Railroads*, the railroad was chartered in 1858. The original rails were wood with iron strips on top. In 1862 a Union gunboat shelled the landing at Tocoi along with the train cars. Union soldiers even took the iron rails to melt down. By 1870 the railroad was back in operation after it was bought by William Astor.

Amos Cummings's article on the Florida railroads appeared in the *New York Sun* on April 22, 1873, and in the *Weekly Sun* three days later.

10

A RAILROAD IN FLORIDA

WOODEN RAILS AND COOKING STOVE LOCOMOTIVES.

From Tocoi to St. Augustine Fifteen Miles in Seven Hours—Two Roosters Aston- ished—Mule Driving as a Science—An Engine Without a Safety Valve—How She Took Water—A Mean Yankee's Land Strike.

Green Cove Springs, April 2.—I have made my second trip over the railroad between St. Augustine and Tocoi. Five years ago passengers landed at Pi- colata, four miles below Tocoi, and crossed from the St. John's to St. August- ine in an old-fashioned stage coach. The country between the old city and the St. John's is a wilderness. It is fifteen miles across, and there is neither a house nor a fence the whole distance. The ground is as flat as a pancake. It is filled with white shells, and covered with tall pines, sickly scrub palmettos, and swamps of mossy cypress and wild orange trees. Deer hunting is good. Tocoi is a dirty-looking slab house, containing three rooms, a half-dozen wooden chairs, and two benches filled with slivers. Other seats are placed without the door, on a sort of platform. Their backs are broken and they are warped by the action of the sun. A South Sea Islander would be disgusted with the place.

A FLORIDA RAILROAD.

A shaky-looking pier runs out into the St. John's river, serving as a bed for a railroad track. Ten miles of the road are laid with wooden rails. The sun has cracked and warped them, and a picket line of spikes raises its heads above them at regular intervals. These serve to jounce and jolt the passengers, mak- ing it extremely unpleasant for invalids. The road is equipped with two horse cars, adorned with broken windows and dirty roofs, a half dozen starving mules, six horses, a home-built baggage car, and an engine resembling an old- fashioned cooking stove.

I arrived at Tocoi at 10 A.M. A dozen passengers disembarked from the boat. We were kept waiting in the hot sun, ladies and all, until 3 P.M., at which time the up-river boat came in. Then the car was packed with passengers until

Steamboats *Hattie* and *Starlight* tied up to the dock at the west end of the St. Augustine and Tocoi Railroad at Tocoi, sometime in the 1870s. Courtesy of Florida State Archives.

it seemed as though it would burst. Trunks and baggage were piled upon the platforms, thus completely sealing the vehicle.

AN UNFORTUNATE COLORED WOMAN.

On the top of the trunks on the back platform sat an old colored woman, with a rooster under each arm. She stood it splendidly until we reached the warped wooden rails, and went bouncing over the spikes. Then the roosters began to complain. All the old lady's efforts to soothe them were useless. They squawked at every jounce, until at last, in turning a curve, the car gave a sudden lurch, and the old lady, roosters and all, plumped into a ditch at the side of the road. Fortunately she was not hurt. With rare presence of mind she clung to the roosters. They seemed disappointed at not getting away. After this the birds kept quiet. They acted as though they thought they had been pitched overboard as a punishment for their noise.

HOW TO FORCE MULES INTO A TROT.

The car was terribly crowded, but the railroad company was well represented. First there was the driver, then the man who sold the tickets before we left Tocoi, next a youth to take up the tickets, and last a gentleman to look after the baggage. The poor fellows seemed to be exhausted with labor. They were worked almost as hard as the assistant librarians of the City Hall.

After going three miles the tandem team of horses gave out with the epizoot.[1] They were then walked five miles, when a pair of mules were dragged out of a crazy stable on the left of the road, and put in the place of the horses. The driver yelled at them like a wild-cat, and whipped them until his arm ached, but he could not persuade them into a trot. He got off the car and clubbed them most unmercifully, but they paid no attention to him. He swore at them, and kicked them, and yelled "Geedap" until he was hoarse and exhausted. The mules didn't even twitch their ears, but moved on as placid as a summer sea. Suddenly Mr. Hugo Wesendonck of New York began humming "Hark, I Hear an Angel Sing." That did the business. The mules stopped for one moment, heard the German's notes rolling over the saw palmettos, and then started off as though they had been shot, leaving the driver in the rear, and setting the car to dancing over the spikes like a marble on a bagatelle table. They never stopped running until Hugo stopped singing.

IN ST. AUGUSTINE.

The frogs were piping, and it was long after dark when we reached St. Augustine. The railroad ends at a shanty over a mile from the city. This is a lovely arrangement for the invalids. It affords them the luxury of being jolted to the hotels in an omnibus packed like a sardine-box. As soon as they are wedged in so that they can't move a finger, the conductor blandly insists upon having fifty cents a head. Meantime the stage rolls off at swift speed, and the invalids, while looking for their change, are banged about the vehicle like so many images. Thus we reached the city. Bear in mind that we saw neither house, fence, nor human being after leaving Tocoi. It is all a wilderness; and this is the only way of reaching a city founded over fifty years before the Pilgrims landed at Plymouth Rock.

A SENATOR'S MAIL.

I returned to Tocoi two days afterward. Before we started there was a row between two post office officials at the rough board shanty called the depot. Two bags, each holding about two bushels and a half, had been left in the shanty over night. Plain pine blocks were strung to the bags bearing the following inscriptions: UNITED STATES MAIL. A. Gilbert, U.S.S. Hon. ABIJAH GILBERT, St. Augustine, Fla.[2] One of the bags was loaded with Pub. Docs., and the other seemed to be filled with seed potatoes. There was Satan to pay because the bags had not been sent to the Senator's house the previous night.

MULE-DRIVING AS A SCIENCE.

We started for Tocoi at 8 A.M. We had the same old horse car, the same mules, and the same driver. The harness was a curiosity. It was a mass of ropes and straps, though it would puzzle a Jersey harnessmaker to discover where the ropes began or where the straps ended. The car was comfortably crowded. Three members of the Legislature were on board bound for Tallahassee. One of them was a native of Minorcan descent, and the others were carpet-baggers, fair specimens of Northern bummers. The carpet-baggers scanned each stranger closely, as though wondering whether he had any money about his clothes. The mules started off on a walk, and the driver began to lash them with a gad.[3] He made the most outlandish noises in his efforts to scare them into a trot. They couldn't see it. Then he pummelled them with the butt of the gad, but the patient creatures seemed to think that he was simply amusing himself, for they did not hasten their speed.

"It takes a nigger to git a mule to go," said a native fisherman, who stood upon the back platform listening to the driver's curses. "I never seen a white man yit who kin manage a mule like a nigger. Somehow-or-a-nuther the mule understands the nigger, and the nigger understands the mule. Thar's a heap o' sympathy 'tween mules and niggers. They'm mighty alike—niggers and mules is."

"Who is the driver?" I asked.

"He's one o' those here Western fellers what come down here for his health—one of those fellers what plants orange trees upside down, and grafts banana bushes with lemons. He says he got tired of layin' around a doin' nothin', and so he hired out to drive mules at a dollar a day. You see the trouble is he don't holler at the mules right. Thar—did you hear that? (The driver made a noise like a small calliope.) That's no way to holler at a mule. The mules don't understand him. Now, if a nigger had those mules, all he'd have to do would be to give one yawp, and away the mules ud go. You see the two races understand each other."

"What races?" your correspondent inquired.

"Why, the mule race and the colored race," answered the fisherman.

A MODEL HARNESS.

Going to the front platform I took a look at the driver. He was a six-footer from Wisconsin. His hair was long, and his face was covered with a bushy beard. The mules were tandem. Two ropes ran from the bits of the front mule through the hame rings of the hind animal, where they were fastened to the reins. They were tied so that the driver had no command over the leader. All the slack came upon the hind mule. When the driver pulled the reins the nearest mule was drawn back on his haunches, while the front mule was perfectly free. The leading mule made several attempts to pull off the hind mule's head and fore legs, while the driver held on to the hind legs. At one time the leader walked off the track. Then the driver jumped from the car and clubbed him on again. It may have been good for the driver's health, but it didn't seem to improve the health of the mules. The driver was totally ignorant of the cause of the trouble.

TWO USEFUL COLORED MEN.

Two miles from the city we came upon the cooking-stove locomotive. She was hitched to a dirt and a freight car. The mules were left behind, and the horse car was attached to the freight car. The passengers were overjoyed. The engine gave a shrill whistle, and the cars began to dance over the spikes. Suddenly they stopped. The passengers were looking out of the windows to see what was the matter, when the locomotive gave a jerk, landing them in a heap at the lower end of the car. They had hardly recovered their feet before the engine kicked again, sending them to grass a second time. This was exhilarating to the invalids. The old cooking stove continued to kick, and your correspondent got off to see what was the matter. He found a negro with a crowbar on either side of the locomotive prying at its wheels. When the steel driver lay on a level with the top of the wheels, its weight would cause them to make a half revolution, and this produced the kicking. Then the colored men would place their crowbars under the wheels and pry away until the driver again struck the centre, when the kicking would be resumed. The train was on a curve, with a slight up grade. The Superintendent assured us that when we got around the curve we would have no more difficulty. The invalids felt consoled. It took only an hour and a half to get around the curve. Then the train ran free for five minutes, when it stopped as though it had been knocked in the head. The negroes alighted and the crowbars were again brought in play. There was another hour's delay, followed by a five minutes' run, and more crowbar exercise. Then the train moved backward sixty rods. As the sun was very hot the delight of the invalids was unbounded.

Drawing of the terminus of the railroad at Tocoi on the St. Johns River in 1877. Courtesy of Florida State Archives.

A STARTLING DISCOVERY.

Finally the cars ceased to move. The passengers went to the front in a body. They had been five hours making six miles. The engineer had uncoupled his locomotive, and she stood about forty feet in advance of the train. It was found impossible to move her either backward or forward. The colored men heaved away at the crowbars, but though the engine fizzed and fumed she did not budge an inch. The passengers gathered about the machine in mute admiration, when one of them discovered that she had no safety valve. A wooden plug was jammed in the place of the valve, and at ten-minute intervals a negro would run out on the side of the locomotive, pull out the plug, and ascertain the depth of water in her boiler. This discovery pleased the invalids so much that they scattered in all directions among the scrub palmettos.

AN INDIGNATION MEETING.

At last matters grew so bad that the passengers held an indignation meeting. It was resolved to throw the locomotive over into a ditch, after which the gentlemen would put their shoulders to the wheel and shove the car containing the ladies to Tocoi. Dr. Westcott, the superintendent of the road, who was tinkering about the engine, was informed of the determination of the passengers. With tears in his eyes and a briarwood pipe in his mouth, he pleaded with them. He told them that the loss of the locomotive would ruin the company. They would never be able to raise it from the ditch. He protested so earnestly that the travelers allowed him thirty minutes to get the old thing in working order. He went to work with a wrench, twisting a nut here and turning a screw there, pounding a bolt on one side and oiling a piston on the other. Within twenty minutes he had her so that she would move backward, but no power could force her forward.

The doctor looked at his watch, and began to sweat with agony. In this dilemma a passenger suggested that they should take out the valves and turn them around. "Then," said he, "she will move forward and not backward, and that's exactly what we want." The valves were turned. It was a success. The locomotive went off like a bird. The superintendent made a spring for the dirt car, missed it, and fell with his foot under the wheel. One of the bones of his leg was broken. The train stopped, and the passengers brought him into the car. His head had struck a spike, and he was covered with blood, but the briarwood pipe was still clenched between his teeth.

TAKING WATER.

A Mr. Rupe of New York gave the doctor some whiskey to build him up, and the train proceeded. She ran three miles and then stopped to take water. She took it out of a ditch at the side of the road. Three negroes sprang from the engine. The engineer pitched a water pail to the first one, he handed it to the second, and the second passed it to the third colored man, who dipped it in the water. Then it went back to the engine. It took twenty minutes and twenty-three pails of water to fill the machine. As she had no tender, I presume they poured the water into the boiler. After she was filled ten minutes were spent in getting up steam. Thrice did the negroes fill her with water before we reached Tocoi. We were seven hours on the way. The boats had all left for Jacksonville. It was Saturday, and there was no way of going down the river until Monday. There was no shelter nearer than St. Augustine. The invalids looked particularly pleased. Fortunately the steamer Hattie hove in sight on her way up the river. Two-thirds of the passengers wanted to go to Jacksonville, but they were compelled to run up to Pilatka and stay over Sunday, or sleep in the open air without provisions. They went a hundred miles out of their way before they reached their destination.

THE WORK OF THE CARPET-BAGGERS.

Such is the Tocoi Railroad. The President and largest stockholder of the road is a New Haven Yankee named Skidmore. He lives in Tocoi. All his efforts seem to be bent toward discommoding his passengers. Even in New Jersey he would be tarred and feathered. Not a day passes but what a half dozen suffering consumptives are forced to pass six or seven hours in the hot sun at Tocoi, because the railroad company is too mean to send over an extra car. The fare is $2.

The people of St. Augustine would build another road if that were possible. The Legislature, however, actually gave Skidmore & Co. six miles of good land on each side of the road as a subsidy for constructing it. This gives them a complete monopoly. The land alone is worth treble what it cost to build the road. Free passes are provided for all the Assemblymen. I was informed that not a native-born Southerner owned a cent of the stock. The dividends are enormous, and as long as they continue so the stockholders think the road good enough. The invalids, however, think different.

The Zen of Fishing and the *Jaws* Phenomenon

Drive around Florida and you will soon notice bumper stickers on automobiles that say things like "The Worst Day Fishing Is Better Than the Best Day at Work." The tacit message behind such statements is that although one may not catch any fish while fishing, it is actually a lot of fun just being out on the water.

I have subscribed to that same self-delusion on many occasions and have often told Scott Mitchell, another archaeologist I sometimes fish with, that we should not feel bad if we did not land any meaningful fish because we are still having fun looking at birds, cow-nose rays, and, occasionally, a sea turtle. The enjoyment also includes getting sun-drenched and very tired from getting up so early to drive to the coast and catch first light on the water.

Don't believe any of it. What would really make a fishing trip a first-rate nature experience would be to catch fish, lots of fish, fish like they used to catch in 1873.

Whenever I read an article like this one by Amos Cummings, I feel cheated. Everyone else ate the cake before I got to it. In short, the fish are gone. Fish populations have been horribly depleted. Fishermen will never again enjoy the spectacular fishing that Amos Cummings did.

Modern sportsmen regularly blame commercial fishing and sport fishing for overharvesting fish. That, of course, means that we sport fishermen are blaming ourselves. I don't mind that—I just wish I could catch more fish. Cummings, in this article, suggests another fall guy to blame: seabirds. Do birds actually eat that much fish?

Cummings also raises another modern issue in this article: the *Jaws* effect. Twenty-first-century beachgoers are scared to death of sharks, a phobia most analysts trace to a late twentieth-century movie. But if Cummings's stories are correct, sharks chewing on residents and tourists is nothing new.

A similar conclusion is generated by other data on shark attacks. One of my colleagues at the Florida Museum of Natural History helps maintains a worldwide registry of shark bites (the International Shark Attack File; see http://www.flmnh. ufl.edu/fish/Sharks/sharks.htm). That database contains more than 3,200 documented shark attacks dating as far back as the mid-1500s. The file makes it clear that shark attacks are not becoming more numerous. Probably the attacks are just better reported. Newspapers love to titillate their readers with stories of shark attacks; chambers of commerce in coastal towns hate them.

All of this makes me think that we need a new bumper sticker, one that Amos Cummings, himself an ardent fisherman, might enjoy: "The Worst Day Fishing in the 19th Century Is Better Than the Best Day in the 21st Century (And Don't Worry about the Sharks)."

"The Fishing in Florida" was in the *New York Sun* on May 9, 1873, and in the *Semi-Weekly Sun* on May 13.

11

THE FISHING IN FLORIDA

OVER 3,000,000,000 BUSHELS OF FISH EATEN IN TWELVE MONTHS.

**The First Channel Bass—A Struggle at Midnight—Feathered and Finny Fisher-
men—The Highway Robbers of the Air—Acres of Man-Eating Sharks—The
Phantom Drum-Fish—A Fish Weighing 1,500 Pounds that Eats Grass.**

Sᴛ. Lᴜᴄɪᴇ, Aᴘʀɪʟ 5.—The gamest fish in Florida is the channel bass, or redfish.
It is a salt water fish, built like a striped bass. It has silvery and red golden
scales, but no stripes. A round mother-of-pearl spot on the neck of the tail is
its most striking mark. Channel bass hang about the mouths of fresh water
brooks in great swarms at certain seasons of the year, and gobble up the young
mullet. In the fall of the year the mullet is a delicious fish. It never takes the
hook, but is caught in a cast-net.

WONDERS OF THE CAST-NET.

Every sea-coast family in Florida below St. Augustine owns a cast-net. Spread
upon the grass this net is about twenty feet in circumference. The edge is
loaded with heavy sliding sinkers, each of which fills the outer stitch of the
net. From the centre runs a strong cord from eighteen to thirty feet in length.
The thrower takes the end of this cord between his teeth, arranges the net in
folds on his right arm, firmly seizes a fold in each hand, swings himself partly
around, and then gives the net a powerful heave. It strikes the water in a
circle, the sinkers instantly carry the rim to the bottom, and every fish beneath it is a prisoner. The fisherman then draws in the net by the cord, while
the weight of the sinkers brings them together, thus preventing the escape of
the fish. The art of throwing the net is acquired only by constant practice. It
looks easy enough, but there is a knack about it that renders it difficult. I have
seen a twelve-year boy send it eighteen feet, when a two-hundred-pound
greenhorn could not even spread it on the water. An adept will throw it from
twenty to thirty feet.

A NEW YORK DOCTOR LAID OUT.

One of the most skilful net throwers on the eastern coast is George C. Acosta[1] of New Smyrna. He occasionally hunts quail (the Floridians call them partridge) with a cast-net. Some months ago a match was arranged between Acosta and a Dr. Gill of New York. Gill was to hunt quail with a breechloading, double-barrelled shot-gun, while Acosta was to use his cast-net. Both had pointer dogs. When Acosta's dog flushed the birds, Acosta arranged his net, crept carefully behind the dog, and whirled the net beyond him, always bagging a fair number of quail. Gill went into the business in the old style. His shot-gun was ringing through the woods the entire day. At night both men returned to Lowd's Hotel.[2] Acosta had five quail to Gill's one.

GREEN CATFISH—CHANNEL BASS.

I caught my first channel bass at Turtle Mound[3] on a Cuddyhunk hook, which was much too small. Standing upon the point of a spit of sand, I cast the mullet-baited hook fifty feet into the water. Five minutes passed before a bite. The fish was fastened and reeled in. It was a two-pound catfish of a delicate green color. In the sun it had the lustre of a green silk dress. A second time I drew in a green catfish. Then half an hour elapsed without a bite. I grew discouraged, and running the line from the reel, walked back to a bunch of stunted palmettos, and laid my rod across them, intending to go to the sea beach and look for shells. I had gone nearly two hundred feet, when I looked back and saw the reel running out at smoking speed. The rod had started over the sand before I reached it. The fish was evidently a large one, and wanted play. He ran up and down the river as though he had been dosed with laughing gas. It was ten minutes before he became quiet, and I began to work the reel. When within twenty feet of the shore, he made a second break, taking two hundred feet of line, I could feel him shaking his head and trying to get the hook out of his mouth as he sped away. Then he ran in upon me like a race horse, faster than I could take in the slack. Dashing into the shallow water, he took a look at his tormenter. It was not satisfactory. Making a wide sweep, he flirted the foam into my face with his tail, and again sailed off into the river, raising a swell upon the surface of the water. For an instant he was quiet, and then there was a circus-horse performance, which lasted over a minute. Finally the fish became exhausted, and was cautiously reeled in. I had no gaff hook, and was about to stick my fingers into his gills and draw him upon the sand, when Dr. Fox, my guide, said, "Catch him under the fore fins; he's got teeth in his gills." I found two pockets or arm-pits under his fins, and pulled him ashore. He was a channel bass, weighing twenty-two pounds.

Within twenty minutes I took in a second one, weighing a little short of fourteen pounds. At Seventy, near Pepper Hammock,[4] I caught a twenty-five-pound fellow.

BAREFOOT FISHING AT MIDNIGHT.

I camped six days on the shore of Banana River, in a wild orange and lemon grove. Before leaving Smyrna Mr. Lawrence of New York (Abe Lawrence's uncle) had given me a small clothes-line over 300 feet long, with a heavy sinker, and a hook nearly five inches long, backed by an enormous shank. Every night at dark I was in the habit of tying the line to the limb of a cabbage tree overhanging the camp fire. Afterward I would bait the hook with half a mullet, take the sinker out in a skiff the full length of the line, and drop it overboard. One night after I had gone to bed there was trouble in the old cabbage tree. The limbs were cracking and dancing over the embers of the camp fire as though the spirits of the air were at work. Buster, our dog, was barking like all possessed. Roused from a sound sleep, it was some moments before I could realize what was the matter. It struck me like a flash. I dashed out of the tent in my bare feet, stood upon the beach in the soft light of a February moon, and spent fifty minutes in getting to the shore a bass that weighed fifty-three pounds. At times I could not hold him. He absolutely drew me over the shore. When I landed him I was dripping with sweat. The splashing of the water and my shouting to my comrades started a regiment of owls, and they filled the woods with unearthly hoots. The owls startled the alligators, and the alligators the herons, and the herons the wild cats, while hordes of drumfish beat a general alarm. Dr. Fox scaled the bass with a grubbing hoe. The most of the scales were as large as silver dollars. The Floridians turn up their noses at a sheepshead, and only use the head and shoulders of the bass. With these, however, they make a delicious stew.

FISHING FOR SNAPPERS.

Next to the bass in point of gameness are the snappers. Of these there are two kinds—the red and black. The color of the first is as delicate as the color of the under fins of a speckled trout. The snapper is a stocky-built fish, something after the shape of a shad, only heavier about the shoulders, and with a larger mouth. The name is an index to the character of the fish. Snappers not only snap up the bait, but they snap off a man's fingers unless he is careful. In weight they run from one to fifteen pounds. When hooked, they break like a kingfish, though with more weight. They whip around as if crazy, and invariably dash under the boat. It requires nerve and skill to land them. The best snapper-fishing is in Indian River Inlet, opposite Fort Capron.[5] The inlet is alive with game fish. There are bass, snappers, grouper, jewfish, and cavallo, or "crevalyea," as the natives call them, in abundance. But the sharks are just as plentiful, and of enormous size. They amuse themselves by walking off with your fish after you have hooked him. They lay claim to about every third fish, and take hook, sinker, and all with the utmost assurance.

EIGHTEEN PERSONS EATEN BY SHARKS.

The water fairly boils with sharks. I counted one hundred and twelve within the space of an acre, none of which were less than eight feet long. Indian river people say that they have seen them twenty feet in length. I saw one that measured over seventeen feet. They would frequently break under the bows of our twenty-one foot sail boat, careening her to one side and at times half lifting her from the water. They flocked about the boat by dozens, and cast hungry looks at the huge yellow dog on the fore-castle. At one time I struck a twelve foot fellow over the snout with a heavy boat pole. He made a great swirl through the water, as if surprised, but saucily darted back to the craft to see what had hit him. Occasionally boatmen plunge lily irons[6] into them, and are towed about the river against wind and tide for miles. Some of the natives declare that they are man-eaters, while others deny it. Jim Paine, of Fort Capron, told me that he had stood in the water for hours while these big sharks were nosing about his legs, but Dr. Fox, my guide, seemed afraid of them, and declared that he had known them to pull an estimable young lady from Savannah out of a boat while she was dragging her hand behind the stern. She was cut into mince meat in five seconds. During the war, it is said, that a boat containing fourteen men disappeared. The water tinged with blood marked the spots where they had been drawn under. Two of the sailors got ashore, but so bitten and in shreds that they died soon afterward.

I was told another story of four men who started to walk up the beach from Cape Florida[7] to St. Augustine. They managed to get across New Inlet[8] upon an improvised raft, but on arriving at Lake Worth Inlet they attempted to swim across. Three of them were gobbled up by sharks. The fourth reached the shore, and travelled on to Jupiter Light, where he told of the fate of his comrades. These reports certainly show that many of the sharks are man-eaters. The most of them are of the shovel-nosed variety. As they are more lively and voracious in the summer than in winter, it is probable that they would attack a man in July or August when they would not touch him in December or January.

THE BEST FISHERMEN IN FLORIDA

are the pelicans and ospreys. A pelican consumes about a peck of fish a day. They flock about the inlets and straits by thousands. Supposing there are 2,000,000 pelicans in Florida—and there are certainly more than that—they would eat 500,000 bushels of fish each day, or 182,500,000 bushels per year. The millions upon millions of white and blue cranes, herons, curlews, gulls, fish-hawks, kingfishers, and other water fowl devour thousands of bushels of fish every twenty-four hours. An experienced Cracker estimates that 700,000 bushels of fish a day are required to feed the birds of Florida alone. This would make 255,500,000 bushels each year. Add to this the billions of fish swallowed by sharks, bass, and others, and the sum total will reach nearly 2,000,000,000 bushels of fish destroyed by feathered and finny fishermen on the peninsula in twelve months. At first glance these figures appear enormous, but let any man make his own estimate and carefully figure it up, and he will find them under instead of over.

THE PRINCE OF FEATHERED GLUTTONS.

The pelican is the prince of feathered gluttons. I shot a dozen of them on the wing. Sometimes the fish would begin to tumble out of their gullets before they reached the ground. In no case did I find less than four large fish in their baggy throats. The lower fish would be half digested. Their throttles are like mill hoppers. They fill the pouch under their bill with a peck of fish. The fish overflow into their throats. As fast as one digests another drops into its place, and goes through the same process. The bird is fat, logy, and very rank. It is full of grease. Handle a dead one in the sun or before a camp fire, and the grease will drip from the body. They weigh from twelve to twenty pounds. Dr. Fox shot a white one measuring nine feet and one inch from tip to tip, and weighing 19¾ pounds. While sitting upon the water they hold their heads well up, with their enormous bills and pouches flattened upon their breasts. They look as grave as country judges—so grave that but few persons can see them without laughing outright. They fly in Indian file, sometimes in strings half a mile long. When the leader flaps his wings the second one follows suit, and so on down the line; and when the leader soars No. 2 does the same, and is followed by the others. Each bird seems to be under strict discipline, and when gathered in great flocks upon the beach they resemble an army massed by battalions. The plumage of the gray pelican is much admired. Every feather is shaded from a black to a beautiful silver gray. The under part of the neck resembles yellow satin, and the back part is a glossy brown velvet.

THE HIGHWAY ROBBERS OF THE AIR.

It is amusing to watch an osprey while he is fishing. An eagle is soaring through the air five hundred feet above him. The osprey is sailing over the water, carefully eyeing its surface. Suddenly he steadies himself against the wind, rolling his wings as though endeavoring to back water. Then he drops through the air like a plummet. There is a splash in the waves, and the osprey rises with a fish in his talons. Meanwhile the eagle is drawing near. As the osprey descends in the air, the eagle utters a threatening cry and swoops upon him. Unable to escape, the hawk finally drops the fish. Before it strikes the water the eagle darts downward like a flash of lightning and catches it, while the osprey flies to a hammock, where his comrades gather round and sympathize with him.

THE DANCING FISH.

A man-of-war hawk or frigate pelican is a peculiar fisherman. He descends upon his prey like a bullet from a height of three hundred feet. He seizes the fish in his beak, and soars aloft into the sky. His mates gather about him, while the lucky fisherman tosses his tidbit into the air so as to catch it by the head, and swallow it, as it comes down. His throat is so small that he can get it in his stomach in no other way. There is a wild swoop, and another hawk seizes the fish, and again it is tossed up in the air, and tossed up indefinitely until one of the birds is so fortunate as to catch it headfirst, when it disappears. I have seen a dozen frigate pelicans keep a fish dancing the air fifteen minutes before it was swallowed.

The most wonderful fisherman on the Indian river is a native named Stewart. He seems to be amphibious. It is no uncommon thing for him to jump into the water and run down a fat mullet, catching it in his hands. The Futch family have two dogs so starved that I have seen them dash into a school of mullet and reappear with fish in their mouths.

THE PHANTOM DRUMFISH.

Mr. Abbey of Abbey, Sturdevant & Co., Fulton street, New York, occasionally visits New Smyrna, and spends a few winter weeks in fishing. His favorite amusement is spearing drumfish. One afternoon he left the wharf in a boat with Mr. Lowd, the proprietor of the hotel. For an hour they had fair luck, and then there was a lull. Mr. Abbey began to grow drowsy. Lowd was rowing the boat. Suddenly an enormous drum was heard at the bow.

"Stop, stop," shouted the fisherman, raising his spear. "There's one right here ahead of us. Wait until his tail comes above water."

Lowd steadied the boat, and Abbey waited for the fish, but none came in sight. The boat moved on. In a few moments a fierce drumming arose at its stern.

"Stop, stop," cried, Abbey, "he's behind us," again balancing his spear. "Steady now. Wait until his tail comes above water."

Lowd waited, but no tail appeared, and there was no sign of any drumfish. A third time the boat swept on. Quickly a vigorous thumping was again heard in front.

"Stop, stop, steady," screamed the Fulton street merchant. "Here he is, straight ahead of us again." The spear was brandished once more. "Now, just wait until his tail comes above water."

The tail didn't come. Mr. Abbey stood in eager expectation, but there was no swell upon the water. The fisherman began to sweat with anxiety. There was drumming on the left and next on the right of the boat. Again it was at the bow, and again under the stern, but no fish was to be seen, although Mr. Abbey declared that it must be a big one. Finally he returned to Smyrna unable to explain the mystery. A few days afterward, however, he learned that Mr. Lowd was so good an imitator of the noise of a drumfish that he frequently deceived the fish themselves.

FISH CAUGHT IN FLORIDA.

Among the fish caught at Smyrna are sheepshead, bass or redfish, the red and black grouper, salt water trout, mullet, kingfish (the natives call it whiting), sea-bass, pig-fish, drumfish, sailor's choice or porgie, sergeant-fish, cavallo, snapjack or bluefish, green and black catfish, red and black snappers, menatee, lady-fish, jew-fish, stingarees, sharks, dog-fish, porpoises, saw-fish, sword-fish, ribbon-fish, pompaneau, different kinds of cuttle fish, two kinds of eels (natives call them congarees), an electrical flounder, similar to an electric eel, flukes, skates, big shrimp, whipparees or clam-crackers, bezongs, toad-fish, blowfish, porcupine fish, cow-fish, mojarra, angel-fish, and spade-fish.

The grouper is a sort of a salt-water perch, and is highly prized for its flavor and gameness. It is generally caught in deep water.

The salt-water trout is not the Northern weak-fish. It resembles a brook trout, but the dots on its sides are black, and not red. It bites like a weak-fish, and is game to the backbone.

The pig fish is built like a grouper. It is a game fish, and derives its name from the fact that it grunts like a pig when thrown from the hook to the bottom of the boat.

The sheepshead are not so large as Northern fish of this name.

The sergeant-fish is a salt-water pike. It is a splendid fighter, and is called a sergeant-fish because it has three strips running across its body similar to a sergeant's chevrons. It grows as large as a muscalonge.

The cavallo or "crevalyea" is a favorite game fish. Its head and fins are tipped with gold. The former is shaped like the prow of an old-fashioned Erie Canal boat. The fish is very narrow at the root of the tail, which has a golden tinge.

The ladyfish is delicate and silvery. When struck by the hook they spring from the water with more energy than a black bass. Their flavor is delicious.

The jew-fish grows to an enormous size, occasionally reaching five hundred pounds in weight. It is of a greenish color, covered with irregular dark spots, and is very game. Why it is called a jew-fish is one of those things that no fellow can find out.

The saw-fish becomes very large, and takes the hook like an old stager. A flat bone, set with teeth on either edge, juts from its nose, giving the fish its name. It is good eating and game.

The ribbon-fish has a snout like a pike. It is a thin fish, strung out like a ribbon, from which it takes its name. It is regarded as a delicacy.

Stingarees are plentiful, and of an enormous size. Some of them weigh 250 pounds. The sting is in their tail. It is a bone several inches in length, bearded in a hundred places like the shank of a hook. The fish can throw it through a man's boot, or even through his body. It is a dangerous fish, and has been known to cause death in a few hours. The natives use the stingaree's tail for toothpicks. They declare that it prevents toothache.

The pompeneau is the pride of Southern epicures. It is caught in a net and has a round body, shining like a plate of silver. Its bones are soft, and it has a flavor superior to that of a shad.

A FISH THAT EATS GRASS.

The menatee, or sea-cow, is a huge amphibious animal. It is found in the St. Lucie river. It has a head like that of a sea lion, and it looks like a gigantic seal. It feeds upon the rank grass growing upon the marshes of the St. Lucie. The menatee has ribs as thick as a man's arms. Last year Dolph Sheldon[9] and Frank Sams caught one alive near the mouth of the river, intending to send it North for exhibition. The animal weighed over 1,500 pounds. Unfortunately it was tied to the boat so firmly that the rope cut into its flesh, and it died before the party reached the head of the Indian river. The porgies devoured the body. Florida is the only place in which the menatee is found on the North American continent. Formerly it was abundant, but it is now nearly extinct, and becomes more scarce every year. Its meat is greatly relished and tastes like the best Fulton Market beef.

The whipparee[10] resembles the stingaree. Its mouth is filled with two ivory rocks, and between them it cracks the clams on which it feeds. It reaches an enormous size.

The porcupine-fish has a round body filled with quills. It is small, and good for nothing.

The cow-fish is a curious fish. It has the head of a pig, with two horns above the ears. On the bottom it is as smooth as a flat iron.

The majarra is the shape of a sheepshead, and has a lustrous brown shading above the tail. It is as handsome as an angel fish, and is good eating.

The spade-fish also looks like a sheepshead, but it has no hard fins.

NO TROUT IN FLORIDA.

All the books on Florida declare the rivers are filled with trout. This is untrue. There is not a fresh-water trout in the State. What they call trout are a kind of black bass, trapped on a troll. They have huge mouths, and are caught by scores in the St. John river. A lady hooked one at Enterprise weighing ten pounds and a half. Compared with sea fishing, however, fishing on the St. John is boyish sport.

Giant Spiders and Lost Civilizations—
The Other Lake Okeechobee

In this article, Amos Jay Cummings writes about an 1874 expedition undertaken by Dr. Edward Palmer and Frederick A. Ober, both of whom garnered fame for their various exploits in the Americas. It was only on my second reading of the article that I realized Cummings was not actually a participant on the expedition. To write his story he must have interviewed one or more of the men who were on the trip while Cummings was in Fort Capron.

Edward Palmer, born in England and living in the United States, was, by accounts, an "adventurous" collector of archaeological, botanical, and zoological specimens for many museums and private collections. Funded by museums and patrons, he made many collecting trips, including a number to Mexico and to the southwestern United States. Specimens collected by Palmer grace many venerable American herbariums.

Ober was an equally famous, some might say infamous, adventurer who wrote a number of books about his travels in Florida, Mexico, and the Caribbean. Among them is *The Knockabout Club in the Everglades; The Adventures of the Club in Exploring Lake Okeechobee* (1887).

An article appearing in *Forest and Stream* magazine (November 20, 1873, 233) and certainly written by Ober, who refers to himself as "our Florida correspondent," briefly outlines the plan to explore Lake Okeechobee and refers to an earlier failed attempt by that same correspondent to reach the lake. Ober claims that on that expedition, which took place in 1872, the correspondent (himself) reached "within one mile of [the lake's] shores, where, entangled in the cypress swamps and deserted by his Indian guide, he was persistently pushing his way through, guided by the sound of waves beating [the lake's] shore after a storm." Even so, he never actually reached the lake.

The article then relates what the correspondent would have found had he reached the lake, relying on an account recently published in the *New York Herald*. That *Herald* story reports an exploration of the lake by Mr. C. K. Allen, of St. Marys, Florida, and four other men. It is one of the tales about Lake Okeechobee written by "literary imposters" that Cummings mentions in his own article.

The *Herald* article, among other things, says Lake Okeechobee was 170 feet deep with several islands, one of which featured a four-mile-long line of 150-foot-high cliffs. The forest on the island was home to a gigantic species of spiders, each two feet long and weighing three to four pounds. According to Allen and his fellow explorers, they also found stone ruins on that same island, along with a mysterious stone circle. Clearly they made the whole thing up.

In a subsequent issue of *Forest and Stream* (March 5, 1874), Ober, writing under the pseudonym Fred Beverly and calling himself "our Florida commissioner," provides a long account of his travails in 1874 in reaching the Indian River region of Florida and his subsequent journey down the coast to Fort Capron, all preparatory to the 1874 expedition with Palmer. Ober's pseudonym—Fred Beverly—was derived from an abbreviation of his own name, Frederick, with the surname taken from Beverly, Massachusetts, where the boat was built that the expedition shipped to Florida and then transported overland to the Kissimmee River, where Ober and his companions launched it and headed south to Lake Okeechobee.

In the March 26, 1874, issue of *Forest and Stream,* Fred Beverly authored a brief letter penned on February 21, the day after the expedition reached the Kissimmee River. The April 16 issue of the same magazine contains Fred Beverly's account of the discovery of the lake. It is datelined "St. Lucie, March 18." That same issue contains a second article, certainly written by Ober but with no author listed, which announced "the complete success of our expedition which was fitted out last December for the exploration of Lake Okeechobee, in Florida, and to present to our readers the *first map* of that mysterious body of water ever published."

In the April 23, 1874, *Forest and Stream,* Ober, writing under his own name, published a list (with notes) of sixty-three species of "birds of Lake Okeechobee" seen on his trip. Two weeks later (May 7, 1874), writing again as Fred Beverly in the same magazine, Ober provides a long description of the Indian River region. He could not have been happy that Cummings's lengthy article on the expedition, including a map, had appeared in the *New York Sun* on April 27. The May 7 article, "Our Okeechobee Expedition," is prefaced by the following statement:

> The *Forest and Stream* Expedition, sent out by this office especially to explore Lake Okeechobee, is the only one that succeeded in reaching that body of water the past winter. All letters purportedly to come from other sources are written by persons who were permitted by courtesy to accompany our commissioner. The only boat on Lake Okeechobee and the lower Kissimmee, was built for our expedition at Beverly, Mass., and taken to Florida by our sailing vessel.—Ed. F & S.

Ober would later publish an account of the expedition, one rivaling Cummings's article in detail. The account appeared in two 1874 issues of *Appleton's Journal* (October 31 and November 7) six months after Cummings's account.

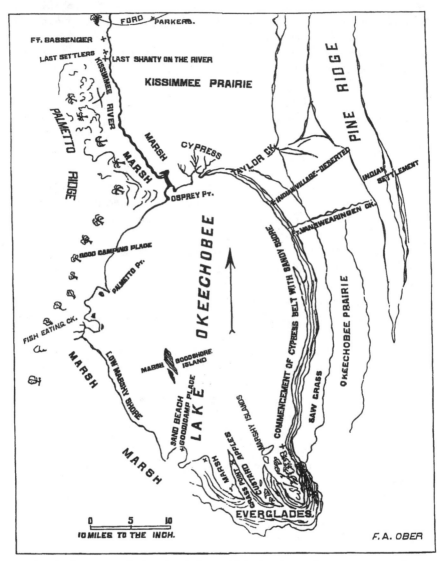

Frederick Ober's map of Lake Okeechobee published in the April 16, 1874, issue of *Forest and Stream* (153).

Ober's story contains information not found in Cummings's article (for example, Ober says there were two students on the expedition, not one), but Cummings's article also contains things not in Ober's version.

Cummings states he received the map printed in the *Sun* from Col. Von Boskerck, one of the expeditions's participants. It is remarkably accurate and I wonder if the colonel (and Ober?) had access to one of the maps of Lake Okeechobee made by U.S. troops during the Third Seminole War. The Ober map does not appear to be a copy of the map Cummings included with his article (that map, redrawn by Scott Mitchell, is included here in Cummings's article, along with Cummings's legend, which is keyed to his numbers on the map).

The map published with Cummings's articles contains a few place-names I have not been able to find anywhere else, probably because the expedition made them up. Other of the names still exist today, though in altered form. Lookout Island is probably Observation Island, and Cummings's Cohanza Bay appears on an 1857 military map (a copy of which is catalogued as PKY 1848 in the University of Florida's P. K. Yonge Library of Florida History) as Cohancey Bay, while on the 1885 Le Baron map it is Cohansey Bay. On more modern maps, it is recorded as Chancey or Chancy Bay. Interestingly, a trail marked on Le Baron's map may show the route the expedition took from the east coast west to the Kissimmee River.

In his 1874 articles, Ober mentions, and dispels, the fantastic stories of lost cities, four-pound spiders, and other mysteries that had been attributed to Lake Okeechobee. He also notes that the existence of the lake was seemingly unknown to many people in the nineteenth century.

Certainly Ober's 1874 *Forest and Stream* expedition was not the first Anglo incursion onto Lake Okeechobee—U.S. military forces had traveled the area as early as the Second Seminole War, and settlers already were making inroads into the region by the latter part of the nineteenth century. But the lake was relatively unknown in 1874. It is not mentioned in Rambler's *Guide to Florida* (1875) or Sidney Lanier's *Florida: Its Scenery, Climate, and History* (1875). Ober's article, and perhaps Cummings's, served to garner attention for what formerly was a little-known feature of interior South Florida. Taken together, the Beverly, Ober, and Cummings accounts provide a remarkable view of Lake Okeechobee at a time when it was still in its natural state.

Last, as a museum curator I cannot help but point out that Erwin J. Shores, the Brown University student who Cummings says accompanied the expedition, apparently did not return home to Providence empty-handed. In the collections of the Haffenreffer Museum at that university there is a pair of Seminole Indian moccasins labeled "Donated by F. Ober to the Museum of Brown University."

THE SHORE OF OKECHOBEE

EXPLORING THE MYSTERIOUS LAKE IN THE EVERGLADES.

A Search for the Mysterious Temple of the Mound Builders—The Wonders of the
Inland Sea of Florida—A Vast Expanse of Dead Water—The Blue Mountains—
A Flea Pit—Narrow Escape of a Friend of Agassiz—The Crazy Snake Bird—
Ruins of an Indian Village—The Carpenter Bee—Mysteries of an Old Cypress—
A Remarkable Island—The Bower of Custard Apples—A Gale—Lost on Lake
Okechobee.

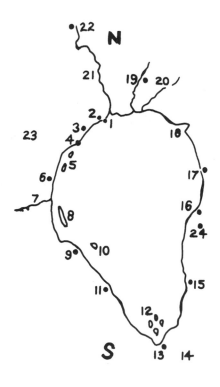

Legend:

1. *Osprey Point.*
2. *Indian Camp.*
3. *Mulberry Camp.*
4. *Palmetto Point.*
5. *Swampy Islands.*
6. *The Carpenter Shop.*
7. *Fish-eating Creek.*
8. *Lookout Island.*
9. *Fossil Camp.*
10. *Grass Island.*
11. *Custard-apple Rookery.*
12. *The Sisters.*
13. *The Beehive.*
14. *The Everglades.*
15. *Shell Beach Camp.*
16. *Hurricane Camp.*
17. *Banana Grove.*
18. *Cohanza Bay.*
19. *Taylor's Creek.*
20. *Taylor's Battle Ground.*
21. *Kissimmee River.*
22. *Fort Bassinger.*
23. *Big Cypress Swamp.*
24. *The Halpattee Okee.*

FORT CAPRON, FLA., MARCH 25.—Lake Okechobee has at last been thoroughly explored. It may interest the American Geographical and Statistical Society[1] to hear that no islands covered with ancient ruins were found upon its bosom, and no rusty convent bells were seen upon its shores. There was no evidence that any white men had ever settled within sight of its waters. The lake is simply a vast platter of dead water, situated near the centre of an immense marsh. It has no outlet except in the rainy season. Then its waters rise until they pour over the encircling marshes into the Everglades, and are slowly funnelled into the Gulf of Mexico and Atlantic Ocean through sluggish sluices like the St. Lucie, Jupiter, Shark, and Withlacoochee rivers. The Coosala-hatchie does not rise in the lake, as is laid down in the [sic] most of the maps of Florida. Okechobee drains the country over a hundred and fifty miles to the north. Its largest source of supply is the Kissimmee river. This river, with its branches, is more than two hundred miles long. It is very deep, and pours a volume of water into the lake.

THE EXPLORERS.

The explorers of Lake Okechobee were Dr. Edward Palmer of Cambridge University, Erwin J. Shores, a student of Brown University; Frederick A. Ober of Beverly, Mass.; and Col. T. B. Van Boskerck[2] of New York city. The Indian river was made the base of their operations. The trip was taken in a flat-bottomed sail boat, cat-rigged, twenty feet long and six feet beam. The Indian river is a bay or salt water lagoon, stretching along the eastern coast of Florida, like Barnegat bay[3] along the Jersey coast. The explorers had their boat hauled from Fort Pierce to the site of old Fort Bassinger on the Kissimmee river, a distance of sixty miles. Fort Pierce is on the Indian river about 220 miles south of St. Augustine. It was formerly a military reservation. None of the forts have been garrisoned since the Seminole war. At that time they were stockades. Two yoke of steers owned by Capt. Elias Jernegan, an old Floridian living in the neighborhood of Fort Pierce, were hired to drag the craft to the Kissim-mee. Jernegan is a nephew of old Aaron Jernegan,[4] a celebrated scout in the Florida war. The country between the Indian and Kissimmee rivers is thinly settled. The inhabitants own large herds of cattle that are driven across the State to Tampa, from which port they are shipped to the Cuban market.

The boat was the property of Ober. The supplies were furnished by Van Boskerck, the University men chipping in as the necessities of the situation required. The Cambridge Professor and Brown student were in search of rare bugs and plants. Van Boskerck joined the party out of a love of adventure, and appears to have been the commander of the expedition. Ober, with true Yan-kee ingenuity, combined business with pleasure. He took along a trunk full of

Engraving of Fort Bassinger, 1883. Courtesy of Florida State Archives.

garters, spring scales, shoe strings, condensed coffee, mouse traps, shirt buttons, shot, spool cotton, itch ointment, soap, powder, blacking, hooks and eyes, and similar knick knacks, and traded them with the families of the cow drivers on the route. He also had a photographic instrument, which coined a few honest half dollars by taking pictures of the "crackers" or natives. Col. Van Boskerck says, "It was hard to say which was the controlling passion in Ober's breast, the spirit of barter and trade or the spirit of the Okechobee."

DEPARTURE OF THE EXPEDITION.

The company left Judge Paine's[5] residence at Fort Capron, three miles north of Fort Pierce, on St. Valentine's Day. On Feb. 15 they camped in the pine woods, four miles west of Fort Pierce. The following night was passed at Jernigan's. The Colonel rode a horse, and amused himself by shooting at everything that crossed his path. He saw a few deer and some pink curlews. Occasionally he ran across a moccasin snake or an alligator but observed no signs of wild-cats or Florida tigers. Dr. Palmer ran down all strange bugs and insects, and grabbed up every odd plant he could find. Ober endeavored to strike up a trade with each man, woman, and child on the route. When these failed him he fell back upon his own party and proposed to swap jackknives with no takers.

Three days were spent in going from Jernegan's to Fort Bassinger. The weight of the boat broke down the wagon. Much time was lost in replacing the vehicle. The road ran into a trail, and at times the path was almost obliterated. The way lay through a marshy prairie, but as there had been no rain and the water was low it was traversed with little difficulty.

Giant Spiders and Lost Civilizations

THE BLUE MOUNTAINS AND—THE FLEA PITS.

What are known as the Blue Mountains attracted much attention. These mountains are clumps of cypress trees that stud the marshes, and stand out in the sky like the Black Hill of the plains. The clearness of the atmosphere gives them the bluish tinge from which they derive their name. The cow hunters, who have never seen a real mountain, point them out with peculiar pride.

Four nights were passed near the habitations of the cow drivers. Some of them live in abject squalor. But few of their houses were floored. Van Boskerck says that he saw ladies chewing tobacco like horses and ejecting the juice with the precision of a rifle ball. They could hit a tenpenny nail on the head every time.

When the company first entered one of the "cracker" houses they were somewhat startled. Four graves yawned at their feet. The holes were quite deep, and it required caution to keep from falling into them. Ober nearly broke his neck while descanting upon the beauties of a pair of ladies' garters which he was anxious to sell, and the Colonel turned a back somersault while drinking a tin cup of coffee. These graves were flea pits. The great curse of Florida is its fleas, and not its mosquitoes. The country is literally sown with fleas, and they seed every day in the year. Cattle drivers dig these pits in their houses. The fleas jump into them and they cannot get out. When the bottom of the pit is covered, a thin layer of ashes is strewn over the insects, and they perish. The ashes is the bed of another strata of fleas. More ashes is poured upon them and the operation continues until the hole is filled with alternate layers of ashes and fleas, when new pits are dug.

ON THE KISSIMMEE.

Two nights were spent at Fort Bassinger. The Kissimmee river is deep, and its water cool and refreshing. Mosquitoes were thick, but the explorers were well provided with bars, and retired early. Van Boskerck says that they were surprised at the scarcity of alligators. The Palatka *Herald* had reported the river jammed with the scaly reptiles. It had asserted that they lay in the hot sun upon its banks in ridges twelve feet high, and that their roaring sounded like the roar of Niagara. The Colonel declares that his party saw but few of the monsters, and those few were exceedingly shy. In numbers and boldness they did not compare with the alligators on the Upper St. John's.

While camped on the shore of the Kissimmee Dr. Palmer had a narrow escape from death. He and Shores had stripped for a bath. The Doctor was standing upon the bank of the river rubbing his bare legs, and wondering whether the water was cold, when the student from Brown University playfully shoved him in. The water was from twelve to twenty feet in depth, and the Doctor could not swim. He shouted lustily for help. Col. Van Boskerck heard him and ran for his gun, supposing that an alligator had caught the Cambridge Professor. Ober was frightened, and began to load his Ballard rifle. The Doctor was sinking a second time when the Colonel reached the river. As he came to the surface for the last time Van Boskerck stretched out an oar. The drowning man grasped it and was drawn ashore. Several hours went by before he fully recovered.

Fort Bassinger is sixty miles from Fort Capron, and the same distance from Lake Okechobee.[6] The boat was launched on the Kissimmee, and the supplies placed on board. The guides were dismissed, and the voyagers started down the river on the morning of Washington's birthday. They trolled for black bass, and caught several fine fish. One weighed over seven pounds. Flocks of parroquets were seen, and the Colonel bagged a few of them. A bird was wounded and captured alive. Its wing was broken. It became domesticated, took up its quarters in the boat, and was quite a pet. The mosquitoes were not more troublesome than in other parts of Florida. The whole country, however, was infested with great cockroaches. Every palmetto fan and boat was a hiding place for these insects, and the boat was filled with them.

IN LAKE OKECHOBEE.

The river between Bassinger and Okechobee was lined with marshes miles in extent, intersected by sluices and lagoons. Occasionally cypress trees dotted these swamps, and tall reeds and wire grass reared their heads upon the edge of the water. Acres of green lily pads danced upon the verge of the stream, and the voyagers passed thousands of floating lettuce or "bonnets." The current was quite strong, and the scenery similar to that on the upper St. John's, though there were fewer palmettoes.

After carefully threading the marshes the explorers reached the lake during the afternoon of the 24th of February. The water stretched to the south as far as the eye could reach, and a line of marshes gradually faded away in the east and the west. The lake is not so large as has been asserted. It proved to be forty-five miles long and twenty-five wide. At high water it may be larger, but its area cannot be much increased. The water was so low that a white sandy beach margined the swamps on the east. There was no high land on the west. The water is bordered by cypress swamps and marshes reeking with decayed vegetation. The lake is shallow. It avereged [sic] about seven feet, and at no place was it more than ten feet deep. The floating vegetation was so rank that it had been churned into jelly by the action of the water. At times the odor was frightful. Shores caught a fever, and is now at Fort Capron, just able to toddle about the house.

THE CRAZY SNAKE BIRDS.

So stale was the water that there were no fish in the lake. For days the troll was spinning without success. Even the alligator shunned the stagnation. The gar was not seen, catfish could not be found, and no frogs filled the mid-night air with music. Birds of rare plumage were unknown. Cranes and herons were very scarce, and the cries of loons and bitterns were not heard. Snake birds or water turkeys were discovered in abundance. They were nesting when the party entered the lake. This discovery pleased the Cambridge Professor. The snake bird is said to be the only bird having a parasitical worm feeding upon its brain. It has been a mooted question among naturalists whether this parasite is generated in the brains or takes up its habitation after the bird is of age and has left its nest. Van Boskerck says Dr. Palmer has solved the problem. He examined young birds just from the shell, and found the brain parasites upon their necks and in their throats. From this fact he concludes that the worm gradually works its way into the brain of the bird, and is not a native of its skull. It might interest some people to know how the parasite gets into the throat of the infant bird before its shell is cold. I am informed that the Doctor is in doubt. Another naturalist may at some future day find it necessary to run over to Okechobee to settle this perplexing point. The snake bird derives its name from its peculiar movements while in the water. It has a long, black, shiny neck, and a head shaped like that of a snake. It hides its body beneath the waves, and contorts its head and neck so that it is frequently mistaken for a swimming serpent. Its feathers are brown and glossy, and are highly prized. It is a tough bird, and one exceedingly difficult to kill. On the wing it holds its neck and head as stiff as though they were strung on a straight steel wire.

THE MYTHICAL TEMPLE OF THE MOUND BUILDERS.

Of all the islands in the lake, there is but one on which a landing can be effected. It is about a mile long and but three rods wide. The most prominent object upon it is a big cypress tree. The water line upon this tree shows that at certain seasons of the year the island is entirely inundated. This is probably the spot selected by the St. Augustine Munchausens[7] as the site of the mythical ruins of the temple of the mound builders. The lake is dotted by a dozen islands, but the others are small marshes and have no camping ground. They are from four to eight miles from shore.

The explorers resolved to turn west from the mouth of the Kissimmee and to go completely around the lake. It was a terrible job. They had no servants, and as the wind came out against them they were compelled to row their heavy boat at least half the distance. Shores was sick and unable to bear his brunt of the burden. The lake was so shallow that in some places they could not approach within three miles of the shore. Where the water was deep and a landing could be made they were in danger of impaling their craft upon the sharp cypress trees beneath the surface. Dr. Palmer was perhaps the most energetic man in the company. He took his turn at the oars, caught bugs by the hatful, dug bulbs by the peck, and did the cooking. He was frequently so exhausted that he went to bed supperless. The water was horrible. It smelt worse than asafoetida.[8] To add to their discomforts they were much of the time compelled to sleep in the boat, as it was impossible to find dry land. Ober slept night after night up in a seat twelve inches wide. The mosquito bars could not be properly hung while on the water, and the insects were fearfully annoying.

A NIGHT IN AN OLD INDIAN CAMP.

As the voyagers turned from the outlet of the Kissimmee they passed a sharp point of a low land. An osprey had built its nest in a cypress tree upon this cape, and was giving the young ones a fish supper. The tongue of land was called Osprey Point. Two miles southwest was an old Indian camp. Here the party passed their first night on Lake Okechobee. The camp fire shone bright and cast a ruddy light upon the lake. Fresh fish caught in the cool waters of the Kissimmee were cooked, pipes were lighted, and mosquito bars spread. The crotched stacks and fluge poles of the Indian tents were standing, and wood was abundant. The Cambridge Professor was busy classifying his bugs, and the Brown student pressing flowers preparatory to a thorough examination. The company retired early. During the night Ober and Van Boskerck felt several bugs crawling under their bars and shouted to Dr. Palmer, who gladly arose and secured the prizes. None of them proved rare curiosities.

The next day, Feb. 25, the wind still being unfavorable, the explorers made but five miles. Their course was again southwest. At dark they were near an old slough made up of rotten lily pads and floating cabbage, torn and ground by the rolling of the waves. The effluvium was sickening, but the expedition was forced to cast anchor. The adventurers slept, or attempted to sleep in the boat. In the night Polly, the winged parroquet, cleared the vessel of cock-roaches and made herself generally useful. At one time she ran a big ma-hogany-colored roach under the professor's bug box. The Doctor awoke and heard the parroquet working at his box. He thought the little creature was after his choice insects. His hair stood on end. He drove the bird forward and securely fastened his box. Van Boskerck declares that the Doctor would rather have lost his gold watch or his breeches than one of his spiders or bugs.

THE CARPENTER SHOP.

The following day adverse winds continued. The men rowed unceasingly, but with all their efforts ran only five miles from the slough. They were fortunate, however, in finding firm ground on the shore of the lake and in making a landing. They camped beneath a large mulberry tree, a few feet from the water. The Colonel climbed the tree, but could see nothing of interest. A big cypress swamp covered the view to the west, and the waters of the lake spread away to the east. The camp was dry, and mosquitoes were not especially troublesome.

They were off early on the morning of Feb. 27, still working with a white-ash breeze.[9] During the forenoon they passed a low cape embowered with cabbage palmettoes. This they called Palmetto Point. Two small islands lay well in shore on the west, but were covered with rushes, and of no account. About noon they struck a lone cypress tree on the main shore. Its trunk was of enormous size, and it was over fifty feet high. The tree was perforated with holes bored by the carpenter bee. This insect resembles a bumblebee, and ruins all the trees in its vicinity. The "cracker" name them borers. They sting ferociously and are not pleasant fellows to handle. The cypress tree was designated the Carpenter's Shop. It stood near the mouth of what is laid down on the maps as Fish-Eating creek. Why it is termed Fish Eating is a mystery. The company tried all sorts of tackle, and could catch no fish. They got no bites except from the mosquitoes, and finally put up their hooks and lines satisfied that there were no fish in the creek. The stream was choked by lily-pads. They went up it about a mile and could go no further. The boat was too large. A portion of the afternoon was spent at a snake bird rookery, and many eggs and fine specimens were secured. Night overtook them in the lily-pads, and they came to anchor.

THE WONDERFUL ISLAND.

On Feb. 28 the course was south and south-east. A low island was discovered about nine miles from shore. It was a mile long and from thirty to forty feet wide. The trees averaged nearly thirty feet in height. One of them, a royal old cypress, was much higher. It stood upon the north shore. The boat was headed for it and good camping ground discovered. The island was a rookery for different kinds of birds.

The party were here two days, and visited all parts of the island. If any interesting ruins were to be seen, they ought to have been found here. In vain they looked for stone pillars and massive arches. They could not find even the Indian pottery so plentiful in other parts of Florida. There were piles of guano and broken birds' eggs, but no ivy-clad pilasters. Van Boskerck climbed the great cypress, and looked out upon a vast expanse of swamp and dead water. Well up on the body of the tree his attention was directed to a number of names cut in the bark. They were the names of a few of Gen. Taylor's[10] officers in the memorable Indian campaign of 1836. Time had dealt squarely with the inscriptions, and the Colonel says he had no difficulty in making them out. While carving his own name he heard a noise a few inches from his head. Looking up he saw a large moccasin snake evidently bent upon forming his acquaintance. Van Boskerck slid to the ground and opened fire upon the moccasin. At the first shot the head was severed, and fell so close to the Colonel's feet that he says he thought the serpent had dropped upon him. The snake was as thick as the fleshy portion of a man's arm.

Lookout Island was the name given the place. It is supposed that the cypress tree was used as a signal station during the Indian war. The view was more extensive than at any other point on the lake.

THE LOST PARROQUET—AN OWL SERENADE.

While at Lookout Island the sprightly parroquet disappeared. It was probably captured and eaten by a snake. The bird was a great favorite. It had become very tame. While in camp it was in the habit of wandering off after bugs and caterpillars, but when night came it invariably returned to headquarters, and slept beneath blankets under the musquito bars. It kept the boat comparatively free from fleas and cockroaches, and its loss was sincerely regretted. The broken wing had become firmly knitted, and the other wing had been clipped to prevent the bird taking French leave. As a buggist it is said to have eclipsed Dr. Palmer.

On the 3d of March the explorers left Lookout Island. The wind was still ahead, and nothing but a steady pull at the oars kept the vessel in motion. Toward night a shell beach was seen west of a small grassy island, and again the tired travellers camped on the main land. The shore was strewn with fossil shells of a common order, and the place was termed Fossil Camp. The blankets were spread in a clean spot. For two or three hours the adventurers slept soundly. About midnight a half-dozen horned owls alighted in a tree over their heads and began a protracted meeting. It was worse than a woman's temperance crusade. The owls were mating. They laughed and hooted, chuckled and screamed, panted and blowed until Van Boskerck declared that they had escaped from a private lunatic asylum. Sleep was impossible. The owls claimed the land and would not be driven off. It was broad daylight before the infernal racket ceased. "If you have ever heard a gang of green Dutchmen laboring at the opera of 'Der Freyshcutz,' you can have some idea of our alarming situation," said Col. Van Boskerck.

SWEEPING PAST THE EVERGLADES.

On the 4th of March the wind sprang up fair and free. Sail was set, and the boat sped along the water like a thistle down. The little grassy island soon disappeared. Before 12 o'clock the adventurers passed a grove of custard-apple trees, used by the birds as a rookery. Late in the afternoon they were at the extreme southern end of Okechobee. Four little islands, known as the Sisters, were huddled in a bay dipping into the Everglades. The entrance to the glades was a thicket of custard-apple trees. The fruit was ripe. Its flavor was delicious, something like our Northern May apple. The carpenter bee had been at work among the trees on the southern shore. So numerous were their perforations at a point opposite the Sisters that the explorers called it the Bee Hive. Van Boskerck asserts that there was but little water in the Everglades. It would have been impossible to force a canoe through the marshes. Saw grass, lily pads, and scattered custard-apple and cypress trees were all that could be seen.

The company tried to land on the Sisters, but failed, and were compelled to camp in the boat. Mosquitoes swept down upon them like a sand storm. There was no withstanding the onset. The insects threatened to fly away with the boat. At 11 P.M. sail was set, and the voyagers went a little to the north of east until they reached a beautiful shell beach. They landed in a bright moonlight, spread their bars, and were lulled to sleep by murmuring trees and chirping crickets.

A GALE ON LAKE OKECHOBEE.

By daylight the wind was blowing hard. The lake was shallow, but the waves rolled from eight to ten feet high, and combed in foam like the breakers of the sea. The sail was double-reefed, and the craft was swung upon the wings of the air. It was late in the forenoon when the explorers left the shell beach. After they had run thirty miles, the wind increased to a gale. It was deemed prudent to camp. The vessel was beached upon a shore of shining sand half way up the western [sic; should be eastern] coast. By dark the leaves of the palmettoes were humming to the tune of a hurricane. The waves rolled upon the beach with such force and noise that it seemed like camping within gun shot of the ocean surf. The camp was dry. It was called Hurricane Camp.

On the 6th of March the adventurers arose pretty well fagged out. The novelty of the trip had worn off, and they worked as though they were performing a hard task instead of experiencing a pleasure. The wind had died out, and the lake was placid. It looked as though another white ash breeze would be required to move. While working along to the northeast a grove of banana trees appeared upon the shore. The beach was white sand, and thirty feet wide. The men went ashore and secured a large branch of bananas. The land appeared to be rich and productive. There were traces of sugar cane, and ruins of houses, either blown down or torn up. But few timbers were left. The plot was the remains of some sort of plantation. It is laid down on old maps of Florida as the site of an Indian village, and was undoubtedly destroyed during the last Seminole war. A camp was made and the vicinity thoroughly explored. Nothing more of interest was unearthed.

LOST ON LAKE OKECHOBEE.

On March 7 the course was north until a large bay was reached. The voyagers took it for Cohanza bay. It is so designated on the maps. Taking a northwesterly and then a westerly direction they struck another fine bay, which they took for the mouth of the Kissimmee. A broad stream emptied into it, and they were sure that they had seen the last of Lake Okechobee and were on their way home. While rowing up this river they saw a man upon the shore. He was the first human being they had seen in fourteen days. In reply to their questions he said that he was a Western man, and was looking around for a cattle range. He was depending upon his rifle for subsistence and seemed to be passing his time very pleasantly. He had been away from civilization over two months, and rather liked it. The Colonel was out of tobacco and asked him if he could spare some. The Western man willingly divided his last plug, remarking as he did so, that he didn't care much for tobacco anyhow.

"How far do you call it to Fort Bassinger?" the Colonel inquired.

"Fort Bassinger is on the Kissimmee," responded the stranger.

"Isn't this the Kissimmee river?" asked the Colonel.

"Oh, no," replied the stranger. "This is Taylor's creek. It was on this creek that Gen. Taylor fought the battle of Okechobee. The battleground is only a few miles off."

The tired explorers made no effort to reach the battle-field. They had taken with them no change of clothing, and were anxious to return to Fort Capron. The Colonel wore a boiled shirt. It was in a shocking condition, and he wanted to get rid of it. So the boat was headed down the stream, and the voyagers reentered the Lake. Kissimmee bay lay two miles further to the southwest. They anchored at the outlet of the river and lay by for the night.

LAST SIGHT OF OKECHOBEE.

In the morning the oars were again brought into requisition, and the travelers began to stem the current of the river. The day was hot, and sweat oozed from every pore. The broad waters of Okechobee were dancing in the horizon behind them, and reflecting the beams of the burning sun. There was a sudden turn in the marshes, and the panting oarsmen had seen the last of the mysterious lake. A steady pull of eight hours followed. When night came no camping ground was visible. The gentle ripple of the water on the bow of the boat and the sweet strains of the mosquito soothed the company to sleep.

The next day, March 9, rowing was resumed. They ran up four or five old sloughs, mistaking them for the river. Each of the sloughs had a stiff current, which misled them. The channel was found at last and they passed the night at an old Indian camp on the eastern shore. The roots of the palmetto trees were blackened with fire, and bunches of dry fans marked the beds of the Seminoles.

On March 10 the channel of the river was maintained without much effort. Good camping ground was discovered in a dry hammock, and the party prepared for a refreshing sleep. Ober thoughtlessly fired the crisp palmettoes. Tongues of flame darted into the sky, and in an instant, the place was as hot as Tophet. The bedding was hastily pitched into the boat, and the four men shoved out in the river, leaving their cooking utensils to the mercy of the fire. It was midnight before the ground was cool enough to land. The fire, however, destroyed the mosquitoes, and a peaceful night's rest was the result.

THE RESULTS OF THE EXPEDITION.

This was the last adventure of any consequence. The following night the party reached the house of Mr. Thomas Doughtery,[11] who hospitably welcomed them. They slept eight in one room and three beds. Doughtery's habitation is on a high bank, twenty feet from the Kissimmee. The water was deep, and a good sized steamer could moor to the bank in front of his house without a wharf. Fort Bassinger was reached at 4 P.M., March 12, eighteen days and nights having elapsed since the company had left it. On March 17 they arrived at Fort Pierce, having accomplished the round trip in just thirty-one days.

The results of the expedition were hardly satisfactory. Dr. Palmer, who was an intimate friend of Agassiz,[12] secured many bugs and insects, but very few worthy of notice. He has any number of butterflies, but none very rare. The trip did not repay him for his time and trouble. But while the expedition may have been unsatisfactory in a scientific point of view it has removed much of the glamour cast over the lake by the stories of the Indians and cracker hunters. The latter pretend to visit Okechobee every summer, and return with wonderful accounts of its beautiful birds and immense alligators. They say that it is the breeding place of the flamingo, roseate spoon-billed curlew, snowy heron, ermine pelican, and other birds of royal plumage. They aver that the lake is filled with enormous alligators and gars, and magnify the difficulties attendant upon an expedition to its shores. Four-pound spiders are said to be common. All this is done for the purpose of selling a few feathers and bird-skins obtained elsewhere to Northern visitors at a high price. Cow drivers declare that no hunter has entered the lake since the Indian war.

This expedition is the first that has placed a boat upon the waters of the Kissimmee, and Okechobee cannot be reached and explored any other way. The Indians occasionally enter it with their canoes, via the Halpatteen-hatchie, the Big Cypress, or the Everglades, but the first high wind drives them upon the shore, and they are glad to crawl back into their native swamps. They fill white men with marvellous stories of snakes forty feet long and winged lizards larger than turkey buzzards and more poisonous than bandy-legged tarantulas. The red man looks upon the white man with jealous fear. The Everglades and contiguous swamps are his last hiding-place, and it is to his interest the pale face should know as little about them as possible.

The best thing accomplished by Col. Van Boskerck and his companions is the exposure of literary impostors. One of these has written a fictitious visit to the lake, which he palmed upon the editor of *Lippincott's Magazine* as genuine, while a St. Augustine man exhibits in his museum specimens of remarkable ruins which he declares were found upon an island in Okechobee, and with which somebody has imposed upon the venerable Judge Daly and the American Geographical Society.[13]

I am indebted to Col. Van Boskerck for the map printed above. It compares favorably with Drew's map as far as the shape is concerned, but in nothing else is Drew accurate.

ZISKA.

Mar-a-Lago–1874

Amos Cummings had some extraordinary adventures in Florida. This may be his best. With two other men he traveled by boat from Fort Capron near Fort Pierce Inlet south past Hobe Sound, across Jupiter Inlet, and down to Lake Worth. Today a similar trip from St. Lucie County to Palm Beach County via the Intracoastal Waterway would be an easy outing in a motor boat. In 1874, it was a life-or-death struggle through an extraordinary land and waterscape.

Without Cummings's article, would modern residents of the towns of Lake Worth, Palm Beach, and West Palm Beach realize what their part of Florida once was like? I don't think so. According to information I found online, some of those residents even think Lake Worth is an artificial lake! Others have no idea that in the nineteenth century Lake Worth was not the saltwater lagoon it is today. What? Yes, it is true. On August 28, 1874, when this article appeared in the *New York Sun* (under the name Ziska), Lake Worth was a freshwater lake, though it may have been a bit on the brackish side occasionally when the ocean slopped in.

What happened in the intervening years? The transformation of Lake Worth from freshwater to salt has been well documented by Palm Beach County engineers. The lake originally was fed not by springs but by drainage from the Everglades on its western side. Its eastern side was demarcated by a narrow strip of land—a barrier island—that separated ocean from lake, giving rise to names such as Mar-a-Lago (Sea to Lake). Today that narrow strip of land is among the most expensive property in Florida.

That same barrier no longer protects Lake Worth from the Atlantic Ocean. The lake has been opened to the sea. Settlers on the heels of Amos Cummings's adventure created an inlet from the Atlantic into Lake Worth. Presto! What had been a freshwater lake became a saltwater lagoon.

Next, contouring of the wetlands along the shore of the lake began, a process that continued for almost a century. The lake, especially the west side, looks nothing like it did in 1874.

The lake's ecosystem probably became schizophrenic in the 1890s, when a canal was completed from Jupiter Inlet to the north end of the lake, allowing freshwater to flow into it once again. Later the canal was expanded, connecting the lake and Jupiter inlet, resulting in more salt water. Another canal was dug from the south end of the lake south to Biscayne Bay. These latter canals are now portions of the saltwater Atlantic Intracoastal Waterway. By World War I, a permanent inlet also connected the lake directly to the Atlantic.

Since that time, various inlets and canals, some of the latter draining interior South Florida, have caused the salt and freshwater balance of Lake Worth to ebb and flow. But salt triumphed, thanks to two well-engineered inlets connecting to the ocean. Lake Worth, like much of natural Florida, has been bent to the will of modern Floridians.

13

ADVENTURES IN FLORIDA

◆

A SUN CORRESPONDENT WANDERING IN THE EVERGLADES.

◆

The Beautiful Lake below Okechobee–Scenes on the Lower Indian River–The City of Pelicans–A Palmetto Hammock in a Blaze–Narrow Escape from a Menatee–In the Jupiter Narrows–A Night in a Mangrove Swamp–The Black Scorpion–A Pig on a Reel–Lost in the Everglades.

Fort Capron, Fla., March 30.—Fifty miles southeast of Okechobee and sixty miles north of Biscayne bay lies a beautiful lake rarely visited by white men. It is about the size of Seneca lake.[1] A narrow strip of land, densely wooded, separates it from the ocean, and the warm Gulf Stream flows unceasingly within rifle shot of its waters. On the west it is locked in by the Everglades, and is approachable only through the watery paths webbing that unexplored region. The lake is bespangled with islands. It sleeps in perpetual summer. The thermometer runs but little below fifty degrees, and frost never seres the green leaves of the trees. Cocoa palms and ever-blooming oleanders adorn its shores, and scores of dark-green India rubber trees knot their banyan-like branches in its outlying thickets. The mastic plum, luscious alligator pear, purple mulberry, ruddy sea grape, mellow pawpaw, oranges, lemons, cocoa-nuts, and other wild fruits are reflected in its bosom. Variegated shells, tinted land crabs, gilded ants, and crickets, snowy owls and herons, roseate curlews, sea-green turtles, and huge ebon alligators are seen at every turn. Strips of morning-glory prairie are dotted with red deer, and tropical jungles are the lurking places of tigers, bears, and wildcats. The wild turkey struts through the woods, and great ivory-billed woodpeckers drum the sturdy oaks. The silvery pompino jumps from wave to wave, and the lake is filled with fish. Such is the bright side of the picture. Its dark side is a haze of fleas, sandflies, mosquitoes, jiggers, deerflies, scorpions, red bugs, snakes, and hurricanes; but despite these annoyances, the country is a paradise for all who enjoy camp life and like hunting and fishing.

LAKE WORTH.

London and Paris are nearer Jacksonville in point of time than Lake Worth; for such is the name of this quiet sheet of water. With the most favorable winds it would take two weeks to reach it. Running to the head of steamboat navigation on the St. John's, the traveller must strike across to the Indian river. After sailing down this estuary to its confluence with the ocean at Jupiter, he must ascend one of the sluggish outlets from the Everglades, and thread many of the almost numberless slews and lily-padded ponds of this extraordinary swamp. Lastly he must draw his boat over an arm of land completely encircling the lake and cutting it off from the glades. The distance from Jacksonville is over 400 miles, and much of the journey through a country with scarcely an inhabitant. The trip to the Indian river is full of interest, but has been so often described that I pass it by.

I left Fort Capron, nearly a hundred miles south of Cape Canaveral, on the 8th of March. My companions were a Mr. Hammond of Conneautville, Pa.,[2] and Mr. Charles Moore.[3] The latter is an old salt. For years he was the only white man living on Lake Worth. Hammond found his way down there last year, and has preempted 160 acres of rich land skirting the beach. We had a month's provisions—a bag of salt pork, several packages of prepared flour, a bushel of hard bread, a few sweet potatoes, and a gallon or more of syrup. The trip was made in a nineteen-foot Whitehall boat, about four feet wide. She had a centre-board and a sprit-sail, and would weigh close on to 300 pounds. Tent, blankets, mosquito-bars, and provisions on board, there was but little room for passengers.

OYSTERS GROWING ON TREES.

Everything in readiness, sail was hoisted and we darted away from Judge Paine's little wharf.[4] Fort Capron sounds large, but the Judge's family are its only inhabitants. The stockade rotted away years ago, and a dim line of earthworks alone remains. It was an important point during the Seminole war. The Judge was then a sutler,[5] and has lived at Fort Capron since that time. His residence is nearly opposite Indian river inlet. Of old South Carolina stock, he upholds its reputation for courtesy and hospitality. A man of noteworthy attainments is the Judge. I am told that he can begin with the first line of Tempest and recite Shakespeare from memory clear through to the last line of Othello. He entertains travellers, and his accommodations are unsurpassed along the river. Indeed his is the only house in Florida where I have been able to procure a gourd of fresh milk.

At Fort Capron the river is from three to four miles wide. Its bottom for twenty-fives miles north is a mass of oyster beds. The bivalves are of great size, and equal to a saddle rock in flavor. I have seen shells fourteen inches long. It may sound tough, but I have also seen the branches of mangrove trees loaded with oysters. During high tide the limbs sweep the water, and young barnacles fasten upon them. Oysters clamp themselves upon the barnacles, and at low tide dangle from the trees. The ocean side of the lower Indian river is strung with mangrove islands. The trees are numerous and at a distance the islands resemble great banks of *arbor vita*,[6] closely trimmed.

A CITY OF PELICANS.

We were off before a stiff norther. A heavy sea was running. Our course was a little south of west. Over the waves danced our boat like a cockle shell. Moore wet the mast every ten minutes to keep the sprit in position. As night approached the wind increased in fury. Each wave was crested with foam. Twelve miles below Fort Capron we passed a singular mangrove island. Every tree seemed to have been white-washed. Standing in the foreground, backed by the dark wavy foliage of the beach, the island looked like a ruined marble temple. It was a pelican roost. The trees were whitened with guano, and the deposit covered the ground to the depth of several inches. Thousands of pelicans crowded the island, and the mangroves bent with the weight of their nests. The males were dumping bags of fish into the throats of their setting mates. It was a city of feather inhabitants, with a fish trade that threw Fulton Market[7] into the shade.

The sun was dropping in the west as we neared the mouth of the St. Lucie.[8] It is a broad, deep stream, emptying into the Indian river about thirty miles below Capron. Its actual source has not been discovered, but it is supposed to take its rise in the Halpattee Okee or some other of the great swamps of the interior. Near its mouth it forks to the north and south. Both branches flow through a primeval wilderness. Not a soul lives upon its banks. At its junction with the St. Lucie the Indian river becomes broad and imposing. Its western shore rises in stair-like ridges, etched with green palmetto scrub and bordered by a thin line of dark spruce pine. The eastern shore is rimmed by high palmettoes and mangroves, and the sullen roar of the Atlantic was wafted to our ears through their murmuring leaves.

NARROW ESCAPE FROM A MENATEE.

Both the Indian and St. Lucie rivers are filled with a coarse, rank grass, which takes root at a depth of from twenty to thirty feet, and rises to the surface. It is called menatee grass, because it is eaten by the wonderful menatee or sea-cow. Florida is the only spot on the North American continent where this animal is found. It is amphibious and herbiverous, and weighs from 800 to 2,000 pounds. It suckles its young, and has a head like a seal, a nose like a cow, flippers like a sea-lion, and a tail like a whale. Such is the description by those who have seen it. Of immense strength, when at bay it can easily knock a boat to pieces. The body is powerfully built. The bones are like iron, and the ribs are short, thick, and heavy, and as white as ivory. The menatee is very shy. Once in a while one is shot. Several have been netted. One was captured a year ago and taken to Savannah alive, but it died within a few months. The meat is eaten by the people living on the upper Indian river, and is said to be sweet and palatable. Indians are extremely fond of it.

While on the way up from Lake Worth, Moore and Hammond had a narrow escape from a menatee. They were sailing at twilight in one of the sluggish and tortuous lagoons leading to the Everglades. While rounding an abrupt curve in a mangrove swamp they startled a menatee. The monster was sleeping under some low branches. Thinking itself cornered, it made a rush for the boat. Fortunately the water was deep, and it slipped under the bow. Its back, however, scraped the keel, and the craft was lifted from the water. The menatee lashed the waves with its tail, barely missing the boat, and raised such a swell that she half filled with water. The pale-faced men baled her out and continued their journey.

Years ago an Indian river hunter was caught in a similar fix. The sky was overcast and the night very dark. A frightened menatee shattered his boat and she went to the bottom. The hunter caught the boughs of the overhanging mangroves and tried to pull himself ashore, but was barred by a network of roots. All night long he clung to the mangroves. Clouds of mosquitoes and sandflies surrounded him and he suffered almost intolerable tortures. At daylight he managed to get into the swamp, and after incredible hardships worked his way to a point opposite Jupiter light, where he made himself heard and was rescued.

FIRING A HAMMOCK.

Darkness was upon us before we reached the St. Lucie. The wind was blowing a gale. We skirted the thickets of the eastern shore, looking for a place to camp. We were moving over a watery meadow, and the boat tore through the rank menatee grass like a thing of life. A landing was at last made in a dense palmetto hammock fringed with mangroves. The ocean howled through the darkness two hundred yards beyond us, but tropical vines and briars hedged us from the beach. Palmetto bones strewed the ground, and dead fans swung from the tops of the trees. The breeze swept upon us a myriad of mosquitoes. To drive them away we fired the hammock. In a minute the ground was a sheet of flame. The blaze caught the dried fans in the lofty trees, and jumped through them like a race horse, creating a second sheet of flame sixty feet above us. A bright pillar of sparks was whirled into the sky and scattered upon the broad bosom of the river. The grove and its copses were illuminated as with a Drummond light,[9] and the oily bones glowed with a white heat. A thousand blazing barrels of kerosene could not have been hotter. Forced back to the boat, we shoved from the shore.

From the water the scene was appalling. Scores of night birds shrieked at the devastation, and hundreds of gorgeous butterflies, driven from their hiding places, floated in the bright light like pieces of golden tissue paper. A colony of coots, terrified at the unusual sight, ran off over the water, leaving a sheet of foam in their wake, and thousands of silvery mullet flashed above the surface of the river. The fire ran against the wind, and skipped through the long branches, forming bowers and arches of pure flame. The leaves, bones, and boots of the trees were full of palm oil, and sent out a blaze of peculiar whiteness and intensity.

A NIGHT IN CAMP.

It was nearly 9 o'clock when we reentered the smoking thicket. The heat was stifling and the air was filled with ashy flakes, but there were no mosquitoes or sand flies. Blankets were spread upon the blackened ground and mosquito bars were reared above them. As there were no signs of rain we did not pitch a tent. A Floridian mosquito bar bears no resemblance to the flimsy nettings used at the North. It is made of coarse unbleached cotton cloth, and is a tent of itself. When suspended above the sleeper its sides and ends are tucked under his blankets, keeping out lizards, scorpions, snakes, roaches, and other creeping things. The bar is a square shelter, and shuts out the air as well as insects. The heat is sweltering. In the dead of winter I have slept all night beneath my bar stark naked. The traveller perspires up to midnight, but after that the air becomes cooler, and he catches a refreshing rest, provided he is not troubled by fleas. Avoid woollen blankets. They are the paradise of fleas. To be sure the insects can be driven out by spreading the blankets upon the hot sand of the seashore, but the seashore is not always available. The best plan is to use cotton coverlets. On this trip I slept between two pieces of sailcloth, and was comparatively free from flea bites.

Bars suspended and blankets spread, we sat down around the camp fire. A few pieces of salt pork were fried and a loaf of bread was cut. It was a plain supper, but heartily relished. Unfortunately we had forgotten our coffee, but Moore found a substitute. He stripped a bay tree and steeped its leaves. This decoction is called Indian river tea. It is used by many Floridians. After pipes were smoked every man crept under his bar. I cannot say that I enjoyed the situation. We were thirty miles from any habitation. The sighing of the wind, the moaning of the ocean, and the rustling of the palmettoes forbade sleep. The fire was still creeping through the hammock beyond us, and the cracking of the blazing fans as they fell to the ground was anything but assuring. Flickering shadows trooped over the mosquito bar, and shrill cries from oyster birds floated on the wings of the gale. It was long after midnight when I fell asleep.

WONDERS OF THE JUPITER NARROWS.

We were off before sunrise. The fire had run nearly a mile, and the hammock was smoking like a volcano. Two weeks afterward we passed the same spot, and the woods were still aflame.

The mouths of the St. Lucie were in sight. They formed a magnificent bay. It was as large as New York harbor. Miles in extent, it was shaped like a crescent and margined by crowded cabbage trees. Its water freshened the saltness of the Indian river. The pelicans had founded another city upon an island shading the bay. They gazed at our craft in wonder, and excited laughter by their judicial gravity. After crossing the bay we approached Jupiter Narrows.[10] The river decreases in width and increases in depth. An old dead tree on the beach, seen through an opening in the mangroves, marked what is known as Gilbert's Bar.[11] Over a hundred years ago this was an outlet to the ocean. It is now a ridge of sand over forty feet high. Here the English fleet landed the expedition against St. Augustine. A flotilla was formed, and they went up the Indian, Hillsborough, and Halifax river, reaching the old city by marching up the banks of the Matanzas. It involved a trip of 280 miles, but the Spaniards were routed, and the peninsula fell into the hands of King George.[12]

By 10 o'clock we were sailing through a labyrinth of mangrove islands. These trees had lost their crookedness, and shot into the sky as straight as so many spars. They were from twenty to sixty feet high. The gnarled roots stood out several feet above the ground, and the trunks rose from them, sending over the water a mass of branches. The moist soil surrounding the roots was dotted with millions of bright red crabs about the size of our Northern fiddlers. Air-plants without number sat in the crotches of the limbs, and their plumes of blue and crimson nodded in the wind. They resemble small century plants, or the top of a pineapple. Moore told a story of a Northern lady who visited Florida, and pointing to the air-plants exclaimed: "Oh, what a country of beauty this is! Look at the lovely pineapples[13] growing on the trees." These plants are a blessing to the thirsty. They are always filled with the purest water. Puncture the bottom with the point of a knife, and a refreshing draught can be obtained in the driest weather.

THE BEARS AND THE PALMETTOES.

It is twelve miles through the Narrows—twelve miles of novel beauty. There are places where the river is but little wider than the boat, and the mangroves and rubber-trees lock their branches over the traveller's head. A bad spot it is to be caught in in a calm. The water is so deep that a boat-pole is of no use, and there is but one marshy island where a camp could possibly be made. It is undoubtedly the worst place for sandflies and mosquitoes on the Florida coast. But for quiet, natural beauty, it is unsurpassed. Schools of porpoises rove through its waters, and the ibis and plumed heron rejoice in its ever-green foliage. Airy butterflies fluttered over our sail, and sparkling dragon-flies darted past us at every breath.

The tops of many palmettoes had been torn in pieces by bears. Bruin climbs the trunks and rips out the heart of the trees. The heart of a palmetto resembles a cabbage. Floridians boil and eat it. When raw, it tastes like a chestnut. Pickled in vinegar, it creates a keen relish. Natives invariably speak of the palmetto as a cabbage tree. It is this heart or cabbage that produces a fresh circle of fans every other new moon. As the lower circle fades and drops to the ground, a new one appears. The butts of the dead fans cling to the tree, and look like straps crossing the bark diagonally in opposite directions. These yellow straps are called "boots." As the palmetto reaches the prime of life, it sheds its boots, and the bark becomes smooth. The tree is then of the same size all the way up. If a man can fancy a bullrush from sixty to eighty feet high, crowned with circles of green fans, he will have some idea of an aged pal-metto. Such trees are frequently two or three hundred years old. The wood is absolutely good for nothing. It can neither be used for fuel nor sawn into boards. It looks like strong, dark cord cut into pieces fifty feet long, rolled into the shape of a stove pipe, and glued together. The tree itself is no larger than the mast of a ship.

HOPE SOUND.[14]

As we glided through the Narrows, the forest shut out the wind, and the water became as smooth as a mirror. Part of the time we were compelled to rely upon a white-ash breeze.[15] By one o'clock we slipped through an archway of rubber trees and entered Hope Sound. The scenery retained its beauty. None of the land, however, was fit for cultivation. The stair-like ridges on the west-ern shore became larger, and the lines of saw-palmettoes changed to a green-ish blue. They rose along the bank like seats in an amphitheatre. Immense piles of white sand, sprinkled with scrubby vegetation, glistened in the sun. The roar of the surf still rolled over the beach. We passed a monstrous alligator basking in the sunlight. His eyes were closed, and he slept as peacefully as an infant. Occasionally a gigantic turtle arose from the water and stared at us. The shore was colored with strange flowers and grasses, and pointed agaves and Spanish bayonets were squatted on hillocks of sand. At one point an isolated settler had built a hut, reminding one of the habitations on the line of the Panama Railroad, but mosquitoes had driven him back into civilization, and his house was in the last stage of ruin. Afar off a sharp eye could see the lighthouse at Jupiter. It pricked the sky like a needle.

Below the Narrows the river is nearly straight; yet its channel is crooked, and without a pilot a stranger might ruin his boat by running upon the oyster bars. Our course was diversified by wooded capes and quiet bays, and we caught an occasional glimpse of the great pine woods that stretch from the mouth of the St. John's down to the Everglades. We approached Jupiter on a free wind. Schools of bluefish began to break about our bows. I got out a spinner and hooked one, but he shook himself loose and carried with him a gang of hooks.

A FISH WITH A GIZZARD—AN UNFORTUNATE HOG.

We rounded a white promontory, and were at the light. Its tower rises from a sand hill until it is nearly two hundred feet above the water. It is of brick and iron, and is considered a first-class light. An old white dwelling house stood at its foot, surrounded by red periwinkles, razor-backed hogs, sickly scrub, and sleepy hounds. A spot more lonely or desolate would be difficult to find. The keepers were courteous, but reserved. They seemed to be under the influence of their dreary surroundings, and spent much of their time on the lofty balcony of the tower, smoking their pipes, drinking in the ocean breeze, and viewing with complacency the flea-fighting crowd below. We landed at the wharf, started a fire upon the sand, and prepared for dinner. A school of mullet broke along the shore. Mr. Armour,[16] the head keeper, spread his castnet over them and drew them in. Moore scaled the fish. While cutting them open I made a singular discovery. Every fish had a gizzard like that of a chicken. It was hard and thick, and filled with sand. Mullets have broad heads, and large, dreamy eyes, and are generally found in shallow water. They never take a hook, and are the prey of almost every fish that swims in salt water. They grow as large as shad, and fatten in the fall, when they are regarded as a great delicacy.

Just before dinner I rigged up a rod and reel, made a cast from the little pier fronting the light-house, and caught several red snappers, fish modelled

The Jupiter Inlet lighthouse and keeper's house in the 1880s. Courtesy of Florida State Archives.

after a black bass and fully as gamey. While we were eating, a pig raised a terrible outcry in a clump of bushes sixty yards away. Everybody was on the alert. It was supposed that a bear had caught the pig, and there was a general rush for rifles. The hounds dashed to the covert, and rolled out warning notes. The cause of the disturbance was soon explained. I had left my fishing-rod upon a carpenter's bench without removing the bait. The pig bolted the hook. As he walked off, the line ran out from the reel, and he was soon brought up with a round jerk. Finding himself securely hooked, he raised an unearthly squeal. It was enough to split the drum of a man's ear. I caught the rod, and began to wind in the line. The pig played like a veteran bass, and handled himself with commendable sagacity, but could not shake the hook from his mouth, and it was afterward cut out.

We found the inlet at Jupiter closed for the first time in six years. The ocean had dammed it with sand, and the only outlet to the Indian river was through the inlet at Fort Capron. In the rainy season, when the water pours from the Everglades, a ditch will be dug in the sand bar and the force of the current will soon reopen a channel.

OFF FOR THE EVERGLADES.

An hour before sundown and we were off for the Everglades. The inside passage from Jupiter to Lake Worth crosses an arm of this marvellous region.[17] Twenty miles is the distance.[18] The path is known to but five white men. They have repeatedly staked it out, but the Indians quickly pull up the stakes. The savages desire to retain an exclusive knowledge of the wonders of the glades, and artfully mislead and mystify the pale-faces. There is but one firm spot between the light and the lake. It is known as "the Indian Camping Ground."[19] We were hopeful of reaching it before dark, although it was eight miles away. No puzzle is more intricate than the bayous and lagoons south of Jupiter. Our course lay toward every point on the compass. Gloomy mangroves shut out all surroundings. Moore was our pilot. He had been through the passage twenty times; but he repeatedly lost his way. Steadily we continued on our course, north, south, east, and west. By sundown we found ourselves back within half a mile of the light. We could hear the dogs barking through the mangroves, notwithstanding we had sailed several miles.

The wind died away, the twilight faded, and we were in darkness. Hammond bent himself to the oars. Fortunately the night was chilly, and unfavorable for sandflies and mosquitoes, but while at the lighthouse we had taken on board a large delegation of fleas. They thrived by industry, and we suffered correspondingly. Through the gloom we blundered. We were lost in a sombre lagoon, bordered by broad ferns of a height truly extraordinary. When the mistake was discovered we had gone over a mile out of our way. Our course was retraced. The watery lanes were more perplexing than the streets of Boston. We would think we were moving along all right when the road would abruptly end. The sky shone in the inky water, and reflected the weird cocoa-plum trees along the shore. Again we turned backward. Moore kept a sharp lookout for landmarks. "Now, we're right," he said. "I remember that dead rubber tree." But there was more than one dead rubber tree, and we were not right. Then the pilot thought that he recognized a crook in a mangrove, or a peculiar malformation of an air-plant. His imagination must have had something to do with it, for it was so dark that I could see neither air-plant nor mangrove. The situation was anything but agreeable. We could hear large fish popping from the water. Alligators crushed through the swamp, and the doleful chant of a death-owl floated over the bayou. Every minute we expected to be knocked to pieces by a frightened menatee.

THE BLACK SCORPION.

It was 9 o'clock when we swept between two small islands roofed with custard apples. As we were swinging around a curve Moore pointed to the right, saying, "Hold on. Keep her in. There's the Indian Camping Ground now." He was right. It was a strip of firm ground, the only oasis in this desert of swampy vegetation. We landed. Groping through the furze[20] I found a few decaying sticks and started a fire. In the flickering light I looked about me. Never had I seen a more dismal spot. One small, scraggy oak was our sole shelter, and under it we spread our blankets. To add to our discomfort a cold northeast wind arose, and the scraggy oak began to dance and whistle. The water splashed drearily against the reeds and the boat kept up an uneasy rocking. The dim light of the fire brought into view the crotched posts and ridge-poles left by wandering Seminoles. They were scattered about us like so many gibbets.

After hanging our bars we squatted around the dying coals and made out a supper. Suddenly Hammond clapped his hand to his leg and uttered a cry of pain. It was startling. In the firelight I saw him turn down his stocking and run his hand up the leg of his pantaloons. When he withdrew it a dark object was clinging to his forefinger. "A tarantula!" I exclaimed. He glanced at it and shook it off in horror. The thing struck me in the head, and I was on my legs in an instant. It fell to the ground, and my appetite went with it. An examination showed it to be a large black scorpion, that had been dragged to the fire in rotten fuel. Its sting was distressing. Hammond's leg began to swell. He was quite cool over it, and after bathing the spot in alcohol continued his supper. Afterward he grew uneasy, and complained of pain for a long time. The bite of a full-grown scorpion is very poisonous. Last year a lady in the Miami settlement having been stung in the neck, died within a few hours. During winter months scorpions are torpid, and their poison lacks the extreme virulence characterizing it in July and August. Moore flooded us with stories of these insects before we turned in. They had their effect. I slept but little. The fleas were lively, and I could not shake off the scorpions.

IN THE EVERGLADES.

Before dawn Moore was puttering around among the pots and kettles. The fire was snapping when he shouted, "Come, boys, get up! We're going to have a Portuguese breakfast this morning."

"What is a Portuguese breakfast?" I asked.

"A hell of a row and nothing to eat," he answered. "Come, get up!"

So we got up, and had a crude meal of fried pork and hard bread.

Blankets rolled up, sail was hoisted, and the Indian Camping Ground receded from view. The water was turgid, and the stream very narrow. Tall canes, broad ferns, and thick sawgrass had taken the place of the mangrove swamps. We were in the glades. I had heard my companion speak of a point called the Rapids.[21] My imagination had pictured them after the Rapids of the St. Lawrence. They were twelve feet wide and twenty long. The total deflection was about a foot, not enough to create a musical ripple. Encircled by canebrakes and lily pads, they relieved the monotony of the journey, and were the only rapids that I had seen in Florida.

All day long were we in this arm of the Everglades. The lagoon became a ditch barely the width of the boat. This ditch was as crooked as a ram's horn, and was intersected by hundreds of similar ditches. All were lined with stunted bushes, choked by reeds and sawgrass. Most of the time we could not see twenty feet from the boat. At times the water was of extraordinary depth, and again it was so shallow that we had difficulty in getting through. The bottom was mucky, but occasionally the muck had drifted, and clear silvery sand was seen. This sand underlies the glades. The turns in the ditches were so short that it frequently took several minutes to push the boat around them. At intervals we burst into little lakes covered with lilies as large as pie plates. I dropped a troll into some of them, and caught a number of fine black bass.

While urging our way through a narrow ditch we were confronted by a smashing alligator. He had a large fish crosswise in his mouth. The path was not wide enough for him to pass, and he could not turn around. He studied a moment, and then made a dead rush for the boat. As he passed under it he lifted us from the water, and we could afterward see him fish and all, crawling down stream along the bottom.

SCENES IN THE GLADES.

I wish I could accurately describe the strange and beautiful flowers peering from the sawgrass and dotting the little lakes; also the many brilliant insects that trooped over us. There were striped mosquitoes with golden fans over their eyes, winged daddylonglegs, green spiders with rows of eyes like the guns of a water battery, horse flies with eyes under their wings, triple-tailed spindles, hog-eyed humming birds, and water spiders as large as gingersnaps. I caught a queer bush spider. He had a shell on his back like the shell of a picture crab. The colors were translucent. There were gilded crickets, red grasshoppers six inches long, fleecy butterflies, and millions of long-waisted insects with mottled wings. But the flowers were magnificent. The colors were of a creamy white, delicate yellow, or charming pink, and they emitted the sweetest perfumes. One in particular merited attention, for it was very scarce. I saw not more than a dozen in the whole trip. Its creamy leaves were shaped like the wings of a bat hooked at the angles, and its pistils seemed to be mounted with Chinese characters fashioned with molten gold. A long feeler, like the antennae of a butterfly, shot out from the centre of the cup.

And so the day wore on. The wind freshened. We shook out our sail, and raised the boom half way to the peak. When caught by a gust we tore through the high grass like a hurricane, leaving a great swath behind us. Frequently we lost our way. At such times Moore would carefully examine the bushes. If he found any broken twigs he was sure we were on the right track. He had profited by a long experience with the Seminoles, who mark the paths in the glades by breaking the limbs of the bushes. Moore's eyesight was remarkable. He would detect a broken twig in the sawgrass where a stranger would not notice the bush.

ON THE SHORE OF LAKE WORTH.

On we went. The channel became so shallow that Moore and Hammond got out of the boat and shoved her along. In the muck up to their waists they travelled for at least a mile. Never did they lose their grip of the gunwale, for at any time they were liable to step into a hole of unknown depth. Twice they had hairbreadth escapes from deadly moccasins. I could see the black, flat-headed vipers slipping through the grass as the boat approached them. It was dangerous work. Cranes, snake birds, majors, bitterns, and other fowl circled from the reeds, and flocks of jackdaws laughed at our hardships. A flock of screaming parroquets flew over us. Glad were we when we again struck deep water. We were wafted over a clear open lake. Then we dragged our boat through a muddy little slew, sailed over a reedy pond, and finally struck a firm shore, carpeted with green grass and littered by the debris of an Indian camp. The most prominent object was a large wooden mortar, in which squaws had pounded their corn. Azure lizards were sunning themselves upon it, and it was filled with streaked crickets. Judging from the number of ridge-poles, the place is a favorite camp for Seminoles. A path trailed over a hundred yards of scrub. I followed it.

Lake Worth was before me, glowing in the sunshine. It stretched to the south until its waters were lost in the horizon. Pompino were jumping from its waves, and a fleet of alligators were floating off the shore. A long, black point pierced the lake on the east, designating the entrance to Little Lake Worth. I say black point—it was as black as ebony, and seemed to be alive. It was alive— alive with alligators. They covered it as gulls cover a sandbar. On this shore we camped in the light of a sunset too glorious for reality. It was the dream of a hasheesh eater.

ZISKA.

Mar-a-Lago—1874

Murder and Mayhem in the Sticks

Did they really happen like that? Are the stories true? In this *New York Sun* article from June 4, 1874, Amos Cummings, writing as Ziska, recounts several Florida murders that he heard about. To a civilized New Yorker, the seemingly senseless killings must have reeked of the barbarism of the Florida frontier.

It probably does not matter if the murders indeed occurred as Cummings described them or if they happened at all. He and his readers believed they did. The Florida frontier was rough country inhabited by rough people, people who thought and acted differently from subscribers to the *New York Sun*.

But what is true is that life in Florida was turbulent. On the fringe of the civilized world, people often were quick to kill, while the law was sometimes slow or less than adequate in response. As the Florida frontier moved south, so did frontier "justice." In his masterful trilogy of frontier life in Southwest Florida—*Killing Mr. Watson, Lost Man's River,* and *Bone by Bone*—author Peter Matthiessen brings to life a way of death reminiscent of the murders about which Cummings wrote in this article and in a second article, "The Terror of the Pines," which follows later in this book. Brute, nasty force at times prevailed.

Murder in Florida has a long history, and it was not committed only by frontier rednecks or folks forced to take justice into their own hands. On Tick Island in the St. Johns River, archaeologist Ripley P. Bullen came upon evidence of a murder that took place 5,500 years ago. His excavations revealed a human skeleton of a Florida Indian with a stone spear point stuck in his or her back bone. Two other people had stone points lying immediately next to their bones. They, too, most likely had been stabbed with spears that had broken off, leaving their stone points embedded in the individuals' bodies.

Evidence for another pre-Columbian Florida murder—one that occurred about a millennium and a half ago at an Indian village between Lake City and Live Oak—was found at the McKeithen archaeological site in Columbia County. We were excavating a mound when we found the tomb of a woman. She was buried with red pigment decorating her hair, and with a small amulet—the leg bone of an anhinga, a bird also known as a water turkey or snake bird—tied up in her hair. A small ceramic bird head was placed near her feet. She had died from a horrible infection, the result of being shot with an arrow in her left hip area. The small stone point that had tipped the arrow was still stuck in the bone.

The elaborate rituals that had surrounded her interment in her tomb within the mound made us think she was an important leader in her village. Who had killed her? Was it enemies who raided the village? Or one of her own people? We do not know. The point, however, was a type common in northern Florida at that time and looked like many others found in the village at the same site.

Has Florida always been a hotbed of murder and mayhem? I don't think so. It was the same as everywhere else. And it is no worse today than it was in the past. In my research for this book, I looked through a lot of old newspapers from Florida and from New York City. Murders, robberies, crimes of passion, and even the depravities of mass murderers are nothing new. Amos Cummings and other nineteenth-century journalists wrote about such crimes every day. We haven't learned a lot in the last thirteen decades.

14

LIFE IN THE PALMETTOES

HOW THE PEOPLE ON THE SUWANEE FILL THEIR GRAVEYARDS.

A Young Virginian Loses his Life—Story of a Dog and a Raw Deer Hide—A Man Trades his Daughter for Another Man's Wife and Twenty Head of Cattle—The Cart-wheel Battery—Eleven Buckshot and a Rifle Bullet—A Moonlight Tragedy.

NEW SMYRNA, FLA., MAY 1, 1874.—While I was stopping in Enterprise a painful murder occurred in Mellonville, across the lake. A young Virginian was spending the winter there. One night while attending a hop he saw a fellow making off with his overcoat. He caught him by the arm, saying, "Hold on, sir. You are making a mistake. You have taken my overcoat." The native denied it. A row ensued, ending in a triumph for the Virginian. During the following day the man met the Virginian on the street, drew a revolver, and shot him. He died within twenty-four hours. The murderer fled down the St. John's. The people of Mellonville knew that they could not afford to allow him to escape. Such a course would decrease the stream of Northern visitors. Prompt pursuit was made. The assassin was captured near Volusia, and brought back to Mellonville on the steamer Lollieboy.[1]

He was forwarded forty miles across the country to Orlando, the shire town of Orange county. It was thought that the Sheriff's party would string him up while on the way, and thus save a bill of expense to the county; but the murderer arrived in Orlando, and was sent to prison. It is now rumored that he has escaped. Whether this is true or false, nobody anticipates a conviction. The victim had no friends in the county and the murderer, though of bad repute, has relatives and can command a little ready money.

HOW A FATHER ENFORCED OBEDIENCE.

A strange murder is reported from the vicinity of Bulow's Creek,[2] below St. Augustine. A man named Cochrane[3] has lived near the Creek for the past three years. He had a wife and two sons, one sixteen and the other eighteen years old. The family had planted a few orange trees, and raised enough sweet potations, shot enough game, and caught enough fish to keep alive. One day the oldest boy killed a buck, skinned it, and placed the hide upon the fence to dry. His dog tore the pelt from the fence, and the boy was picking it up when the father approached him. The old man was in ill humor. He peremptorily ordered his son to shoot the dog. The boy demurred. He said that he owned both the dog and the hide, and if the former tore the pelt, no one was injured but himself. It was a hard thing to get a good deer hound, and he didn't intend to kill this one without a better excuse. Harsh words followed. In his rage the old man rushed into the house and reappeared with a loaded rifle. "Now you can take your choice," he shouted, "you've got to shoot the dog, or I'll shoot you."

The son refused to kill his dog, and the old man raised the rifle and fired. The boy dropped to the ground, shot through the abdomen. His blood welled out over the deer hide. He lived about a quarter of an hour. His brother bewailed his fate so loudly that the old man threatened to put an end to him. But the brother was too quick for him. He ran to the house and secured the powder flask and bullet pouch, saving his own life and preventing a double murder. Cochrane acted as though he had been moved by a sense of duty. He procured a coffin, dug a grave, hired a clergyman, and invited the neighbors to the funeral. The boy was buried, and the old man shed tears over his resting place. He appeared to be a sincere mourner. To a settler who asked him if he was not sorry for what had happened, he said, "I reckon I haint. I got shut of the boy because he didn't do just as I told him, and I'll get shut of the next one if he don't mind just what I say to him." The crime was so atrocious that the authorities were compelled to notice it. A warrant was issued, and the Sheriff of St. John's county set out to serve it. When the bereaved father heard of it, he took an affectionate leave of his wife and remaining son, and rifle in hand sloped for Okechobee. The Sheriff took his track, and has succeeded in arresting him. Such were the particulars given me on the Halifax river.

LIFE ON THE SUWANEE RIVER.

As I came down stairs the other morning I saw Capt. Frank Sams,[4] a noted hunter, seated on the edge of the stoop, swinging his feet into a rosebush. "Look here," said he, "you think you know something about Florida murders. The Lang and Cochrane stories aint a patch to the beauties of the Suwanee country. Out there they make a wholesale business of it. Some time ago two men named Locklier and Mundy lived near the mouth of the Suwanee river. They raised cattle for a living. Locklier had an average-looking woman for a wife, while Mundy was a widower with a mighty fine daughter. The two men got quite thick, and used to cow-drive together and eat in each other's houses. After a time Mundy took a fancy to Locklier's wife, and Locklier took a fancy to Mundy's daughter. So they struck up a trade. After palavering around, Mundy offered to give his daughter for Locklier's wife and twenty head of cattle. Locklier took him up straight, and the bargain was made."

I asked the Captain what kind of girl the daughter was.

"Well," he replied, "I've heard that she was a plump little filly, about eighteen years old. Locklier's wife was a little skinny, but she was a good driver and worked well in harness with her husband. The daughter never made any objection to the bargain, and the wife, like most of the women, was glad of anything for a change. So Mundy drove off the twenty head of cattle and the old woman, and Locklier shook himself down in the cabin with the daughter. Things were all snug. Well, in about two weeks Locklier's wife got sick of it. She declared that her husband was bad enough, but he was an angel alongside of Mundy. She went back home, and swore that she wouldn't live with Mundy any longer under any circumstances. Then Mundy came up to Locklier's house and wanted his daughter back. The daughter by this time had fallen in love with Locklier, and you couldn't have driven her out of his cabin with a pack of dogs. Locklier said she shouldn't go unless the old man drove back the twenty head of cattle. Mundy said he'd see Locklier in hell before he brought back the cattle, and threatened to shoot him if he didn't turn over his daughter. Locklier told him to shoot and be dodrotted.[5] So they parted bad friends."

THE CART-WHEEL BATTERY.

I interrupted the Captain by asking what the neighbors thought of such proceedings.

"Well," he replied, "they didn't have many neighbors. What they did have were like themselves. They looked upon the whole thing as a bona fide bargain, and if one or the other got cheated it was no outsider's business. As I was a saying, Mundy declared war. He threw up a sort of parallel around Locklier's house and bombarded it with a double-barrelled shot gun. All day long he laid around the house, waiting for a shot. Locklier was afraid to go out or to even show his face at a window. For hours he would sit on a chair with his old rifle across his knees and watch the door. Whenever the latch moved he would blaze away without waiting to find out who was coming in. Two or three times he came near shooting his wife when she was out after a pail of water. You see he knew Mundy meant business, and he wasn't going to let him get a twist on him. Mundy skirmished around the house until dark. Then he travelled home and got a good night's sleep; but by daylight Locklier again found him intrenched outside the door.

"This arrangement lasted several days, and Locklier began to get tired of his imprisonment. One night he took a couple of stout-cart wheels standing near his cabin, boarded them in on three sides with two-inch plank, and when Mundy put in an appearance the next morning confronted him with this movable battery. The tables were turned. The old man had to fall back. Locklier followed him up the road with his battery, shelling him at every jump. Mundy was driven into his headquarters, and his antagonist took the part of besieger. A dozen shots were exchanged before sundown, and at dark Locklier drew back to his house under cover of the battery. Before the roosters stopped crowing he was again moving up the road toward Mundy's house, shelling his way every few rods, and driving the old man and his shot gun to cover."

THE MOONLIGHT TRAGEDY.

"Well, the war was kept up this way about a week, but at last it had come to an end. One bright moonlight night Locklier thought he would quietly wheel his battery up the road and see if he couldn't catch Mundy outside of his fortifications. So he laid his rifle before him and set the wheels agoing. He had shoved them about a quarter of a mile, and was just turning a curve in the road when he heard a scraping noise on his left. Mundy had flanked him. By the light of the moon he could see the old man on his knees behind a fence, shoving the barrel of his shot-gun between the rails and getting his head down to take aim. Locklier had no time to lose. He snatched his rifle and sighted it. They fired together. Mundy fell dead behind the fence with a rifle bullet in his head, and Locklier tumbled into his battery with eleven buckshot in his breast. He lived about four hours, and declared if he hadn't been listening to the crickets he would have seen Mundy before the battery passed him. The wife and daughter buried the two men, divided the twenty head of cattle, and got all the property."

FIRE AND SWORD.

Sams's story is literally true. This Suwanee country has always borne a hard name. It is out of the beaten track of travel, and is in a measure inaccessible. During the war it was a favorite retreat for Confederate deserters. Its inhabitants defied the conscription. They virtually seceded from the Confederacy, and ravaged adjacent territory with impunity. They made repeated raids into Madison county, Ga., murdering and plundering the inhabitants without mercy. So outrageous were their depredations that the rebel Government was compelled to send an expedition to punish them. It was commanded by Col.

Canfield,[6] a brave South Carolina soldier. He swept the district with fire and sword. Drum head courts-martial[7] met almost hourly. Over a score of the most notorious desperadoes were hanged, and the country was restored to law and order. Canfield's name, however, became a terror to the inhabitants, and to this day they curse him as bitterly as the Irish curse Cromwell.

ZISKA.

Go 'Gators!

In this June 1, 1874, article, Amos Cummings, writing as Ziska, again provides his *New York Sun* readers with stories of Florida murder and mayhem, blaming the lax law enforcement at least in part on corrupt state officials. In one murder case, he also implicates a Florida alligator, though at best I suspect the 'gator could only have been prosecuted for destroying evidence.

Florida and alligators, like the Sunshine State and oranges, are inseparable. Florida's Indians ate the reptiles for thousands of years before Europeans showed up. Alligator scutes—the bones that give alligator tails their distinctive bumpy ridge—are ubiquitous in most archaeological sites; less common are alligator teeth. French documents from Florida in the 1560s describe how the Indians killed the reptiles using spears, clubs, and arrows.

Among the earliest Spanish accounts from Florida are mentions of *los lagartos* (the lizards). That Spanish name for the alligator, *el lagarto*, gave the animal the word we use today: alligator (say *el lagarto* ten times in rapid succession).

Over the years, Florida's alligators have taken a beating. Once they numbered in the millions. In his article "Adventures in Florida," Amos Cummings wrote of a "fleet of alligators" on Lake Worth, and he noted that the mouth of Little Lake Worth appeared black because it was "alive with alligators." In Florida in 1874, alligators were everywhere, and local residents and visitors had no compunction about plugging them with rifle bullets for fun. But it probably was the trade in alligator hides—the belly skin can be tanned to make a fine leather—that began about that same time and continued into the twentieth century that greatly reduced Florida's alligator population.

The situation became so bad that alligators were awarded protected status in the early 1960s, and laws were passed to control the movement of hides within the marketplace. Poachers went out of business. Since then alligator populations have rebounded, and estimates place their number in Florida at more than a million. Their protected status also has been lifted, though they remain a species of concern, mainly because of the inability of most Floridians to distinguish between an alligator and their endangered crocodilian cousins.

Today the hunting of wild alligators is carefully monitored and licensed. Alligators also are farmed. The animals taken from hunting and those raised on ranches provide sufficient hides for the market, not to mention tail meat, considered by some—mainly adventuresome tourists—to be a delicacy.

Today the biggest threats to alligators appear to be habitat destruction and degradation. As humans expand, alligators have fewer places to live. In a few areas, notably Lake Apopka, Florida's third-largest lake, pollution from agricultural activities has turned lakes into chemical stews, places not even an alligator would or could live.

Despite all, alligators persevere. Go 'Gators!

15

THE TERROR OF THE PINES

A SINGULAR MURDER NEAR THE SHORE OF OKECHOBEE.

The King of Saxony's Gardener Cut up and Fed to Alligators—The Robbers in the Pines—An Assassination that would Appal an Arab or a Modoc—One Result of Carpet-Bag Rule in Florida.

NEW SMYRNA, FLA., MAY 1.—Remarkable in everything, Florida is more than remarkable in the peculiarity of its murders. But few of its assassins are arrested, and of these few scarcely one is convicted and executed. This is undoubtedly owing to the political situation. The Governor, under the carpet-bag Constitution, has the selection of all sheriffs, county clerks, justices of the peace, and judges. They hold office subject to his pleasure, and can be removed without an instant's notice. Some of the appointees are notorious gamblers and ruffians. A Columbia county officer is credited with five cruel murders, but as long as he retains his political influence and picks Republican primaries in the interests of his office-seeking chief, just so long will he hold his position. If a prominent politician or one of his friends is concerned in a murder, the Justice of the Peace must await his cue before issuing a warrant, and the Sheriff will not attempt an arrest without an official hint. This is a rule and not an exception. If the guilty man is arrested political considerations form the Grand Jury, and no indictment is found. Should the Grand Jury, however, make a presentment, there still remains a chance to nurse the traverse jury and fasten a political screw to the neck of the Judge. Failing in all these points, the prisoner can either escape from the rickety county jail or fall back upon the clemency of the Governor. Since the war Jackson, Columbia, and Orange counties have been the theatre of scores of murders, and of but one execution. While Hart[1] was Governor, one of his near relatives was arraigned for a shocking crime. The victim was a little negro girl, daughter of his washerwoman. The punishment was death. Though the evidence of his guilt was clear, he was acquitted. The Governor's political friends justified the verdict on the ground that it would be atrocious to hang a relative of the Governor for the sake of a small "nigger wench."

One crime, however, is promptly punished. It is that of cattle stealing. The pine woods of the great peninsula are a vast cattle range. The cattle bear nicks and brands chosen by their owners and registered in the office of the County Clerk. They roam the pine woods until spring, when the cow drivers turn out, corral the calves, nick and brand them, and allow them to rejoin the parent herds. Woe to the shiftless rascals who help themselves to the beeves. When caught they receive no mercy. The majority are strung to the nearest tree. "Kill a man and you are safe; kill a beef and you are gone up," is a common saying in Florida.

THE STORY OF LANG.

Over thirty years ago a man named Lang came to the Indian River country. It was then a trackless wilderness; even now it is but little better. Lang was well educated, and could have adorned a high station in life. He was a thorough botanist, and at one time supervising gardener to the King of Saxony.[2] It is said that he was driven into exile by domestic troubles, but whatever the cause he invariably left his cabin and plunged deeper in the wilderness whenever a white man settled within twenty miles. He was over six feet tall. Physically he had no superior south of the latitude of St. Augustine. For years he lived upon the shore of Lake Worth, nearly a hundred miles from any post office. The only path to his place was an intricate channel through an arm of the Everglades known only to himself and the Seminoles. To this day but five white men can pilot a boat by the inland passage from Jupiter light to Lake Worth.[3] Lang's home was a flowery paradise. It was below the line of frost. Oleanders, cocoanut trees, palms, agaves, guavas, and other tropical fruits and flowers clustered about the door of the cabin and bloomed in the neighboring hammocks. The German lived alone. Months passed without seeing a human being. He forgot the day of the week and the date of the month, and contracted the Indian habit of computing time by the number of moons. Twice a year literary hunger drove him back through the Everglades into the shadow of civilization in search of reading. He has been known to travel twice to Sand Point[4] and back to borrow and return a book. It was a trip of 600 miles in a sailboat, subject to whims of the wind.

THE LONELY CABIN ON THE ST. LUCIE.

About four years ago the richness of the hammocks around Lake Worth attracted the attention of a land hunter. He announced his intention of making a clearing. That was enough for Lang. He pulled up stakes and departed, giving his beautiful home to a jolly old sailor named Moore.[5] Lang returned to the Indian river. Association with the people of the scattered Jupiter settlements partly drew him from the shell of isolation which he had so long occupied. Attracted by the charms of a young woman living with her parents up in the pines back of Lake Jessup, he married her. Then the old longing for retirement returned. Away up the St. Lucie river—a haunt of the mysterious menatee—he found a small hammock in which he erected a palmetto cabin. It pleased him, for he and his wife were the only human beings living along the river. His nearest neighbor was distant a day's journey. A clearing was effected, and a little garden became green with vegetables. Wild orange trees were transplanted, and limes, bananas, and guavas were put into the ground. There were no lazy hairs in Lang's head. He worked hard, and barely made a living. Domestic affliction dropped upon him. A child was born, but its prattling was silenced by death. Its body was buried beneath the wild flowers, and its father and mother were its undertakers, pall bearers, grave diggers, and mourners.

Lang detested visitors, yet he was extremely hospitable when they came to his house. Last January two stout young men suddenly appeared in the door of his cabin. His wife recognized them as Tom Drawdy and Allen Paget,[6] who lived miles away in the direction of Lake Okechobee. The former bore a hard character. He had lived in Volusia county but had been driven into the Okechobee country by Sheriff's warrants. He was accused of cattle stealing and other crimes, and had at one time been a prisoner in Enterprise jail. His sisters rescued him by knocking down the watchman and chopping open the doors of his prison. Paget belonged to an Okechobee family whose reputation was but little better than that of Drawdy's.

THE TERROR OF THE PINES.

The two men lounged about Lang's house, and finally accepted his invitation to dinner. On rising from the table they picked up their rifles, and asked the German to put them across the river. Lang readily consented. He had a sail boat and a row boat. Hatless and shoeless, and entirely unsuspicious, he went to the boat followed by Drawdy and Paget. Lang took the oars and shoved from the shore. His wife, who was within a day or two of confinement, saw him for the last time. She heard the report of a gunshot, supposed that it was shot at a deer, and paid no attention to it. When the sun went down and the waters were blackened in the shadow of the tall palmettoes, she became alarmed that her husband did not return. The long dark night was spent in listening for the sound of his oars. At daylight she managed to cross the river. The boat was found upon the opposite shore. Drops of blood scattered upon its bottom told too surely the fate of her husband. A hat belonging to one of the murderers had caught upon one of the oar locks. The horrified wife hunted for Lang's body, but did not find it. She returned to the desolate cabin, rolled up her blankets, and made for the nearest settlement in the sail boat. Her fatherless child was born soon after her arrival at Lake Jessup.

Visitors to Lang's cabin since the tragedy say that the garden has been destroyed, the oranges trees removed, the flowers above the grave of the dead child trampled under foot, and the settlement wiped from the face of the earth. This is supposed to be the work of the murderers.

People residing within fifty miles of the St. Lucie speak of the murder in whispers. They are afraid to open their mouths. While all were anxious that the particulars should be made public, none were willing to volunteer any information. They required a pledge of secrecy, through fear that the murderers might retaliate. The whole country is cowed. At Fort Capron no one would talk about the deed, and I was compelled to glean any information from other sources. Though not at liberty to reveal its origin, I believe that the statement can be verified.

THE CAUSE OF THE CRIME.

Among their friends and acquaintances Drawdy and Paget make no secret of their crime. They rather glory in it. They acknowledge that they broke bread with a man and assassinated him within fifteen minutes while he was doing them a favor. An Arab or an Indian would turn his face from such men. But it is said they offer an excuse for the murder. One of the murderers had entered Lang's house months before and found fresh beef upon the table. As they knew he owned no cattle, they were satisfied he had been butchering other peoples's beeves. So they visited his house with the intention of killing him for cow stealing. This explanation seems to be satisfactory to settlers at Lake Worth, who give Lang a bad name, but those further north, who knew him more intimately, declare that it will not hold water. They say they can't see why one cattle thief should kill another for stealing cattle. They speak in the highest terms of the victim, and credit him with minding exclusively his own business.

Another cause for the crime is given. It is said that Lang's wife passed the period of her first confinement in the house of a well-known citizen named Jonergan.[7] After her recovery a difficulty arose over the settlement of the bill. Jonergan wanted more than Lang was able or willing to give, and the two men parted in enmity. In conversation with others they spoke bitterly of each other, and the ill-feeling grew with the lapse of time. As evidence that this quarrel was the real foundation for the crime, men point to the fact that Drawdy married one of Jonergan's daughters soon after the crime.

FOOD FOR ALLIGATORS.

The sequel almost surpasses belief. The murderers appear to have been frightened after their bloody work. They pitched the corpse over-board, and fled in such haste that one of their hats was left behind. Their relatives, fearing an investigation, visited the scene of the murder and found Lang's body stranded on the shore. They loaded it with heavy weights and sank it in the bed of the river. While revisiting the place for the purpose of removing some of the orange trees, the corpse came to the surface and again bore mute witness to the enormity of the crime. It floated upon the water with the weights attached. The dead man was secured and cut in twain. A stone was tied to each piece, and both were heaved into the St. Lucie. But Lang was powerful even in death. The stones were too light and the dissevered body a third time sought the light of heaven. It was then chopped in pieces, and the chunks dropped into the alligator holes dotting the marshes near the river. Thus all trace of the crime was washed out.

There have been no special efforts to secure the murderers. I hear that the Governor has offered a reward of $500 for their apprehension and conviction. Unfortunately the county is without a sheriff. I am told that Mr. Stewart,[8] the first incumbent, happened to be an honest man and a Democrat, and has been removed. I have not heard that a successor has been appointed. It would not be very astonishing if the Governor should commission either Drawdy or Paget. Events more strange have occurred during the carpet-bag domination in Florida. Unnaturalized foreigners have been appointed Justices of the Peace in this same county. Nobody seems anxious to secure the promised reward, payable in State scrip. Meantime the assassins are roving about the settlements with revolvers lashed to their hips, threatening death to all inquisitive strangers. They live in the unsettled region around Okechobee, and it will require more than a sheriff's common posse to capture them. They will probably remain safe so long as they refrain from robbing or attacking the Savages, Hodges, Houstons, Osteens, Prevatts, Stewarts,[9] and other prominent families of Eastern Florida. A shot at one of these men would bring upon them decisive retribution. The whole clan would turn out, and the wretches would be hunted down like wild beasts and exterminated root and branch. Until that time they may remain the "Terror of the Pines."

ZISKA.

Go 'Gators!

"Life 'twixt Plated Decks"

Sea turtles are magnificent creatures. They also are few in number. On fishing trips in the Atlantic Ocean off Florida's coast, I always enjoy those infrequent instances when I can catch a glimpse of one swimming past the boat.

In his famed poem "The Turtle," Ogden Nash documented some of his subject's interesting qualities:

> The turtle lives 'twixt plated decks
> Which practically conceal its sex.
> I think it clever of the turtle
> In such a fix to be so fertile.

Unfortunately for sea turtles, they also are good to eat. Early sailors in the Caribbean found them storable sources of meat that could be put on board a ship and kept alive for days before being consumed. As is evident from this Ziska article published in the *New York Sun* on August 6, 1874, sea turtle populations also took a heavy hit from people living in the Indian River area in the late nineteenth century.

Today we have a conservation ethic. Coastal dwellers on Florida's Atlantic coast routinely turn out their outside lights so turtles aren't confused when they come ashore. Civilian patrols police the beaches and dunes to make certain that turtles coming ashore to lay eggs are not harassed and that hatchlings can find their way to the sea without passing through a gauntlet of tourists.

Archie Carr, the famed University of Florida naturalist, along with his colleagues and students, spearheaded the sea turtle conservation effort. In 1986, the Archie Carr Center for Sea Turtle Research was established at the University of Florida to carry on his work. Today the center promotes sea turtle education and conservation along with active research programs to help us better understand the world's sea turtle populations and how they may be saved. Among other things, the center charts turtle gene pools and tracks tagged turtles using satellite telemetry to learn about the movements of populations.

In the late nineteenth century, there was no conservation ethic, and people treated sea turtles as an inexhaustible resource. Yes, as Amos Cummings documents, bears also ate sea turtle eggs. But the numbers of eggs taken by bears could not have been as great as the number taken by humans. Imagine feeding your mules five thousand turtle eggs, as Cummings describes in this article! Thank goodness sea turtles are both clever and fertile. Otherwise sea turtles might have joined that list of animal species that never made it to the twenty-first century.

16

THE HOME OF THE TURTLES

SCENES ON THE OCEAN BEACH IN EASTERN FLORIDA.

The King of the Sands—Green Turtles and their Captors—Gaffing the Leather-Back—The Tortoise of the Lower Peninsula—Egg Hunting on the Indian River—How the Bears Find a Turtle's Nest—The Fattening of Dr. Wallace's Mules—Sand Storms on the Beach—Moonlight Scenes—Pacetti's Monstrous Loggerhead.

Jupiter Inlet, Fla., June 1, 1874.—The past two months the bears have flocked to the sea coast from the great pine woods and cypress swamps of the interior. They are drawn to the ocean beach in search of turtle eggs, for which they have a keen relish. The turtles break from the sea on the night of May 7. From that time until the 1st of September they throng the beach. After depositing their eggs beneath the burning land they settle down among the coral rocks that appear above the water at low tide. There they are caught by the few people living along the coast between St. Augustine and Key West, who are thus furnished with a delicacy almost unknown in Northern latitudes. Some of the fishermen carry their turtles to Key West, but the market there is generally overstocked, and the business is by no means remunerative.

CATCHING GREEN TURTLES.

Of all the turtles frequenting the beach the green turtle[1] is the most highly prized. In early spring many of these turtles are caught in nets in the Indian, Hillsborough, and Halifax rivers. The water is salt and subject to the action of the tide. The nets are stretched across the channels of the rivers. As the turtles come lumbering along with the current, they are entangled in the meshes and captured. The fisherman drops his prey in what is termed a "crawl," where it is kept awaiting the market demand, or until its captors hanker for turtle steaks or soup. The turtle crawls are distinguishing features of the salt water rivers. Cypress stakes are driven into the sand and water some rods from the shore in the form of a square. The water is from two to three feet in depth, and

Loading a big sea turtle (350 pounds) in Key West, 1885.
Courtesy of Florida State Archives.

flows through the intervals between the stakes. At a distance the crawls look like pig pens at anchor. The word "crawl" is probably a corruption of the Spanish *correl*. The natives persist in pronouncing and spelling it c-r-a-w-l.

While in captivity the turtle seems perfectly at home. He is purely a water hog. As long as his stomach is filled he is happy. He is fed a peculiar grass resembling pulse[2] that is found upon the bottom of the rivers. It is this grass that gives the green turtle a delicious flavor. Like the canvas back duck, he subsists entirely upon a vegetarian diet. The loggerheads[3] and other varieties eat fish, and are not so eagerly sought.

THE KING OF THE SANDS.

The beach is the summer resort of the coarser-grained turtles. A few green ones troop along in their wake, but they are outnumbered by the loggerheads and shellbacks.[4] The king of the sands is the great trunk-backed turtle.[5] He carries a shell built up from his back like a tower, and presents an interesting appearance as he crawls along the sand. Beachcombers say that their shells are from two to five feet thick. The flesh is regarded as a great luxury, and single shells are sold to curiosity-seekers at prices ranging from fifty to a hundred dollars. The trunk-back, however, is becoming very scarce. None are taken north of Lake Worth. They keep below the line of frost. In size they are enormous. Mr. Charles Moore, of Castle Rag,[6] tells me that he has trapped them weighing from six to eight hundred pounds. It is hard to say what causes the peculiar conformation of the shell. Mr. Moore thinks they are centenarian loggerheads, and that each ridge is the weight of a certain number of years. Their necks are shrivelled, and they bear the marks of old age on their faces. They bite ferociously, and could easily nip off a leg or an arm.

THE LEATHER-BACK AND THE GOPHER.

Turtles caught on the beach between Jupiter and Cape Sable average from 100 to 350 pounds. Many people eat the loggerhead. Some declare that they prefer it to the green turtle. The descendants of the Minorcans[7] cook it in a way that destroys the fishy taste and renders the meat extremely palatable. Its breath is fetid and disagreeable, but there is nothing offensive about a green turtle.

The most delicious of all is the leather-back.[8] This is a small turtle, found in both fresh and salt water. At the edges its shell is as soft as jujube paste, but increases in solidity as it mounts the back. The centre of the back is of a circular form, about the size of a trade dollar, and as hard as ivory. The leather-back is taken while sleeping upon the surface of the water. None are sent north. They are caught by a long-handled gaff-hook, the point of which is jerked through the soft portion of the shell. Along Lake Worth these turtles are found in abundance. They are of a dark color, lacking the light grassy hue of the green turtle and the delicate yellow of the loggerhead. It is not uncommon to see a turtle floating upon the water fast asleep while a pair of gulls are making love upon its back.

I have heard Floridians speak highly of a land turtle which attains a large size in the lower part of the peninsula. It lives in holes in the ground. They call it a gopher.[9] It resembles the common land turtle of New York and New Jersey, and is protected by a hinged door of shell, both fore and aft. Negroes and Indians go into ecstacies over its steaming soup.

HOW A TURTLE MAKES A NEST.

The inhabitants of the coast, however, prize its eggs far above the turtle. Females begin laying eggs on the 7th of May. Old turtle catchers assert this date with much positiveness. They say that no turtle was ever known to drop an egg before the 7th. The females generally come upon the beach at night. Their course upon the sand is marked by the trailing of their tails and flippers. The trail from the water to a point above high tide is as straight as a line. Approaching a chosen spot, the turtle makes a gentle swerve to the north, and sounds the sand with her flippers. Satisfied of the desirableness of the situation, she begins to dig a hole. To do this her hindflippers alone are used. Her work is remarkable, if not artistic. The hole is shaped like the inside of a large jug. Its neck is small, but its interior is circular, and from fifteen to twenty or more inches in diameter. The sides are smooth and rounded through the use of the flippers. No workman in a pottery could turn out a job more true.

Frequently the turtle is dissatisfied with the labor. Probably she finds the ground undermined by the bright-eyed sand-crabs that dance along the shore. In that case she makes a curve to the east and marches directly to the water, emerging at some other point and going through the same performance. Sometimes she digs four or five holes before she begins to deposit her eggs.

HOW THE FEMALE LAYS HER EGGS.

Her nest finished, the female turtle settles down to her work. Up to this time she invariably takes to the water at the approach of a stranger. After she begins to lay, the presence of an army would not frighten her. A man could stand upon her back, and she would keep her position until the last egg was dropped. Dr. Frank Fox,[10] a well-known hunter of New Smyrna, tells me that he once saw a bear take his stand behind a turtle on the nest. Bruin caught the eggs in alternate paws as they fell, and devoured them with a smack of the chops that could be heard at the distance of a hundred yards. Bears have been known to watch turtles for hours, and then tear them in pieces because they showed no disposition to lay.

The eggs are deposited at a depth of from fifteen to eighteen inches. They are not oval, but round, and nearly the size of a hen's egg. The shell is flexible, and white as snow. It is as elastic as rubber. Dent an egg with your thumb and the indentation will last for hours. Egg hunters always carry a bag, in which they drop the eggs. A bag of eggs can be thrown across a horse, the horse ridden at full gallop, and not an egg be broken.

APPEARANCE OF THE YOUNG TURTLES.

In filling their nests the females display marvellous skill. The eggs are deposited in layers so arranged that there is not an inch of room to spare. No human hand could show such a knowledge of packing. Beachcombers are frequently astonished at the quantity of eggs taken from a small nest. They say they have repeatedly tried to replace them as they found them, but in no instance have they succeeded in getting more than two-thirds of them back in the hole. From seventy-five to 150 eggs are found in each nest. The general average is 130. Dr. Fox says that he has unearthed 170. Last year, however, Dr. Wallace[11] of Turtle Mound discovered a hole containing 210 eggs. This is probably the largest nest ever found on the Florida coast.

When the female has filled her nest she covers the hole with moistened sand, and packs it down with her flippers. No garden roller could make it more solid. The spot is then sprinkled with loose sand, and the old turtle returns to the sea. The eggs hatch within thirty-five days. The summer sun is very warm, and the sand becomes so hot that it blisters the feet. When the young ones break the shell they swarm to the surface and take a bee line for the water. Instinct points out the direct route. Men have driven shingles around a turtle's nest and awaited the hatching of the eggs. Though out of sight of the water, the little ones would crowd the side of the inclosure nearest the ocean, and die there unless released. When dropped behind a sand bank they turn to the east, and travel in that direction with the confident eagerness of a Masonic neophyte. When hatched, they are a little larger than a silver half dollar.

APPRECIATIVE BEARS.

An egg hunter usually walks the beach before sunrise and after sunset. If the tide is low, he finds the nests by the trails leading from the water. The deposit is always found on the curve of the trail above high water mark. The packed sand indicates its locality. Many turtles, however, make what are called false nests. They take great pains to leave a clear trail, and pack the ground on the curve without dropping an egg. After thus endeavoring to mislead the enemies of their young, they slip off to some quiet spot and lay. This ruse deceives men, but never bears. Bruin has a keen nose, and is always up to snuff. He never wastes his time on a false nest and never fails to stop at a good one. When that is found he makes the sand fly. As he gradually scoops it out, his head disappears and his hind quarters stand up against the sky. At such times, his joy overcomes his fears. All cautiousness is thrown aside, and he relapses into the enjoyment of his delicacy. A daring man might walk up and pinch his hind leg without fear of discovery. More bears are killed while nosing the nests of turtles than at any other time. Nothing but a rifle ball will keep a bear from a turtle hole.

While at Lake Worth I heard a story of two egg hunters who went out on the beach just after the sun had set. One of them discovered a nest and was about to rifle it, when his companion said, "Let us go on and find another one before dark. We can dig this up on the way back." The egg hunter replied that he was afraid some bear might get ahead of him. "Oh, throw your coat on the nest, and no bear will dare touch it," said his comrade. The coat was thrown down. They found a second nest three-quarters of a mile down the beach. Its eggs were secured and they were on their way home, when they saw a huge bear come out of the palmetto scrub and walk along the shore, sniffing for eggs. The men were unarmed. The bear raised his head and saw the coat. In a jiffy the garment was torn into carpet rags, and the sand was flying from the nest. The egg hunters heard the smacking of Bruin's chops with sorrowful faces, and never again dropped a coat upon a turtle's nest.

HOW A DOCTOR FATTENS HIS MULES.

Millions of eggs are destroyed every year. Coons and opossums train in the wake of the bear, and scour the beach. Opossums have been caught so stuffed with eggs that they could hardly walk. When a settler lives near the beach, his hogs fatten themselves upon the nests. Mankind comes in for the smallest share. Dr. Wallace gathered 5,000 eggs last year before the season was half over. Of course, he had more than his family could eat. The eggs threatened to spoil on his hands. One night his mules were without corn. He dumped a peck of turtle-eggs in their manger. The beasts seemed to like them better than grain. After that the Doctor fed them eggs once a day throughout the summer, and the animals became as fat as butter. Soon afterward his dog developed a taste for them, and between his dog, mules, and family the Doctor had his hands full to keep up the supply.

The eggs can be kept from five to six weeks. They are used for all cooking purposes, and are said to be more nutritious than hen's eggs. For pies, custards, and similar delicacies they are all that can be desired. Fried, boiled, scrambled, or knocked into an omelet, they are savory and palatable. No effort has ever been made to ship them North, where they would undoubtedly be appreciated.

MOONLIGHT SCENES ON THE BEACH.

Hundreds of turtles are caught on the beach by moonlight. They cannot walk quite so fast as a man. It requires peculiar skill to handle them. They are seized by the shell above the hind flipper, and turned on their backs as quick as an old Californian would turn a flapjack. There is a knack about it that is not easily acquired. An expert has a quick eye and a quick motion. He is as supple as a hickory sapling. If the turtle is large, he throws himself over with it, thus turning a complete somersault. If the monster is not thrown in the

Fishermen flipping sea turtles near Tavernier Creek in the Florida Keys, 1871. Courtesy of Florida State Archives.

twinkling of an eye, it raises itself to its legs and shoves for the water, leaving its pursuer flat on the sand. A beachcomber weighing no more than a hundred pounds can pitch over a three hundred pounder apparently with the greatest ease. Strangers are advised not to experiment with the logger-heads, as they are wicked when annoyed, and are apt to bite. A story is told of a fat man who endeavored to lift a large green fellow into his boat. The turtle seized him by the slack of the stomach, and the man set up a roar that startled all the bears in the vicinity. Fortunately his pantaloons were tough, and he escaped without serious damage.

Last year Bartolo C. Pacetti[12] saw a logger-head near Mosquito Inlet weighing more than five hundred pounds. The turtle was filling a nest, and was of such a size that it was useless to think of turning it by main strength. In this dilemma Pacetti scooped a great hole in the sand at the side of the nest. As the monster rose and started for the sea he exerted all his strength and tumbled it into the hole. It struck upon its back and set its flippers in motion. Pacetti says that for five minutes he thought the sky was filled with ashes. The sand flew in all directions, and the turtle would have covered a regiment if it had had the opportunity.

HOW A PHILADELPHIA DOCTOR CATCHES THEM.

Once on its back a turtle is helpless. It will throw sand faster than a fanning mill can spout chaff, but it is securely anchored, and will lay there until it dies, if not removed. Beachcombers turn their turtles by moonlight, and secure them in the morning.

Some of the inhabitants take their turtles in the heat of the day with a cast-net. I spent one day hunting them with Dr. Wm. Wittfeld,[13] formerly of Philadelphia. The Doctor walked along the surf at low tide, carefully watching the sunken coral rocks. The turtles would rise between the rocks and blow like porpoises. In an instant the cast-net was in the air. As it spread on the water and sank the turtle was meshed, and the Doctor rushed into the sea, caught it by the flipper and dragged it out. These turtles were small green ones. Their meat was tender and juicy, and the Doctor preferred them to those caught in the rivers. They fed upon the delicate seaweed growing between the coral formations.

During the summer Col. Titus[14] of Kansas and Nicaragua fame visits the beach below Cape Canaveral, and spends six weeks in turtling. He has tents and servants, and camps out like an old veteran. As he is entirely crippled by bullets and rheumatism he can do but little besides overseeing the job. I hear that he is one of the most successful turtlers on the Indian river.

With all its enemies on land, the turtle has a ferocious assailant in the water. Enormous sharks, cruel and voracious, frequent the coast and inlets of Florida. They attack the largest turtles, biting off their heads and flippers without ceremony. During the latter part of April I caught an old loggerhead near New Smyrna. It had been stranded at high tide in the slue of a sand bar, and was not able to get out. A shark had bitten off one of its fore flippers. It weighed about 170 pounds.

ZISKA.

Law and the Natural Order

Life in Florida in the 1870s was not all orange trees and sea turtles or farming and fishing. There also was death, sometimes tragic and unexpected. In this poignant article, Cummings provides still another view of Florida, one that reveals the harsh reality underlying the dictum "if in danger, they must perish." The article, signed by Ziska, was published in the May 4, 1874, *New York Sun*.

Cummings records the name of the swimmer who was in danger and who did perish as Mr. F. A. Law of the town of Sunrise City. He was a visitor to Florida and had checked in at a local hotel. Local residents told Cummings that Mr. Law appeared to be of "more than ordinary intelligence," about fifty-five years of age, and very wealthy. After his death, a search of his pockets turned up a gold watch, a comb, a pocketknife, and $502 in cash. There also was a blank check drawn on a Concord, New Hampshire, bank.

Attempts by local residents to find our more about Mr. Law went for naught. A hundred and thirty years later could I be any more successful? Yes, a bit, though I had the advantage of the Internet.

Indeed, as the local residents told Cummings, the only town called Sunrise City in the United States in 1874 was in Minnesota. At some point the "City" was dropped from the name. Today Sunrise is a small town in Chisago County. Both I and Mr. Steve Nielsen, reference associate of the Minnesota Historical Society, working separately, consulted the 1870 federal census of Minnesota and came up with the same conclusion. The man who drowned in 1874 was Mr. Charles F. Law, a resident of Sunrise City, Minnesota, in 1870. In that year, according to the census, Mr. Law, a lawyer, was fifty-one years old. He also was quite wealthy. Value of his real estate was $37,000, making him the wealthiest individual in Sunrise City. Law, whose birthplace is listed as New Hampshire, was not married.

Numerous Internet searches for Charles F. Law produced only one mention of that name. A Charles F. Law was involved in a real estate transaction in Effingham County, Illinois, in 1849. The circumstances are vague, but they would not be inconsistent with that Mr. Law being an attorney and the same person as our drowning victim.

With these clues and the information that the Sunrise City Charles F. Law was born in New Hampshire and carried a check from a Concord bank when he died, I delved again into the census records and consulted David Smolen, special collections librarian at the New Hampshire Historical Society's Tuck Library. But to no avail. I found no other record of Mr. Law in earlier census records from either Illinois or New Hampshire. I did find several families of Laws in the 1860 census in Merrimack County, New Hampshire, of whom three individuals lived in the town of Concord. Were they relatives of Attorney Charles F. Law? Possibly, but I could not verify that.

It is easy to imagine that lawyer Law left Concord to seek his fortunes on the frontiers of the United States, then only a century old. Perhaps he traveled first to Illinois and Minnesota before heading south to Florida to check out real estate and other prospects. There, not far from where modern pioneers send space shuttles and Mars landers into space, Charles Law met his fate.

17

THE FATE OF A STRANGER

AN EXCELLENT SWIMMER'S LAST SWIM IN FLORIDA.

Dr. Wittfeld's Lookout on Banana River—The Mysterious Sail—A Gale from the North—"Night is Coming On, If They are in Danger they Must Perish"— Eleven Days Hunting for a Corpse—The Prey of Buzzards—Buried above High-Water Mark.

New Smyrna, Fla., April 18, 1874.—Dr. William Wittfeld,[1] formerly of Philadelphia, is clearing up an orange grove in the wilds of Florida, about twenty miles southwest of Canaveral light. He has a sightly hill, crowned by an Indian mound, overlooking the broad Banana river and the ocean on the east, and the Indian river on the west. It is situated on Merritt's Island, twelve miles from its southern extremity. Two houses woven from palmetto fans stand upon the Banana shore. One is the Doctor's kitchen, and the other is his residence. Strangers and travellers are provided with comfortable quarters in a frame house upon the hill, which commands a view of the most charming landscape in Florida.

THE MYSTERIOUS SAIL.

As the Doctor arose from his dinner table on the 16th of last January he saw a sail in Banana river, off the point of George's Island.[2] It was opposite the mouth of Newfound Harbor, a bay running up the side of Merritt's Island. The weather was cold and cloudy, and there were signs of a strong norther. The Doctor eyed the craft closely, but did not recognize her rig. She was a small sailboat, and was skipping along the water with a fair spread of canvas. He passed on to his wood pile, and brought an armful of wood into the kitchen. As he came out he thought he would take another look at the sail and see if he couldn't place her. To his utter astonishment she had disappeared. He commanded a view of the river for miles, yet no sail was in sight. In his perplexity he was more than half inclined to believe that the craft was an imaginary one, probably a mirage from the ocean. He called his wife and children. They had seen the same sail, and were as much mystified as the head of the family. The wind was already pouring from the north, and white foam began to fly from the crest of the waves. The family stood upon the shore and peered over the agitated water, but could see nothing but startled pelicans and storm-stricken curlews.

"Well, wife," exclaimed the Doctor, "this is strange. There must have been a sail. We certainly saw one. Probably the wind is so strong that they are reefing."

So they waited, but no reefed canvas was spread above the waves. Finally the Doctor gave it up. He concluded that the occupants of the boat had lowered their sail and cast anchor, intending to ride out the approaching storm.

THE LITTLE BLACK SPECKS.

Within half an hour the children told their father that they could see a boat, but so far off that the men in it looked like little black specks. The Doctor went to the river and gazed over the hissing salt water. The wind was tearing through the broad palmetto leaves above him, and ominous rifts of clouds were scudding to the south. At last he thought he saw the boat. It was but for an instant. The heaving waves snatched it from view, and the Doctor saw it no more.

"If there is anything the matter," he declared, "those men are in a bad box. It would be better for them to cut loose and drift ashore."

He proposed to row out in his clinker-built boat and find out whether they were in trouble, but the children cried and his wife objected. The storm, she said, was increasing in fury, and if anything should happen to the husband what would become of the family? She had no doubt that the men were safely anchored, and would laugh at the Doctor if they thought he betrayed any anxiety on their account. At all events, she was opposed to his risking his life on an uncertainty. The Doctor listened to her and went about his business.

The gale grew in intensity. The spray blown from the combing waves spread over the wide river like a fog. The wind clouds swiftly chased each other to the south, and the branches of the tall palmettoes thrashed the air like insane giants. The children could see the boat no longer, and huddled beneath the palmetto roof.

IF IN DANGER, THEY MUST PERISH.

About half past four o'clock the wind perceptibly slackened, but was still very strong, rolling the waves to an unusual height. The storm was not yet over. Again the children discovered the boat and its black specks. Its position was unchanged. As it rode upon the swell of the water the Doctor regarded it long and earnestly.

"Those men may be anchored," he said, "but I must go and see. Night is coming on, and if they are in danger, they must perish."

He threw off his coat. Despite the entreaties of his wife and children the clinker-built boat was drawn over the shallow flat along the shore, and the Doctor took the oars. It was a dead pull against the wind for fully three miles. The boat was tossed upon the waves like an egg shell. She shipped the combing of the seas, and made a little headway. Drenched to the skin, the Doctor clung to his oars. At one time the wind freshened; and his arms became numb with the strain. His boat began to turn in the trough and drift toward the south. The thought of the probable peril of the strangers and the anxiety with which they might be watching him, nerved him to a renewed effort. It was almost dark when he approached their boat. At the distance of a hundred yards she was plainly visible. Two men were apparently very comfortably seated in her stern, watching his frantic attempts to reach them. It was not until he was within twenty feet that he saw that their boat was capsized and they were crouching upon her keel. The anchor had caught, and their craft was held as firmly as though she was tied to a rock. At every surge the men were submerged. The Doctor forced his boat alongside, and hallooed to them to get in. He received no answer. The strangers were chilled by the cold north wind, and could neither speak nor move. Ten minutes more and they would have been lost. With much difficulty the Doctor managed to steady his boat, while he drew them in over the gunwales.

A STARTLING INQUIRY.

In an instant they were off before the wind. The wet strangers lay upon the watery bottom of the boat, with white faces and chattering teeth, while the Doctor plied the oars. Not a word was spoken. A blazing fire kindled by the children lighted them to the shore. As the rescued men dragged themselves to the blaze they were in a pitiable plight. One of them shed tears. His companion shivered over the fire until its warmth revived him and took the stiffness from his limbs. The Doctor's wife made a pot of steaming coffee and provided them with dry clothing. They were profuse in their thanks. The Doctor cheered them up, the little children brought them chairs, and they were soon in better spirits.

"Where is Law, Doctor," inquired one of the strangers.

"Law?" repeated the Doctor. "Who's Law?"

"Why, the man who swam ashore and told you we were in danger," was the reply.

The Doctor was astonished. "Swam ashore?" he said. "Nobody came ashore here. The children first discovered you, and called my attention to your boat."

THE FATAL SHEET ROPE.

Then their story came out. It appeared that early in January an elderly gentleman arrived at Col. Titus's hotel in Sand Point,[3] and registered himself, "F. A. Law, Sunrise City." He was of more than ordinary intelligence, and seemed to be very wealthy. After spending a few days in Sand Point, he hired a sail boat, and in company with Mr. Crook of the Titus House and another gentleman started on a pleasure trip around Merritt's Island. Up to a point south of Cape Canaveral the voyage was exceedingly pleasant. Then there was a succession of blustering cat squalls, and the wind shifted to the north. It blew so strong that a double reef was taken in the sail. The sheet rope was probably fastened to one of the stern cleats instead of being held by the boatman's hand. After passing George's Island, a heavy wind struck the boat and she was careening on her side when one of the men started to go forward. He stepped to the leeward and the boat went over as quick as thought. The anchor fell from her bows and held her fast. The three men clung to her sides and clambered upon her keel, where the storm burst upon them in all its fury.

It was singular that neither of them thought of cutting the anchor rope. Had this been done they would have drifted to the shore of Merritt's Island, about two miles south of Wittfeld's. Opposite the doctor's house, Banana river is four miles wide. A thin strip of sand and scrub palmetto cuts it off from the ocean. The boat capsized within a mile of this beach, and a good three miles from Wittfeld's residence. It would have been comparatively an easy matter for an average swimmer to reach the ocean beach, as the water is so shallow that a man can wade almost three quarters of a mile. The nearest resident on that side, however, was a Mr. H. H. of Providence, R.I. His house was fifteen miles away.

A GOOD SWIMMER'S LAST SWIM.

The situation of the voyagers was critical. Two of them could not swim. The wind became colder, increasing in violence, and the waves repeatedly washed them from the keel. Crook pointed out the direction of Dr. Wittfeld's plantation, and after half an hour's drenching, Law determined to try and reach it. Unless he did this all three must perish. He was a good swimmer, but three miles in such a wind as that was a long swim. He promised to send his comrades help as soon as he reached the shore. His coat and shoes were taken off, and he was about to strike out when his companions urged him to peel off everything, even to his undershirt, and endeavor to gain Merritt's Island in a naked condition. This he refused to do. For a long time the shivering men saw him buffeting the waves. Half the time his head was out of sight, and at last it altogether disappeared. Later in the afternoon, while the keel was poised on the top of a high wave, they discovered him over a mile to the westward. He was wading in water waist-deep with his arms above his head. They thought that he had made the edge of the channel, and felt sure that he would soon reach the shore. The truth was that he had struck a bank putting out from the point of George's Island. After leaving this bank, he had a square mile to swim before he could reach the shoal water off Merritt's Island, and this mile was across the mouth of New-Found Harbor, where the swell of the water was the heaviest.

This was the last that was seen of the swimmer alive. The two men eagerly watched the shore for signs of relief. When they observed the Doctor's boat under weigh they rejoiced, for they were sure that Law had arrived at the island and had informed him of their peril. It was with a sore heart they learned that the swimmer had not made his appearance.

A LONG HUNT FOR A CORPSE.

The night was very dark and the gale was still howling through the palmettoes. A rousing fire was built further down the shore, in the hope that the missing man would see it. It was supposed that he had reached the island and lost his way in the dense thickets and tall saw grass. The Doctor lighted a lantern, and walked the sandy beach for a mile, looking for footprints, but found no clue to his fate. In the morning the search was renewed. The whole day was spent in the hunt. No discovery was made. It was evident that the swimmer had been drowned. His soggy clothing had proved fatal. Meantime his two companions secured the capsized boat, and on the third day returned to Sand Point.

Fearful that the body might float ashore and be eaten by the hogs and buzzards, the Doctor continued the search. He explored the shores of New-Found Harbor and the rocks of George's and Brady's islands,[4] but without success. Day after day was spent looking for the corpse, and the Doctor thinks that he traveled over 150 miles. He had no neighbors, and there was no one to assist him. On the eighth day, while sailing near the southerly point of George's Island, he detected a strong, putrid smell, but was unable to trace it to its source. The wind was in the southeast. He remarked the scent on the subsequent day, but again failed to ascertain its origin. Meanwhile he was neglecting his own interests. Weeds were choking the growth of his early vegetables, and hogs and bears were making inroads upon his patch of sugar cane. His wife urged him to give up the hunt and attend to his work. He determined to devote one more day to the search, and if nothing was discovered to drop it.

THE TELL-TALE BUZZARDS.

The morning of the tenth day broke with a stiff norther. A search in such a breeze was impracticable. On the eleventh day, however, the wind again veered to the southeast. As the body had lain in the water over the allotted nine days, the Doctor thought that the norther might have cast it upon the shore. At any rate he made up his mind that this should be the last day of the hunt. He headed his boat for George's Island. Its shores, as well as those of Brady's Island and the long peninsula opposite, were carefully gone over. He saw nothing, and smelt nothing. An hour before sundown he turned toward home. When opposite Fisherman's Camp, a point within half a mile of his house, he saw a dozen buzzards balancing themselves in a bay tree overlooking the beach. He anchored his boat, for the water was very shallow, and waded ashore. Six or seven red-eyed buzzards loped up the beach and sought a foothold with their companions in the tree.

The corpse was stretched upon the sand. A drove of gaunt black hogs were rooting the ground within twenty rods of it. It had apparently been thrown upon the beach by the norther of the previous day. The Doctor had passed the spot a score of times, and had observed nothing. The body was swollen and decomposed. One arm of the shirt was torn away, and there was a large rent in the side of the same garment. Dr. Wittfeld thinks that during the man's drowning struggles he must have caught upon some root or snag on the bottom of the river, which held him down until the shirt gave way. This would account for the mysterious effluvia during a southeast wind.

BURIED ABOVE HIGH WATER MARK.

The body seemed to be that of a man about fifty-five years old. The hair was gray, and there was a circular bald spot upon the top of the head. Buzzards had eaten away one side of the face, and torn a hole under the armpit. A gold watch, comb, pocketknife, and $502 in money were found in the pockets. The corpse had been in the water so long, that it was ready to drop in pieces. Fortunately the Doctor had a piece of an old sail in his boat. In this he carefully wrapped the dead man, and dragged him above the water line. After driving away the hogs, he hastened home, and returned with a spade and pick. With these he dug a grave in the sand, and after sewing the corpse in the old sail covered it with palmetto boughs, and laid it in the ground until he could procure a coffin from Sand Point. When this was done the stranger was exhumed, placed in the coffin, and buried above high water mark. There he rests awaiting orders from friends or relatives.

The dead man's watch stopped running at 4:30. Its owner had been swimming three hours and a half, and sank beneath the waves at the moment the Doctor started to rescue his friends. The Doctor dried the gold watch in the oven of a cooking stove, but the salt water had corroded and ruined it.

WHO IS THE DEAD SWIMMER?

Every effort to trace the dead swimmer's identity has failed. He was registered: F. A. LAW . . . . . . Sunrise City.

The only Sunrise City in the Post Office Directory is located in Minnesota. The Doctor wrote the particulars of the disaster to the Mayor and Postmaster of that place, but has received no answer. A check upon a bank in Concord, N.H., was among the money found upon the body. Seth Eastman, the Cashier or President of the bank, was informed of the accident, and questioned concerning the dead man's antecedents. Mr. Eastman has taken no notice of the letter. And so the case remains a mystery. From remarks dropped in Sand Point it is believed that Mr. Law possessed considerable property. He spoke of several large mills in which he was interested, besides mentioning other business pursuits. It is hoped that his heirs and relatives may hear of his sad fate, and come forward and claim his remains.

ZISKA.

The Not Forever Glades

When Amos J. Cummings signed his name to this *New York Sun* article (published April 23, 1893), the wetlands of South Central and South Florida were in full retreat, beaten back by Hamilton Disston, Col. James Kreamer, and others. To Cummings and most Americans of the time, the men were heroes. Tens of thousands of acres of wetlands had been drained and opened to farming. Former wetlands from Kissimmee southward, as Cummings describes, were being planted with sugarcane, rice, and a host of other crops. New towns were springing up; South Florida was open to development. There were fortunes being made; Florida's economic future was secure.

Though an economic downturn in the mid-1890s left Disston heavily in debt (distraught, he killed himself in 1896), others were happy to jump into the breach. Florida politicians and developers were only too eager to continue Disston's dream. In the early twentieth century, the Army Corps of Engineers set to work channeling the Kissimmee River, a project that both increased prospects for navigation on that once slow-flowing, meandering river and provided opportunities for drainage of more wetlands north of Lake Okeechobee.

Elected governor of Florida in 1904, Napoleon Bonaparte Broward promised to drain still more lands, creating an "Empire of the Everglades," and the next year the Florida legislature set up a Board of Drainage Commissioners to accomplish the task.

Between 1907 and 1927, the Everglades Drainage District did its job, building a host of canals and levees that drained lands south, southeast, and west of Lake Okeechobee. Though the drainage system did not always work as planned, sugarcane and truck crops spread across those lands that were "reclaimed."

Then, in September 1926, a disastrous hurricane struck South Florida, passing over Lake Okeechobee and flooding the area. Nearly two thousand people were killed; entire communities were washed out. In response, renewed efforts to ditch and dyke South Florida were initiated. Flood control and water management became major themes of combined federal and state agencies. President Herbert Hoover toured the area, and soon a new system of locks and levees that tamed Lake Okeechobee itself was named for him.

Governor Napoleon Bonaparte Broward (*back right*) and ex-Florida governor William S. Jennings (*back left*) on a tour of an Everglades drainage project in 1906. Courtesy of Florida State Archives.

Despite the best efforts of the water management agencies, periods of drought interspersed with flooding rains played havoc with the artificial landscape. In 1947, nature tried desperately to reclaim her wetlands when 100 inches of rains caused devastation to the economic interests that had moved onto the land. A new agency, an ancestor of the South Florida Water Management District, was born, along with more canals, levees, pumping stations, and some two thousand water control structures.

What once was a true marvel of nature—the flow of water from Central and South Florida down across the peninsula and west into the Gulf of Mexico—today is a complex, highly engineered, and very expensive proposition, one that does not always work to distribute water as it should. And because of runoff from farmlands, parts of the Everglades are polluted with an assortment of chemicals, fertilizers, and other things toxic to plants and animals.

Today, in the twenty-first century, a multibillion-dollar engineering project is once again under way, this time to help restore some of the Everglades while serving the needs of water control. The project is truly monumental in scope; it will be the most complex ecological engineering feat in human history.

Will it be successful? I hope so. But as we learned with the 1926 hurricane, Hurricane Andrew in 1992, and Hurricanes Charley, Frances, and Ivan in 2004, nature sometimes can throw us for a loop.

If Amos Cummings were around today, would he be back in Florida, covering the story of the Everglades restoration? I bet he would. Being the outdoorsman he was, I would also bet that he would have one of those stickers on his car bumper that read "Nature Bats Last."

THE NEW SUGAR KINGDOM

◆

RECLAIMING THE FAMOUS CYPRESS SWAMPS OF FLORIDA.

◆

Hamilton Disston's Success—Where Bass were Caught Ten Years Ago Now Lie Thousands of Acres of Vegetables and Fruits—The Future of a Once Dead State.

JACKSONVILLE, FLA., APRIL 20.—The development of the Southern States since the war has been marvellous. Alabama, Georgia, and Tennessee have heretofore taken the lead. Their coal, iron, marble, and timber have contributed largely to the wealth of the country. In no State, however, is development now more marked than in Florida. Millions of dollars worth of tobacco are raised every year in the northern part of the State. Her phosphate beds are proving as rich as the coal and iron beds of Tennessee and Alabama. The State is dotted with orange groves, and along Key Biscayne Bay millions of cocoanuts drop to the ground every year. Bananas and pine-apples thrive in profusion, and now new products are to be thrown on the market. The State also bids fair to outstrip Louisiana in sugar product, and to raise more rice than South Carolina and Georgia combined. Her swamp lands are proving as great a source of wealth as her phosphate beds. These lands are gradually being drained.

The great arteries of Florida are the St. John's and Kissimmee rivers. They rise in a nest of lakes in the interior of the State. The St. John's, like the Nile, carries its water to the north until it reaches the sea. The Kissimmee, like the Congo, turns in the opposite direction. It pours its burden into the great lake of Okeechobee, and from thence through a canal into the Caloosahatchee River, reaching the Gulf of Mexico at Punta Rossa. The great lakes in Florida, like those in Africa, have been surrounded with vast stretches of saw-grass. This is the case to-day at Lakes Winder, Poinsett, and Washington, away at the source of the St. John's. It is estimated that thirteen years ago over 12,000,000 acres of land were covered with saw grass. The water in this grass was between two and six feet deep. Each lake was surrounded with cypress trees, and behind the cypress stretched vast savannas of saw grass, in most places as far as the eye could reach. Below Okeechobee this saw-grass country was known as the Everglades.

When Zachary Taylor fought his battle with the Seminoles, on the shore of this great lake,[1] some of his engineer officers saw the possibilities of the future. They ascertained that these swamp lands were at such a height above the ocean that they could be easily drained. They made reports proving their assertions and filed them in the archives of the War Department at Washington.

Fifteen years ago these reports attracted the attention of Col. James M. Kreamer[2] of Philadelphia. The Colonel visited Florida not long afterward. He is an expert topographical engineer. He became convinced that the saw-grass lands were the richest lands in the State, far richer than its hammock lands. Upon his return to Philadelphia he interested Hamilton Disston in the project. Disston paid a visit to Florida, making a careful survey of the land from the source of the Kissimmee to Okeechobee, and from Okeechobee to the Gulf. Satisfied that there was a fortune in the reclamation of these swamps, he made a deal with the State. He agreed to drain these lands if the State would give him half of the reclaimed land. By a subsequent deal he bought the State's right to the other half of the reclaimed lands, paying therefor upward of $1,000,000.

Everybody regarded the scheme as visionary. Old Floridians laughed at Disston, and Northern capitalists regarded him with awry looks. All sorts of stories were told about the scheme. The public got the impression that Disston was trying to drain the lakes themselves, with the Everglades thrown in. The Philadelphian found it almost impossible to interest outside capital. He was forced to bear the financial brunt of it alone. It was not until he had spent over a million dollars of his own money that other capitalists joined with him. Of Scotch descent, his financial shrewdness and judgment were unquestioned. Men said that if Disston put so much of his own money in the scheme, there must be something in it. They went over his work, made their own investigations, and invested.

Work was first begun in the spring of 1881 between Okeechobee and the Caloosahatchee river. A canal was dug from Okeechobee into Lake Hicpochee and from there into Lake Flirt, the head of the Caloosahatchee. The elevation at Okeechobee was twenty-two feet above the Gulf. The water pouring from Okeechobee into the Caloosahatchee drained the great stretch of saw grass to the west of Okeechobee. Through this outlet to the Gulf the swamp lands along the Kissimmee, reaching hundreds of lakes nearly two hundred miles north of Okeechobee, were drained. There were scores of these lakes, each surrounded with immense stretches of saw-grass. More than this, the saw-

Offices of the Disston Land Companies in the 1880s, probably near Kissimmee. Courtesy of
Florida State Archives.

grass stretched on either side of the Kissimmee for many miles, being occasionally broken with Indian mounds and hammock land.

The greatest of the lakes above Okeechobee were Kissimmee Lake, Istok-
poga, and Lake Tohopekaliga. There are twin Tohopekaliga lakes. Surrounding these twin lakes were a hundred other lakes, all environed with saw-grass.
Col. Kreamer got the elevation of each lake, and by a system of canals drained
nearly all of them into the Kissimmee River, the water passing down the Kissimmee through Okeechobee and out into the Gulf. Several lakes north of
Tohopekaliga are being drained into the St. John's instead of the Kissimmee.
Col. Kreamer says that 1,200,000 acres of land have already been reclaimed
along the Kissimmee and its tributaries, and that before his operations are
concluded, they will reclaim 7,500,000 acres.

The draining of the land, however, was nothing unless the land was worth
draining. It has turned out to be as rich land as was ever exposed to sunlight.
Lakes Tohopekaliga and Okeechobee have been lowered eight feet. The vast
stretches of saw-grass around them have been drained without injury to navigation. The cypress trees, once six feet in water, now stand around Tohopekaliga on a ridge, and the shore of the lake roads away from it is as white and
as hard as the ocean beach. Back of the cypresses in the place of the saw-grass

savannas are immense sugar and rice fields. A railroad runs from Kissimmee, on one of the twin lakes, to Runnymede,[3] near the shore of the other lake. This road runs through the sugar and rice fields. It crosses the great canals draining the land. The main canal is twenty-six feet wide, from five to seven feet deep, and with a current running at least four miles an hour. The soil is a rich black loam, formed from the decaying saw-grass of centuries. It has a uniform depth of eight feet. It is almost as black as carbon. It is a rich mould that never cakes. There is no sand in it. One mule will put a plough through it without trouble. Thirty-six mules work 1,500 acres of this land at what is known as the St. Cloud plantation.[4]

Gov. Warmoth,[5] who was lately a visitor at this plantation, expressed great surprise when he saw how easily the land was worked. He said that one mule in Florida would do what it took four or six mules to do in the Louisiana plantations. There the land is sticky and mucky. He foresees a great future for sugar planters along the Kissimmee, and could hardly believe Disston when he said that he had 275,000 acres of just such land in one body, without a break, already drained around Okeechobee. Claus Spreckels,[6] who has also visited the plantation, is reported to have said that if he could have secured this land twenty-five years ago he could have made more money out of it than he had made in all his Sandwich Islands sugar lands.

I visited Runnymede and the surrounding plantations on St. Patrick's Day. As we left Kissimmee, away out across the sea of black loam loomed the towers of the sugar mill on the St. Cloud plantation. Fifteen hundred acres of cane had been planted. It was about twenty inches high and had been slightly touched by frost. This is said to be beneficial rather than a damage to the crop, as it prevents a too luxurious growth and gives stock to the cane. Certain it is that the stocks and leaves were of a rich-dark green, and that the plants were thriving like corn in June on the Missouri bottoms.

The great sugar mill stands upon the back of the canal tapping Tohopekaliga. It is furnished with the finest machinery and is fully equal to the best sugar mills in Louisiana and Cuba. It cost $250,000. Tramways run from the mill into every section of the plantation. The cane grows even more luxuriantly than the saw-grass which preceded it. Without the tramways it would be almost impossible to convey it to the mill.

Along the banks of the canal stand the houses of those employed on the plantation and in the mill. There were little peach trees around the dwellings, and beneath the peach trees squads of urchins were filling the air with their shouts. Along the bank of the canal walked a barefooted negro, fishing rod in hand. He was drawing a home-made spinner through the canal, and had a string of big-mouthed bass swinging from his shoulder. Not one of these bass would weigh less than three pounds. There were a dozen of them, and he had caught them all in the canal.

It is a run of three miles to Runnymede, near the further shore of the lake. Here there is an excellent hotel, and near it a United States experimental station. The latter stands upon reclaimed land. The superintendent is trying experiments with tropical fruits and vegetables. There were Spanish onions in his garden, turnips as big as bowls in a tenpin alley and as mellow as apples, new Irish potatoes, cabbages, carrots, beets, yams, lettuce already run to seed, and cassava.

The cultivation of cassava may become an important industry. It grows in ridges like sweet potatoes. The tubers are sometimes several feet long, and there are as many as a dozen on a stalk. When scraped they are whiter than a potato, and when raw taste like chestnuts. Mules, horses, cows, and other stock are fed upon the cassava. It takes the place of hay and corn, and grows almost wild, even in the sandy soil beneath the pines. It requires very little cultivation. Cattle fatten readily upon it. The mules upon the plantation are fed with cassava. They were as fine looking mules as any in Florida. The cassava is chopped before it is fed to cattle. The discovery of this fodder cheapens the production of sugar and rice, as it costs very little to maintain the mules employed on the plantation. But this is not all. The cassava, as experiments at the agricultural station have demonstrated, makes starch superior to corn, and alcohol unrivalled in purity. S. W. Wiley of the Division of Chemistry, in the Department of Agriculture, says that the fresh cassava root has yielded in his laboratory 25 per cent of first-class starch. He thinks the percentage can be increased. The field from which his sample was taken yielded four tons of roots to the acre. This yield was below the average. He thinks that an average of five tons per acre can be counted on in the pine woods soil. This land is the cheapest in Florida, and there are millions upon millions of acres of it. Mr. Wiley says that glucose made from the cassava starch is equal in every respect to that made from corn starch. The treatment consists simply in rasping it to an impalpable pulp and washing the starch out on bolted cloth. The starch requires no chemical treatment. It is absolutely free from nitrogeneous substances. It makes an excellent tapioca when properly treated. Cassava is a more economical source of starch than maize. At four tons of root to the acre the yield would be 2,000 pounds of starch. The yield from thirty bushels of corn would be only about a thousand pounds.

In the garden of the hotel at Runnymede were many vegetables. There were strawberries and pineapples already developed, and better than all, new Irish potatoes, equal to those grown in Holland. Nor were they grown upon reclaimed swamp land. The potatoes were brought to perfection because the vines were covered with dead grass. This retained the moisture of the air, and gave them an exquisite flavor.

Probably the most astonishing of the products of the reclaimed swamp land is peaches. Back of the ridge of cypresses surrounding the lake, and bordering on the sugar plantation, were two thousand peach trees. They were under the charge of an experienced peach grower from Delaware. These trees were planted so close together that very little sunlight reached the soil beneath them. This soil was a rich black loam, carefully worked, so carefully that not a blade of grass or a weed was seen. The foliage of the trees was a dark green, nearly as dark and as glossy as the leaf of an orange or magnolia. The trunks of the trees were as clean and as smooth as the trunk of an orange tree in good condition. There were no knees upon the roots of the trees. The Delaware man was in ecstasy over them. Not a tree had developed the least sign of a disease, and there were no insects nor worms to fatten on them.

The trees were five years old. They were planted upon ground that eight years ago was eight feet under water. The peaches were about three-quarters grown, and the trees were loaded with them. Within six weeks they would be ready for market. They were the Early Bidwell and Chinese peaches, better known as "peentos." Last year these peaches netted $157 an acre, and this in the face of the fact that the freight to New York was $2,000. If enough of them were raised to make freight an object to the railroad companies, it is said, it would not amount to one-fifth of this sum. They are the first peaches to arrive in the Northern market. On any other land but this swamp land peaches in Florida do not amount to much. The trees grow very large, but the leaves are yellow, and the fruit is small and shrivelled.

Near the peach orchard was a stretch of land shaped like an oblong saucer. It lay beneath the tall cypresses that formerly fringed the lake. Years ago, before it was drained, it was the favorite fishing ground of old Jake Summerlin,[7] a well-known Floridian. The cypresses to which Jake had tied his boat while fishing were still standing. In two hours, he said, he had frequently caught fifty large bass there. A variety of fruit trees now occupies the ground. Among them are pears, apricots, guavas, mangoes, pomegranates, plums, figs, bananas, pineapples, and grapes. The pear trees were Le Comptes, and the grapes Niagaras, with one or two other varieties. All were in a thriving condition. The pineapples were nearly ripe. The pears looked as thrifty as the peaches, and the leaves of the grape gushed dark green from the red vines.

Near these fruit trees were immense agaves. Upon their leaves darted tiny ichneumons[8] in pursuit of insects. Scores of small green frogs were sleeping between the leaves. At night they fill the air with music. The lake was only ten rods away. A cool breeze was wafted through the cypresses. Further along toward Runnymede stood the dwellings of Italian laborers employed on the plantation. They were on the cypress ridge, overlooking the great lake, which appeared to be as round as a shield. There were a dozen or more of these cottages. In the trees above them swarms of blackbirds with scarlet epaulets emitted their dripping melody, while beneath them mules and cows nipped the herbage which sprang from the soil where once the saw-grass grew. These cabins are to be removed and winter cottages are to be placed upon the cypress ridge. Many building lots have been sold and exquisite dwellings are now being erected by persons of wealth and refinement who spend the wintry months in Florida.

Back of the ridge lay the St. Cloud plantation and rice fields as far as the eye could reach. The rice lands are just being brought into market. One of the Charleston Ravenals[9] has leased 1,200 acres. It was being planted in rice in March. With the canals from the lake it is easily inundated. The crop is a sure one, and Mr. Ravenal is satisfied that he can get two crops a year from the rich soil. It is free from the dangers that threaten rice fields near the sea coast. An east wind with a neap tide frequently backs the salt water up the streams in South Carolina and Georgia, injuring and destroying the crop. There is none of this danger in Florida. The water is drawn off as easily as it is let on. Aside from this, the rice fields along the Kissimmee are entirely healthful. It is said to be fatal for a white man to spend a night upon a South Carolina rice plantation. The drained lands in Florida produce no such fatality. There are no fevers or agues along the Kissimmee.

The drainage of the saw grass and the ploughing of the fields seem to have destroyed the mosquitoes and sand flies. Nor is there any miasma arising from this upturned virgin soil. It is so rich that the new and rank vegetation absorbs all the gases and prevents malaria. The Italians and negroes who work the fields have no use for a doctor. The first year they were taxed to support one, the same as under the Louisiana system. The second year they refused to pay the tax. No one was sick. A Mr. Supfer and his family from Kansas, who had suffered from fever and ague for years in Kansas, came to the Kissimmee about four years ago, and have lived there winter and summer ever since. The chills and fever departed, and the family regained their health. They live on the borders of the rice fields. Mr. Ravenal, not satisfied with their story, visited nearly every white resident, and is satisfied that there is no more healthful spot in Florida than these rice fields.

There is no trouble in securing laborers. Mr. Ravenal has brought with him enough negroes from South Carolina to cultivate his plantation, and there are many Italians at work. The superintendent of the sugar plantation says he has no trouble in securing as many as he wants. Once there, they take up little

A steam engine of the Jupiter and Lake Worth Railway, 1893. The railroad, owned by the Indian River Steamship Company, was called the celestial railroad because its stations were named Jupiter, Mars, Venus, and Juno; Jupiter was at Jupiter Inlet, and Juno was at the north end of Lake Worth. Courtesy of Florida State Archives.

plots of land and settle down for life. One reason for the healthfulness of the Kissimmee region is its situation. The easterly winds are laden with salt from the Gulf Stream, and the westerly winds carry salt moisture from the Gulf of Mexico. There is so much salt in the air that the grass absorbs it, and it is never necessary to salt the cattle. The grass upon the reclaimed land is very rich and nutritious. A natural sward leads from the ridge of cypress to the sandy shores of the lake. Bermuda grass becomes as thick as a mat, and lawn mowers were already at work in the middle of March. The drainage of water from the cypress ridge seems not to have affected the trees. They stand there like giants, waving their moss-draped branches. The leaves are of a livid green, and the trees are apparently in their prime. The cypress spreads its trunk as it reaches the water. Some of these trunks remain on the ridge, resembling the tepees of the Sioux, the trees rising a hundred feet above them, making a magnificent shade.

So much for this new kingdom of sugar and rice. The work of development has only just begun. Its possibilities seem marvellous. Dredges are still at work draining numerous little lakes near the divide of the St. John's and the Kissimmee. All the drainage is carried into either the Okeechobee or the St.

John's. With the work already done, steamboats have run from the mouth of the Caloosahatchee through Okeechobee up the Kissimmee, and into Lake Tohopekaliga. The natives asserted that the current would not be strong enough to carry away the silt. Experience has proved that this is not so. The only trouble, if there is any trouble, will probably be found in the canal leading from Okeechobee into the Caloosahatchee. But there is twenty-two feet fall from Okeechobee to the Gulf. With the occasional use of a dredge it will certainly be easy to keep the canal open and navigable.

When the Kissimmee and the Okeechobee lands are thoroughly drained, it will be an easy matter to drain the Everglades and the immense swamp lands of the Halpatiokee, Allokehatchie, and the saw-grass regions along the sea-coast. Within thirty years twenty million acres may be reclaimed, and untold wealth be garnered in sugar, rice, and vegetables from lands that fifteen years ago were under eight feet of water.

In addition to this, thousands of acres of phosphate land have been discovered in this saw-grass region. Within a year, 150 acres of this phosphate land has been sold to an English company for $25,000.

All this wealth would amount to nothing unless brought to market. Railroads are already projected and are now being built to place the lands in close communication with the world. Mr. Flagler is exte 3nding his road from Rock Ledge down to Biscayne Bay, where he will be in touch with Havana and Nassau. The Plant system is being extended along the western coast. With these railroads through southern Florida, and her natural advantages of soil and climate, the State bids fair to become one of the richest States in the Union.

AMOS J. CUMMINGS.

More Murder in Paradise

Two things drew me to this article. First is the recounting, with national pride, of all the nonindigenous plant species that were introduced into Florida. Who knew at that time that we would be trying to pull many of them out by the roots a century later? The second is the mention of a "beautiful sago palm" transplanted to New Smyrna, Florida, from "the little place made memorable by the murder of the Packard family a year ago last December." What was the Packard family murder that had taken place in December 1891? Was this another example of the mayhem that always seems to lurk below Florida's veneer of swaying palms and tranquil gardens of exotic greenery? It was.

It did not take me long to coax the story of the murders out of my computer. Using the Internet, I logged on to the University of Florida library and clicked on the ProQuest Historical Newspapers database, which gave me access to articles from the *New York Times* (1851–2001) and *Washington Post* (1889–1986). When my initial search for articles published in December 1891 mentioning the Packard family failed to turn up a single citation, I switched to "Florida AND murders" and in fifteen minutes had found eight articles dealing not with the Packards but with Packwoods (Cummings had gotten the name wrong).

National coverage of the murders broke in the December 13, 1891, issue of the *Washington Post* in a three-paragraph-long story on page one headlined "With Their Throats Cut, Four Persons Found Murdered in Their Florida Cottage," and datelined "December 12 from New Smyrna, Florida." Miss A. H. Bruce, Mrs. L. D. Hatch and her son, and Master Frank Packwood had been found on the afternoon of December 12 (a Saturday) murdered in a small cottage they had rented for the winter six miles south of New Smyrna.

According to the story, "The throats of all four were cut from ear to ear and they had been dead apparently from eighteen to thirty hours." Though there was no "clew" to the murderer, several suspicious tramps had been recently in the neighborhood. A posse of fifty men, some mounted and some walking, had set out from New Smyrna for the cottage, which was owned by the Packwood family and was "seven miles from the nearest telegraph." Local residents must have been in a turmoil.

The *New York Times* picked up the story on December 14 with more detailed coverage, datelined "Jacksonville, Florida, December 13." Though information was limited because it was not possible to establish telegraph communication with the scene—local people must have had to go to the cottage, then return to New Smyrna to telegraph Jacksonville—the *Times* spelled out what was known. The cottage, owned by Frank J. Packwood of Louisiana, was in an orange grove on the Hillsborough (now Indian) River. Packwood's son, four years old, was among those killed. The Hatch boy, also a victim, was six.

The scene was gruesome. The victims had been shot, stabbed with a butcher knife, their throats cut, and the skull and face of one of the women had been smashed, possibly with the butt of a double-barreled shotgun found in the cottage. Robbery was thought to be the motive. One rumor abounding was that Frank J. Packwood had been killed also, but the murderer had hid his body so people would think he (Packwood) was the guilty party.

Packwood's nephew who lived in Jacksonville offered additional background for the story. He said that his uncle actually had lived year-round at the cottage for at least fifteen years. Packwood's first wife, Miss Bruce of New York, had died, leaving behind their young son, Frankie. After her death, Miss Bruce's sister, Miss A. H. Bruce, had moved south to live in the cottage and help to take care of the son. The Jacksonville nephew had never heard of Mrs. L. D. Hatch.

The same day the *Post*'s follow-up story contained much of the same information, with the additional note that the perpetrator apparently had entered the cottage on Friday night, December 11, by smashing in a window. The next day more stories by the *Times* and *Post* established that Mr. Packwood had left the cottage on the morning of the crime to go to Maitland, Florida, for two days. Mrs. Hatch, whose husband was a carpenter and orange grower and lived near New Smyrna for about fifteen years, had moved into the cottage to spend the day and a night with Miss Bruce.

The crime had been discovered on Saturday morning by Irving Jenkins, an African-American man, who had come by to do errands. One piece of evidence was footprints outside the smashed window, some made by a box-toe boot, size 7 or 8. Because the prints were deeper on the inside, it was theorized the murderer was bow-legged. The trail of prints led away from the cottage through a hammock to the road, which suggested the murderer knew his way around the area. The person may not have been a tramp after all. It also was discovered that the pistol and shotgun used in the crime belonged to Mr. Packwood, who, it was reported, had his suspicions about who might have committed the crime.

Another rumor was that the murders were done by a jilted lover of Miss Adeline H. Bruce. The *Times* believed Miss Bruce at one time was "prominent in musical circles" in New York City. The *Post* cited evidence—a ham cooking in a pot on the stove and dough still rising in the kitchen—that the crime had occurred early Saturday morning.

A slightly bow-legged tramp wearing size 8 box-toed boots, a man named Dorsey said to have been near New Smyrna at the time of the murders, was apprehended in Augusta, Georgia, on December 25 or 26. He was reportedly nervous when a story about the murders was read to him. Florida authorities sent to question him must have soon dropped him as a suspect, since no follow-up stories were published. Most likely, bow-legged tramps all over the Southeast were feeling nervous.

Then on December 31, the *Post* reported a new suspect, Irving Jenkins, the man who had been first to sound the alarm. Captain W. O. Cooper, a Pinkerton man who had been working on the case, was said to have evidence implicating Mr. Jenkins and expected him to confess shortly. Jenkins was arrested and was being taken to county jail at Deland, Florida, where his cell was to be guarded by twenty-five men, presumably to prevent a lynching. Cooper was not making any public statements until he spoke with county officials who had offered a $1,000 reward.

I believe that Irving Jenkins is the boy whose name appears in the 1870 federal census for Volusia County. At that time he was nine years old, one of seven children whose parents had come south to Florida from South Carolina and Georgia. In 1870, his family was living near Enterprise, Florida.

Did Jenkins commit the crimes? What happened to him? I do not know; my computer won't tell me the answers to those questions. The December 31 *Post* story is the last one I could find about the Packwood cottage murders. With an African-American man in custody, the northern newspapers lost interest. Racism or justice? There was plenty of both in nineteenth-century Florida.

19

HUNTING WITH A BOTANIST

◆

A CONGRESSMAN'S EXPERIENCE IN THE SWAMPS OF FLORIDA.

◆

The Superintendent of the Botanical Garden in Washington Searching for Novelties—His Adventures at Keystone Bluff and Along the St. John's—A Bamboo Grove—A Day Among the Palms—Observations of the Insectiverous Plants—The Dog Banana and Its Uses—Information Obtained from an Unlearned Colored Botanist.

WASHINGTON, MAY 13.—South on a hunt; not for deer, nor for bear; for neither ducks nor quail; but for plants. The huntsman is William R. Smith, superintendent of the National Botanic Garden, a countryman and an enthusiastic admirer of Robert Burns.[1] He accompanied Commodore Charles Wilkes in his expedition to Japan,[2] and since then has been in charge of the Botanic Garden. Under his supervision it has grown to its present proportions. Its reputation is world wide. Mr. Smith is plain and unassuming. He has enjoyed intimate relations with prominent Senators and Representatives for nearly forty years. He has a broad Scotch accent. Like his friend, ex-Attorney General A. H. Garland,[3] he is eminently practical, and never dons a dress suit. Although in commission at the Garden for nearly half a century, he had never visited Florida.

I.

We start from Washington on the day before the great naval parade in New York harbor.[4] The weather is cold and the sky overcast. Overcoats are a necessity. The cars are hardly warm enough for comfort. Our trip is over the Atlantic Coast line. We leave Washington at 11 A.M. Over the Rappahannock and over the James we roll into North Carolina. We see the muddy waters of the Roanoke and the Neuse, and before dark are beyond the Great and the Little Pedee.

The botanist leans against the window sill thrilled with ecstasy. Each shrub and tree attracts his attention. The lowliest flowers awaken a lively interest. At times he feels like jumping from the platform of the car to examine some rare specimen. Botanizing by rail, however, requires a keen eye and occasionally a hot wheel. Mr. Smith longs for the latter as he catches glimpses of what he thinks are Venus's fly traps (*Dionaea Muscipula*), a rare curiosity which he says are found growing wild only in the sandy bogs of North Carolina. The hot wheel, however, fails to materialize, and as twilight draws her curtain the disappointed man of science is borne into the Palmetto State.

In the night he crosses the Santee, the Combahee, the Edisto, and the Savannah rivers and their attendant swamps. Long before daylight he is threading the piny forests of Georgia. He crosses the Ogeechee at daylight, and is running over the Altamaha at sunrise. An early riser, he experiences new spells of delight. He sees, for the first time, a palmetto growing wild. It is what the natives term a "scrub palmeetto." Mr. Smith promptly classifies it, but gets no opportunity to examine it. The hot wheel never comes to those who long for it. It is in reserve for those who dread it. Rare plants and shrubs flit from the gaze of the botanist. His pulse beats faster, and he longs to begin work. But the train is on time, and there are no mishaps. At Waycross, seventy-five miles from Jacksonville, he springs from the car to examine two palmettos near the depot. They are about thirty feet high. Mules, switching their flanks with their tails, stand in their shade. The sandy soil below them is strewn with the bright black seed of the trees. In an instant the botanist squats between the mules and begins to pick up the seed. So busy is he that the train gets under way before he is aware of it, and he comes within an ace of being left. He says that he gathers the seed, not for the Botanic Garden, but for friends in Europe. Nothing can daunt his enthusiasm. He bemoans treasures beyond his reach, and gravely proposes to get out of the train at the next station and walk to Jacksonville, botanizing on the way. But the hot sun forbids it.

II.

We arrive on the St. John's at 9 A.M. It is twenty-two hours since we left Washington. This train shows the influence of the Pennsylvania Railroad Company on the old coast line. Sixteen years ago it took forty-eight hours to reach Jacksonville from Washington. To-day it is done in far less than half the time, and with royal accommodations.

Our headquarters are at Keystone Bluff, on the St. John's River, two miles below Jacksonville.[5] It is the winter residence of Charles H. Cummings, at whose suggestion the expedition was organized. He places at the service of the botanist a naphtha launch, and entertains him right royally. The botanist proposes to ascertain what foreign plants and flowers will thrive in the climate of

The *Keystone*, Mary Packer Cummings's yacht, was built in Nyack, New York, in 1893. Mrs. Cummings used the steam-driven yacht for transportation between Jacksonville and her estate, Keystone Bluff, on the St. Johns River until her death in 1912. Courtesy of Florida State Archives.

Florida, and to collect native specimens for the Botanic Garden in Washington. The launch is used day and night, a glowing moon appearing after the hot sun goes down. The rivers and creeks around Keystone Bluff are carefully explored. Landings are made in the saw grass in the swamps, and on the pine bluffs. Two large boxes of native plants are collected and forwarded to Washington. It is an expedition exceeding in interest any hunt for birds or animals. Its results must prove interesting to botanists as well as to those who know little or nothing of the vegetable kingdom.

The first search was for palms. Four different kinds were found growing near Keystone Bluff. The first was the palmetto proper (*Sabal Palmetto*).[6] It thrives luxuriantly along the St. John's and throughout the country, attaining a height of sixty or seventy feet. When about twenty years old it loses the boots or straps which clasp the trunk and give the tree such a novel effect.

There are millions of these trees in Florida, but they are being rapidly thinned out. Some inventor has discovered a process by which the heart-leaves of the tree are turned into paper. They are said to make a parchment equal to the parchment of the olden time. There was a shipload of these hearts at Jacksonville awaiting transportation to the manufactory. Each heart represented a tree. The heart is in the top of the trunk. From it the palms arise and radiate. As the lower ones fade and drop, a new layer appears at the top. When large trees are transplanted, signs of decay are apt to appear in the heart. The new leaves turn a sickly yellow, and the fibers are loosened. The water leaks into the heart, and it dies. At such times it can be drawn out of the tree like a cork from a bottle.

The natives call the tree a cabbage tree. The heart is the cabbage. It is chopped from the top of the tree, boiled or pickled, and served upon the table. "Palmeetokyabbage," as it is called, is a luxury among the wire-grass population. Nor are they alone in the appreciation of this luxury. The Seminoles in the Everglades use it freely. A favorite feast with them is a sniped-nosed, mule-hoofed, razor-backed hog boiled with palmetto cabbage. It makes a sort of chowder. Each guest takes his turn at the cauldron and helps himself. Very few whites are honored with invitations to these feasts. Bears vie with men in destroying the palmetto cabbage. They climb the trees, and tear out their hearts, greedily devouring them.

Whether these trees can grow fast enough to supply the bears, Indians, and other natives with cabbage, and the paper makers with pulp, may soon become a serious question. No tree less than fifteen or twenty years old bears a cabbage worth the chopping out. The trees from which the paper makers are obtaining their pulp are from fifty to a hundred years old.

The palmetto is of slow growth. It has a value far beyond that placed upon it by the paper makers. When twenty feet high, well-established in tubs, it will bring $150 from dealers in London. Mr. Smith says that it requires some skill to handle them, but he believes that a fortune might be made in shipping them. The suggestion was made many years ago by Mr. Van Houtte,[7] the eminent ornamental horticulturist of Belgium. The botanist indignantly denounced the destruction of the tree in Florida for food and other purposes. He said that the same murderous operation was being practised in Australia. The Australian cabbage palm (*Coruplio Australia*)[8] was being destroyed. The natives kill trees 100 years old to secure a mess of the prized cabbage.

In speaking of edible roots and trees in Florida, the botanist ventured the assertion that if the Confederate army had known more about the vegetation of the South it could easily have prolonged the war. Its defeat was due mostly to the failure of its supplies.

The most abundant palm found by Superintendent Smith in Florida was the saw palmetto (*Sabal Serrulata*).[9] It thrives on the main shore, but it grows luxuriantly along the ocean beach. In the piny woods it has a rich green color, but along the beach the green has a light blue tint. It is more of a shrub than a tree. The roots rise above the ground where its growth is rank, like the roots of a Spanish bayonet. Men have crawled beneath them hundreds of yards near the ocean dunes to set traps at bear wells in obscure places. The stems of the palms are almost triangular in shape and have sharp teeth set along the edges of the triangle, like the teeth of a saw. No man can force himself through a dense thicket of saw palmettos without tearing his clothes into strips. These palms bear berries larger than cherries, with pits in proportion. Bears feed upon them in June, when the turtles disappear. The natives also eat them and brew beer from them. They are oily and have a rancid flavor. Only a native can stomach them.

The third palm found by Mr. Smith was *Sabal Adamsonii*,[10] or dwarf palmetto. Some call it the swamp palmetto. It is much taller than its brother, the saw palmetto. The stem is shorter, but the leafy stalk longer. In color it is like verdigris, and it is a tolerably handsome plant in a tub.

The last native palmetto seen was *Chamaerops Hustrix*, or needle palm.[11] It is also termed the porcupine palm. Its stem is short and proliferous. The leaves are circular in outline, with numerous tooth divisions, on triangular petioles, with rough edges. The spines come from the spokes of the leaves, and are from six to nine inches long. They are as sharp as needles. They are numerous, erect, and very strong, and readily force attention from the unwary traveller, who takes the plant for the more common swamp palmetto. The needle palm grows in low shady woods, and is the most interesting of the native palms of Florida. Mr. Smith eagerly sought the seed, as he said the palm was highly prized in Europe.

III.

Aside from these four natives, we found many foreign palms thriving in the Floridian climate. The botanist was delighted with the beautiful date palms (*Phoenix Dactylifera*) of St. Augustine. Three of them are over a hundred years old, and a fourth is well along in its second century. Several varieties of this palm and several distinct species were found in the old city. The variety *Canariensis*[12] seemed to do well. It is a native of the Canary Islands, and is one of the best for tub culture. There is a specimen in the garden of the Ponce de Leon so singularly beautiful that the eye never tires of gazing at it. It shades the fountain.

Other species of date palms luxuriating in the soft air of the old Spanish city were the *Reclinata*, the *Spinosa*, and one that looks like a *Farinifera*.[13] The first two are natives of the Cape of Good Hope, and the last is from India. All were swinging their leaves in the garden of the Alcazar.[14]

Mr. Smith learned that the sago palm (*Sucas Revoluta*)[15] is fast becoming acclimated in Florida. It is found growing out not only in Jacksonville, St. Augustine, Sanford, and Tampa, but it revels in little dooryards all down the east and west coast. There was a beautiful sago palm on the little place made memorable by the murder of the Packard family a year ago last December.[16] It has been transferred to the yard of the Ocean Hotel, New Smyrna, where it is universally admired. The leaves of the sago palm are now used in large quantities by florists for funeral decorations.

Another rare cycad was seen in the magnificent garden owned by Mrs. Alexander Mitchell near Jacksonville. Mrs. Mitchell is the mother of United States Senator Mitchell, the successor of Senator Sawyer of Wisconsin.[17] She has a rare selection of plants from every quarter of the globe. The cycad came from Malabar.[18] Botanist Smith expressed his satisfaction on learning that it had survived the cold winter. He said that in New Ireland the natives use the nuts of such trees for food. If cultivated extensively in Florida, this food might take the place of the cabbage palmetto and preserve many a fine tree.

At Mrs. Mitchell's place he also found a grove of bamboos in a surprisingly thrifty condition. Young bamboos were springing from the ground by the middle of April. They shoot up like asparagus in a single night. Within three days they become over six feet high. The growth is longitudinal only, the cane gaining nothing in thickness from the moment it emerges from the ground. We saw one ten inches in circumference and ten feet high. It was only five days old. This was the *Bambusa Bacifera*,[19] a native of the East Indies. There are several of the species in Mrs. Mitchell's garden. One, and a very strong growing one, had been injured by the frost. The others were variegated and black bamboo.

Nothing could be more deliciously cool than the shade of this bamboo grove. There was no vegetation beneath the trees. They shot up twenty or thirty feet high, leafing far above our heads. Nor was the grove for ornament alone. The canes were utilized. They were used in trellis work and in training rustic arches. A bamboo bridge spanned a little stream in the garden, and rare beds of flowers were fenced in by them.

Mrs. Mitchell escorted the botanist over her garden, extracting and giving information. Probably no woman in the United States has a greater love of the beautiful in nature; certainly none has spent so much money in its gratification. One plant she highly prized for its exquisite odor. It was the *Cineraria*,[20] cultivated in every conservatory North. It was doing surprisingly well in Florida in the open air, despite the cold winter.

IV.

The most interesting part of the expedition, however, was the search for *Sarracenia*,[21] plants that feed upon insects. It began in the forenoon of an exceedingly hot day. The sun fairly scorched the shirts upon our backs. We went up Arlington Creek on the little naphtha launch. It threaded the saw grass and the swamps like a thing of life. A quiet light in the eyes of the botanist betokened an eventful day. He saw the white flowers of the *Thalia*[22] nodding at him from the saw grass and filling the air with perfume. The water, however, was so shallow that he could not reach them with the launch.

Two miles further, and we landed on an island in the shade of a thrifty bay tree. The leaves when crushed in our hands smelt like bay rum. The soil of the isle was dry and sandy with wet wastes near the river. The ground had evidently been under cultivation. Prickly ash[23] was there in profusion. A negro stood near the shore watching our movements. There was no house in sight. When he saw Mr. Smith examining the leaves of the prickly ash his curiosity was excited.

"Dat ah am de toothache tree, gemmen," he said. "Et cures de chills an' fever, an' it am better dan quynyne. But my, ain't it bitter. Yo' wants to chew de peel ob de orange to get de taste out ob yo' mout—'deed yo' does."

He said that his name was Edward King, a native of Florida. He had been employed by some rural botanic physician to gather herbs for the Northern market. The employment jibed with his natural inclinations. He had a name for nearly every herb and shrub, and named the disease for which it was a specific. The botanist gladly availed himself of his services, and gathered some interesting information. Black as a coal, King followed him, listening in astonishment to the botanical names of the various plants and trees.

Mr. Smith found two small orchids in bloom and several other rare plants. Seizing the velvety leaves of a shrub shading the hot white sand, he said, "That's the leather tree."

"Oh, no it ain't, sah," the negro replied. "Dat ah am de dog banana. I seen it many a time agone. It's got little bananas on it, like yo' little finger, about two inches long. Dey gits ripe in de summer. De dogs eats 'em and likes 'em. Some people eats 'em, too. I can eat almost anyting, but I draws de line on dem dog bananas—'deed I does. I leabes 'em for de dogs."

The professional botanist then examined the shrub more critically. He soon found other specimens. Thereupon he readily admitted his mistake. There were scores of them in sight. The plant is known to science as *Asimina Grandiflora*.[24] Its flowers are a yellowish white, with outer petals two inches or more in length. Another species, five feet high, was found, called the *Parvi-*

flora.[25] It had a greenish-purple flower and bears small pear-shaped fruit. There was also a third species known north as the Papaw. All grow on dry, sandy soil and flower in March and April. They belong to the custard-apple family. The botanist was anxious to secure seeds of the dog banana to send to botanic institutions in Europe and elsewhere.

Another discovery that gave him great joy was the coral flower (*Erythrina Herbacea*).[26] He said that he had been looking for it growing wild for twenty years. In a jiffy he tore up a big root of it. It was as thick and as long as a man's arm.

"That's forty years old," the botanist observed. "I have raised them from the seed, and know how long it takes them to grow. A seed sometimes lies in the ground two years before it comes up. I know many a man who would like to have this root."

The negro laughed, and named the disease which the root would cure. It was very common just after the war. Afterward Mr. Smith was about to plant the shrub as a curiosity at Keystone Bluff, but Mr. Cummings's gardener protested. He said that years before the plant had grown so rank near his orange grove that he found it almost impossible to exterminate it. The roots were as difficult to remove as the roots of the saw palmetto.

v.

The search for *Sarracenia* or insect-feeding plants, ran along the edge of a swamp back of the creek. They were found in great profusion. The first discovered were what Mr. Smith calls, "whiskey shops." They were the trumpet leaf, known to science as *Sarracenia Variolaris*.[27] The darky declared that they were a sure cure for small-pox. The plants are perennial marsh herbs. They are vegetable cups about a foot high, tapering like a long champagne glass, and carefully hooded, so as to preserve the liquor inside. The hood arches the cup like the hood of a bath robe. Yellow flowers arise from the root between the cups. The entrance to the cup is under the arch. There are transparent spots upon the back of the hood, something like the spots on good cigars. The cup contains a liquor intoxicating to insects. An ant or a bug crawls up the outside and disappears beneath the arch. There is probably a thimbleful of liquid in the bottom of the oblong cup. The insect finds a sugary substance beneath the hood, which apparently increases his appetite for the liquor below. Possibly it serves the same purpose as a pretzel in a saloon. At all events the bug or fly descends and sips the fluid, until, stupefied with intoxication, it sinks and finally dies.

Upon opening one of the cups we found therein flies, ants, bugs, little green grasshoppers, and other insects, in a wet, compact mass at the bottom. They had evidently met their fate without struggling or even entering a protest. Attention was called to the transparent spots on the back of the hood. Mr. Smith could not divine their object. The colored botanist, who had been a close observer, gave him information somewhat startling. It was the fact that these whiskey shops are open day and night. The transparent spots serve as windows, and let in the moonlight. Thus the little shop is illuminated, and a train of night customers succeeds those who patronize the still by day. The colored botanist had discovered the secret while out at night hunting raccoons and opossums. He had seen June bugs and other insects that fly by night crowding to the bar.

Our observations confirmed the negro's statement. His theory is undoubtedly true. Dr. Gray's interpretation of Darwin is that there is always a purpose in nature. These transparent spots, serving as windows to countless whiskey shops, seem to prove it. Indeed, the colored botanist said that he had placed a lantern at the side of the plants on nights when there was no moon. The light of the lantern shone through the tiny windows, and in an instant the bar was open for business. The insects crowded into the shop and its proprietor silently robbed them of their lives. The plant is nourished by the operation. It feeds night and day, and the flies, ants, and bugs rot and fertilize it.

The liquid may be pure nepenthe, but it has the deadly effect of morphine. The insects seek it like old topers. It is said that a British Admiral once died on a foreign station. His body was placed in a cask of rum and shipped for England. The sailors of the vessel detached for this service became very drunk every night, to the surprise of the officers, who wondered where they got their grog. Finally an old tar, who had been arrested, let the secret out. His messmates, he said, had "tapped the Admiral." The insects who patronize these small vegetable saloons are like the British sailors. When the liquor in the cup is all absorbed, and the V-shaped bottom is choked with dead insects saturated with the fluid, the late comers, finding no beverage, tap the bodies of those who have preceded them. Thoroughly intoxicated by this process, they die in their turn.

An insectivera, seen in great abundance along the line of the railway, was *Sarracenia flava*, also a trumpet leaf.[28] It has the shape of a trumpet, and an opening for insects much larger than the plant just described. The leaves are large, erect, and narrowly winged. The lamina are yellow, orbicular, pointed, downy, red at the base, and veined with purple. The trumpet is shaped so as to prevent the adulteration of its liquor by rain or dew. It bears the same flower as the variolaris, and its victims are full as numerous. Each, however, distills different liquor, and has a different class of customers. Both shops thrive in Georgia and South Carolina, despite their restrictive liquor laws. The effect of the liquor on insects is plainly seen. It would be interesting to know whether it would intoxicate men, if enough of it could be procured. It has a sweet taste, something like cider. Cows nip the plant greedily; nor does it seem to affect their milk, which has as fine a color and as good a flavor as Orange county milk.[29]

After an earnest search we found a whiskey shop bearing a red flower as its sign. There were very few of them. It was the *Sarracenia psittacina*, or parrot-beaked pitcher plant.[30] Mr. Smith has named it "the Sunday saloon." He says its customers creep in by a back door. Once inside they stand at the foot of a tiny hill, and the liquor runs down to them. They drink, drop, and never return. We afterward saw many of these singular plants along the railroad in Georgia, between Waycross and Savannah, while returning to Washington. The leaves are short and spreading, and the tube is slender and broadly winged. It is marked with white spots and is netted with purple veins. The beak is incurved and the orifice of the tube is almost closed.

All these plants protect their liquor from the dew and rain. There is one species, however, which does not do so. It is the *Sarracenia purpurea*, or Huntsman's Cup.[31] It has purple flowers, and is broadly winged. It grows in nearly all of the Florida swamps. The throat is contracted and covered with brown hairs, projecting downward. The botanist has dubbed it "the lager beer saloon." The insect crawls over the hairs and descends the cup to drink the beer. Becoming partly intoxicated it tries to climb out. The down-growing hairs act as a sort of cheveaux de frise.[32] The fly cannot surmount nor thread them. It finally drops into the water below and is drowned. This is the one insectiverous plant that drowns its victims. The Kew guide book says that they all do so, but Mr. Smith says it is clearly a mistake.

Another insectiverous plant is called the Sun-dew (*Drosera*).[33] It kills mosquitoes, and is abundant in the swamps of Florida. It is one of the species of plants of which Mr. Darwin made such interesting investigations. It has from two to six leaves, usually in a horizontal position. Sometimes, however, they have a vertical extension. They are more broad than long. The upper surface is covered with gland-bearing filaments or tentacles. The average number of glands on each leaf is about 190. They are surrounded by drops of viscid secretion. These drops glitter in the sun, and give the plant its name. Insects are caught in the gummy secretion, and the tentacles are brought into play to secure them. The plants are of a red color, and are almost mossy in appearance.

Near these the *Pinguicula*,[34] another insectiverous plant, was found. Its palate is hairy, and the margins of its leaves usually roll inward. It captures its victims with a glue-like secretion, and is said to absorb them by rolling its leaves around them.

VI.

So much for the insect-feeding plants. A score of other curiosities were found before the scorching sun and the red-bugs drove us back to the launch. The search was continued until May 4, when we returned to Washington, instructed and delighted.

AMOS J. CUMMINGS.

Making History

Who gets their names in history books? The answer, of course, is: important and famous people. But just how important and how famous is a matter of debate. For instance, in my research for this book I found numerous biographical sketches and other information relating to Amos Jay Cummings. I thought finding information about William R. Smith, the superintendent of the United States Botanic Garden in Washington, D.C., Cummings's botanical guide for this and the previous 1893 article, would be similarly easy. But that turned out not to be the case. Superintendent Smith somehow slipped below the radar of most recorded history, and I found nothing about him in biographical dictionaries or similar source books.

Ten years ago my search probably would have entailed a trip to Washington, D.C., to search old records. But today that was not necessary. I simply "googled" Mr. Smith using the Google World Wide Web search engine, and there he was. The Internet makes us all famous. Databases and other information accessible through the World Wide Web can put us in touch with millions of people who lived in the past and who did not get their names in history books or biographical compilations. When I discovered the ease with which one can access nineteenth-century federal census records online, I was astounded. Now we can all achieve at least some semblance of fame.

My online searches for William Smith and the National Botanical Garden put me in e-mail contact with W. John Kress of the United States National Museum's Department of Botany and Joan K. Sansbury, librarian and curator of the House of the Temple Library and Museum in Washington, D.C., both of whom graciously provided background about botanist Smith. From their information, I learned Smith was a Scotsman and a 32nd degree Freemason. Not only interested in plants, Smith assembled a well-known collection of publications about and by the Scottish poet Robert Burns.

After Smith's death in 1912, industrialist Andrew Carnegie, trustee of Smith's estate and a patron of his Burns collection, gave the collection to the Ancient and Accepted Scottish Rite of Freemasonry. Today the collection is in the Robert Burns Room in the Library of the Supreme Council in Washington, D.C.

Smith began working at the U.S. Botanic Garden in 1853, initially as a gardener. He was promoted to superintendent in 1863 and held that position until his death. While employed at the Botanic Garden, Smith lived in a small cottage within the garden's grounds and often gave tours to U.S. congressmen. Most likely, Amos Cummings availed himself of Smith's hospitality while he was a member of the United States House of Representatives.

People are not the only things immortalized on the World Wide Web. The oak at Keystone Bluff that Cummings mentions in this article also is on the Web. Long famous locally, the Episcopal Great Oak Tree has achieved national prominence. One can even order acorns from it and plant a descendant of the very tree under which William R. Smith sat more than a century ago.

This article, signed Amos J. Cummings, was published in the *New York Sun* on May 21, 1893.

20

ANOTHER BOTANICAL HUNT

A CONGRESSMAN'S ADVENTURES IN THE GARDEN OF FLORIDA.

The Superintendent of the Botanical Garden Studying the Naturalized Plants of the South—Japanese Plants in the Lead—A Street Shaded with Camphor Trees in New Orleans—Experiments with the Japanese Persimmon—Guavas Touched with Frost—Mrs. Jefferson Davis Makes a Discovery—Plenty of Tea Plants but No Tea Plantations in the South—Rice Paper.

WASHINGTON, MAY 20.—It is a great thing to go on a hunt with a botanist in Florida. Roseate mornings, glowing sunsets, and charming landscapes no longer awaken your admiration. Your attention is riveted upon wonders before unnoticed. The tiniest plant may awaken the keenest interest; gorgeous water lilies have histories of their own; trees growing in the wildest hammocks may boast of an origin remoter than that of the proudest king or emperor.

It is a greater thing, however, to go on a hunt with the Superintendent of the Botanic Garden at Washington. A forty years' experience in raising and propagating plants from all parts of the world makes his observations of more than ordinary interest.

The discoveries of W. R. Smith in the swamps around Jacksonville were rendered more interesting by his researches in the gardens of winter residents along the St John's. One of the objects of his visit was to ascertain what foreign plants and shrubs flourished in the soil and climate of Florida, and thus to learn what others might be acclimated.

I.

There was a broad field for such an inquiry. Within the last few years thousands upon thousands of dollars have been spent in cultivating rare plants on grounds within five miles of Jacksonville. Mrs. Mitchell, widow of Alexander Mitchell of Milwaukee, has a place three miles above the city that is of itself a veritable botanic garden. It contains plants from Australia, the Cape of Good Hope, South America, the East and West Indies, and nearly every other part of the globe. There are curiosities here which she herself brought from the Borghese gardens in Rome, from Egypt, from Havana, and from other places. Some have been cut down by the frost, while others thrive as well as in their native soil.

Six miles below the Mitchell garden is the winter residence of Gen. A. S. Diven[1] of Elmira. The General has served his country on the battlefield and in the halls of Congress. He has one of the most charming places along the St. John's. Rare plants and shrubs, stately trees, thrifty orange groves, and a fountain throwing the purest water twenty feet high are among its attractions. In this paradise the General receives his friends and points out the attractions of his plantation.

Between this place and that of Mrs. Mitchell is Keystone Bluff, the most sightly of them all. It is the winter home of Charles H. Cummings. Its choicest treasure is a live oak of wondrous growth and beauty, whose reputation is becoming national.[2] It has found as enthusiastic an admirer in William C. Whitney[3] as in William R. Smith. Both gentlemen drifted upon it unawares while walking in Mr. Cummings's orange grove. Mr. Smith took off his hat in awe, and Mr. Whitney sat upon a bench in its shade, lost in admiration for several minutes. The tree has a spread of 142 feet. It is nineteen feet around the trunk, and the largest limb is seven feet ten inches in circumference. Aside from this tree, there are some more botanical gems on the bluff. Its proprietor, however, does not pretend to vie with Gen. Diven or Mrs. Mitchell in gardening. He revels in his river view and his green swards. He picks the gray moss from his oaks and dotes upon his orange trees.

It was in these and adjoining gardens that Mr. Smith made his observations. In all he was a welcome guest, and in all he saw rare plants which had been propagated by himself and sent out from the Botanic Garden. The conditions for the growth of such plants were better at the three places named than in some others. Artesian wells are flowing in each of these three gardens, and the supply of water is abundant. Mrs. Mitchell has a fountain and a pond where water plants grow in rare luxuriance. Gen. Diven rejoices in probably the only cascade in Florida. It pours over a prepared rocky bed from the bluff into the St. John's, making refreshing music in the warm moonlight. Mr. Cummings has a bathing pool as fine as that in the Alcazar in St. Augustine. His well flows more than five hundred gallons a minute. The water gushes from a source over 700 feet under ground. It is as clear as crystal, but impregnated with sulphur. The temperature is 72°. The sulphur readily evaporates, leaving drinking water as pure as that of a mountain spring. The water is carried to every part of the grounds, refreshing the grasses and plants through revolving sprinklers.

Gen. Diven and Mrs. Mitchell have wells that evidently tap the same reservoir. They use the water freely upon vegetation, and decisive results are obtained.

II.

The botanist did his work thoroughly. While he found some foreign shrubs growing wild, there were many others flourishing only under cultivation. Most were useful, and a few ornamental. He expressed surprise at seeing so many plants from Japan and China. All were doing well. Among the most thriving was the camphor tree (*Laurus camphora*).[4] These trees were sent South from the Botanic Garden seventeen years ago. There are many now in Florida, but they are mostly to be found in private gardens. Mr. Smith says that they will soon become naturalized and propagated throughout the South, like the orange, the indigo plant, the tapioca, and the alligator pear. In New Orleans they are already found in profusion. One of the streets of that city is shaded by them. On Jan. 5, 1883, a ten inch seedling, one year old, from the Botanic Garden, was planted on the grounds of Mr. R. Maitre in the Crescent City.[5] The tree is now thirty feet high. It has a circumference of fifty-two inches. Photographs of it have been taken and are being distributed. Mr. Maitre sells many of these trees, and supplies the Botanic Garden with seeds every year. Probably 10,000 trees have been propagated from this one specimen since it was planted in Louisiana. We found fine, healthy specimens of the tree in every garden visited around Jacksonville. It yields the genuine gum camphor of the materia medica.

The trees sent South from Washington seventeen years ago were propagated from plants brought from Japan by Commodore Perry. No State in the Union shows more fully the work done by the Commodore than Florida. Her soil and climate suit the Japanese plants remarkably well. Mr. Smith says the balsamic properties of the camphor tree are undoubtedly healthful. It purifies the air and counteracts miasma far better than the eucalyptus. The roots, as well as the leaves, have an aromatic odor. In Japan the camphor is obtained by cutting up the tree and boiling the chips in a trough. Inverted bowls are placed over the trough. The steam is carried into these bowls; the vapor condenses and crystallizes. There is another process, by which the chips and the branches are placed in covered iron pots. Straws and rushes are attached to the inside of the covers. The camphor volatilizes and condenses on the straws. It is scraped off and purified before it is ready for market.

If the tree becomes common in the South, it is not likely to be used to obtain camphor. It will probably be sent to the saw mill and converted into lumber. As a veneering for the interior of bureaus, clothespresses, and trunks, it is unrivalled. There are no moths in camphor trunks. Indeed, the tree is one of the greenest and cleanest in the South. It repels insects, and is free from worms, webs, and grubs.

This has been a hard winter upon trees and plants in Florida. Many have been injured by the frost. Even sugar plants as far down as Kissimmee were touched. Camphor trees, however, came out unscathed. They were never in better condition than they are to-day.

Once planted, the camphor tree will take care of itself. Mr. Smith says that the birds will scatter its seeds as they do those of the cousin, the sassafras. Its future may be indicated by what has happened in the past. Thirty years ago wild orange trees were found in great abundance in the swamps and hammocks of Florida. They have been thinned out by those who transplanted them for grafting. The Spaniards and English, under Turnbull, over a hundred years ago, had immense indigo plantations on the East coast. With the fall in the price of indigo these plantations were ruined. Yet wild indigo is to-day found all along the coast from Mayport to the Indian River. The cocoanut groves of Lake Worth are the product of nuts that came ashore from wrecked vessels. A few trees were growing wild there twenty years ago. Now there are said to be over 100,000 of them. What will make the camphor tree of great advantage to the South is the fact that it is of rapid growth. If properly planted, with a moderate degree of care it will make quick returns.

III.

Nor was this the only useful native of Japan found in Florida. The Japanese persimmon (*Diospyros Khaki*), untouched by frost, was flourishing in many places around Jacksonville. Its fruit is beginning to be sold in Northern markets. It resembles a tangerine. There are numerous varieties of the Japanese persimmon. The best are propagated out from the cuttings of the roots or grafts. Those raised from the seed do not produce the same superior variety of fruit. This singularity was discovered accidentally in Norfolk, Va., some years ago, where the tree flourishes moderately well. A drain was cut through a garden where some trees were growing, and the roots of them were severed. Those on the opposite side of the drain were found to be sprouting vigorously. They produced the same quality and variety of fruit as the original plant.

The Southern darky goes into ecstasy over this fruit. He regards it as far superior to the native persimmon. The pulp is yellow, fleshy, and refreshing. It makes a delicious preserve. The tree grows from 12 to 20 feet high. As it is hardy in the south of England and on the Channel Islands, its adaptation to the climate of Florida is not surprising.

The guava (*Psidium guava*)[6] did not stand the late Southern winter as well as the Japanese plum. All were more or less injured, with the exception of what is known as the *Psidium Cattleyanum.*[7] This seemed to stand the winter better than the other kinds. The plant has been cultivated largely in California. Down the East coast, and in the lower parts of Florida, the guava thrives under proper cultivation. Each family has three or four trees, and turns the fruit into jelly very much as people in the North do the currant, apple, and other fruits. These guava jellies, unlike the most of those imported, are unadulterated. No man has ever tasted guava jelly who has not tasted that made by Florida housewives. The guava is not a native of Florida, but of the West Indies. The seeds were undoubtedly brought to the East coast by the Spaniards centuries ago.

The guava is planted more extensively along Key Biscayne Bay and the Miami River than in the northern part of the State. Here it thrives in a latitude below the frost line. Northern energy and native industry are having as good results in south Florida as in Alabama and Georgia. In time to come, south Florida promises to be a perfect Eden for the production of the comforts and necessaries of life.

The guava, like the pineapple and the banana, makes good returns on a small outlay of labor. Humboldt said that the banana feeds more people than any other plant that can be named. He added that it was a custom in some tropical countries for those who were to be married to start a banana plantation nine months before the wedding. The banana fruits in nine months, and continues to bear every month in the year. At the end of forty years the plantation, with moderate care, is better than nine months after it was begun. Within this time a small plantation, six by eight feet, in one of the green houses at the Botanic Garden in Washington has turned out 200 bunches. These bunches have been plucked and eaten by some of the most distinguished men in the country. Among them were Senators Morgan, Seward, Pearce, Fessenden, Collamer, Conkling, Crittenden, and Beck.

Another Japanese plant is the *Magnolia fuscata*, known in the South as the banana shrub, an evergreen, slow growing, powerfully scented when the sun shines. There is a magnificent specimen at Mrs. Mitchell's, untouched by the frost.

A delicious, sweet, white-flowering vine, with a long botanical name, *Trachelospermum*,[8] was growing nearly everywhere. It covered trellises and arches, and perfumed the night air near every residence. It was in full flower in the latter part of April, although the books say that it flowers in July. Like the other plants, it was brought from Japan.

Another Japanese plant which showed evidences of the severity of the winter was the Loquat or Japanese medlar (*Eriobotrya Japonica*). It is a good-sized tree of the apple family. In Japan it is cultivated for its fruit, which is about the size of a small plum. Hanging from the tree in clusters, it has the flavor of an apple. The plant is cultivated in Australia and in southern Europe, and undoubtedly thrives better in southern than in northern Florida. In northern Florida it requires a sheltered situation, as it is apt to be affected by the cold winds.

This plant was brought to America by Commodore Perry. It was evidently considered a great rarity, for one of Perry's fifty glass cases of plants was filled with it. It had hardly found its way to the Botanic Garden before Mrs. Jefferson Davis, whose husband was then Secretary of War, saw the glass case. She is an admirer of plants and a thorough botanical scholar. Throwing up her hands in astonishment she said:

"What did they bring that here for? It is already growing rank in Mississippi. I can bring you bushels of seed if you want it."

Next fall she brought a peck of the seed with her own hands to the superintendent of the garden. He raised the plants and distributed them throughout the country. It would be interesting to know how the seed was introduced into Mississippi. It was probably imported in the olden time by some wealthy planter and had become common.

IV.

Every few months Northern newspapers contain articles descriptive of a tea plantation in the South. We saw no such plantation nor could we locate one. There were plenty of tea trees, however, around Jacksonville.[9] Mrs. Mitchell has some magnificent specimens in her garden. The most thrifty were seen in the beautiful winter home of Gen. Alexander S. Diven. No attempt to set out a tea plantation has been made. The shrubs grow in a cluster in the shade of a magnificent live oak, near his orange grove. He has also set them out along the paths of his garden. The ground beneath the clump was covered with tea seeds. They resemble small hazel nuts. Mrs. Diven some time ago prepared the leaves according to formula and sent them to the Cincinnati Exposition. She received a premium in return for her efforts. This year she is doing better still. She has sent quite a quantity to the World's Columbian Exposition.

Gen. Diven takes great pride in showing specimens of the tea to his visitors. It has a fine leaf and looks like the black tea of commerce. One thing is certain: The leaf was free from poisonous dyes. None of it was steeped, however, and we had no opportunity to test its quality.

Almost every place of note in Florida has one or more tea shrubs growing upon it. No one seems to think it worth cultivation except as an ornamental shrub. Any effort to grow it with a view to making money by its sale seems to have been abandoned. Whatever the advantages of climate and soil, it cannot enter into competition with the tea grown in China under the present conditions of labor in the two countries. In the Celestial Empire workmen receive not more than six cents a day. In Formosa, where much of our tea comes from, the laborers are paid even less. Somewhat similar conditions exist in India, where tea is successfully raised for commerce.

The tea bush is a pretty evergreen, and nearly allied to the camellia. It produces a profusion of little white flowers in the winter and spring, at the same time as the camellia. The shrub never thrives in low, wet land. In China flowers are cultivated to mix with the tea to give it an aroma. Among these are the sweet olive (*Olea fragrans*)[10] and the *Murraya exotica*,[11] a relative of the orange family. The flowers of the former are so highly prized in China, that they are said to be worth $40 a pound. This where men work for six cents a day. These flowers are mixed with teas of the higher grades only.

The *Olea fragrans* and the *Murraya exotica* are doing well in Florida. The former is called Lan-hoa by the Chinese, who use its foliage as well as its blossoms to perfume their teas. The flowers are very small, and pure white, emitting a delicious fragrance. They are known in the South as the tea olive. There are two of these plants sixty years old in the Botanic Garden in Washington. They are in the Japanese end of the conservatory, and their fragrance delights every visitor.

v.

One of the most interesting of Japanese plants thriving in Florida is the *Aralia papyrifera*,[12] or rice paper plant. It passed through this trying winter without any severe injury. It is a small tree of the ivy family. It grows to a height of ten or twelve feet. The stem is from three to four inches in diameter. The interior is full of white pith like the pith of the elder. This is the plant from which genuine rice paper is manufactured. Its leaves are soft and downy, shaped somewhat like the leaves of the castor bean.

The plant producing this paper was long unknown to botanists. The Chinese carefully guarded the secret, so as to monopolize the manufacture of the paper. The paper is made from the pith of the tree. It averages about an inch in diameter. After being removed, it is cut into pieces about three inches long. By the aid of a lath and the use of a sharp instrument it is reduced into a thin roll, and it is this roll which becomes the rice paper. Whether the rice paper used in the manufacture of cigarettes is the genuine Chinese rice paper or the product of some other fibre is a secret known only to the manufacturer.

At Keystone Bluff the botanist saw the sacred bamboo (*Nandina domestica*)[13] in flower for the first time. It is a native of China and Japan. Temples, altars, and private houses are decorated with these plants on Chinese and Japanese holidays. The bright pink buds delighted Superintendent Smith. He had nourished the plant for years in the Botanic Garden, but had never brought it to flower.

A fine specimen of the *Cryptomaria japonica*,[14] a valuable timber tree of Japan, was also seen. It is winter killed in Washington, but seems to be doing well in Jacksonville.

Botanist Smith laughed when he saw *Boehmeria nivea*[15] growing along the St. Johns. It is known as grass cloth. It recalled an early adventure of the Superintendent of the garden. Thirty-five years ago he was busy scattering the plant over the United States. He had seen small quantities of cloth manufactured from it, and determined to secure enough to make a suit of clothes. He thought that it would be just the thing for warm weather, as it was light, white, and enduring. On the day that the suit was sent home from the tailor's he was invited to dinner at Silver Springs by Gen. Jackson's great friend, Francis P. Blair.[16] A number of Congressmen were invited to dine with him.

Mr. Smith went on horseback, and, as the day was very warm, wore his grasscloth suit and a white beaver. A thunder storm came up. When half way to Silver Springs he was caught in a drenching rain. The white beaver was ruined, but the grasscloth suit was a sight to behold. When wet it is perfectly transparent. The only thing that protected the botanist from curious eyes was his under-clothing. His companions roared with laughter at his condition. He was so chagrined that he dismounted, tied his horse to a fence, entered the woods, and communed with nature until nightfall, when he returned home.

AMOS J. CUMMINGS.

Epilogue

MOS CUMMINGS's death came on May 2, 1902, the result of double pneumonia following kidney surgery in a Baltimore hospital. At the time he was still serving in the U.S. Congress. Newspaper obituaries all claimed he was sixty years old; more likely he was sixty-three. Cummings had become ill in Washington in mid-April and was operated on April 26.

His death elicited a national outpouring of accolades, many of which are pasted in his last scrapbook, today in the New York Public Library. Notices of his death list his New York City residence as 32 Charlton Street in west Soho.

Cummings received a state funeral in the Hall of Representatives in Washington, only the third member of the U.S. House to be so honored. That funeral was followed by another in New York City, attended by the Tammany Hall executive committee. A memorial service held under the auspices of the Columbia Typographical Union of Washington was held May 11, 1902, at an opera house in Washington, D.C. Samuel Gompers, president of the Federation of Labor, was among the audience estimated at two thousand. Another memorial service was held June 22, 1902, in Carnegie Hall, under the auspices of International Typographic Union Local 6, Cummings's old union. At one time, Cummings was the only member of the House who also was a union member.

Contained in the last scrapbook are page after page of small, Chinese fortune cookie-sized rectangles of paper, each with a short poem printed on it. Apparently they were left by mourners at Cummings's funeral. Also in that last scrapbook on the last page was perhaps the most poignant remnant of Cummings's literary life. While in that Baltimore hospital with death at hand, Amos Jay Cummings was handed a pencil and a piece of his letterhead from the U.S. House of Representatives Committee on Library for the Fifty-sixth Congress. In a shaky, barely legible hand, he wrote his last thoughts: "for this is a great world and God moves in a mysterious way."

Notes

Introduction

1. Bagalls, also begalls or bergalls, are sea perch (*Tautogolabrus adspersus*); Rockaway Beach is at the western end of Jamaica Bay.

Chapter 1. Florida's Orange Groves

1. Douglas Dummitt (or Douglass Dummett), as noted in the introduction to this article, was one of the early settlers in what today is Brevard County. His orange grove, from which oranges were first shipped in 1828, was at the southern end of Mosquito Lagoon on northern Merritt Island just south of the old Haulover Canal (Eriksen, *Brevard County*, 33; also see the *Map of Brevard County* (1885), drafted by J. Francis Le Baron, a copy of which is in the University of Florida's P. K. Yonge Library). It was one of East Florida's most celebrated groves during the mid-nineteenth century, and as early as 1865, it enjoyed "world renown" (Eriksen, *Brevard County*, 33). Several of the prominent and colorful individuals Cummings encountered in his travels had been awarded the honorific title captain, colonel, or judge.

2. Cummings is referring to the Seminole Indians, who were living in portions of Central and South Florida following the 1823 Treaty of Moultrie Creek.

3. A long, narrow bay on the inland side of several equally long and very narrow barrier islands on the coast of New Jersey north of Atlantic City.

4. Brought to Florida by the Spaniards, oranges were adopted by the Florida Indians. Archaeologists often observe wild orange trees growing on or near Seminole Indian sites, though it is likely that earlier Indians in Florida helped to spread the trees throughout much of Central Florida. William Bartram saw many stands of wild orange trees in his eighteenth-century journey along the St. Johns River.

5. William J. Hardee graduated from West Point in 1838 and served in the U.S. Army in Florida during the Second Seminole War. He was promoted to general in 1861 during the Civil War.

6. John Eriksen's book (*Brevard County*, 68) shows a map that places "A. Jackson's" land north of the old Haulover Canal and north of Dummitt's lands. As noted in my introduction to this article, I believe Jackson was married to Kate Dummett, a daughter of Douglas Dummett. Andrew and Kate are buried in the Laughing Waters cemetery

with other Jacksons and Dummetts (Eriksen, *Brevard County*, 70). That cemetery is also the resting place for the Campbells, one of whom, mentioned in the introduction to this article and in the article itself, was almost certainly married to a Dummett daughter.

7. Rev. Garnet, a former slave who escaped to the North, was a famed abolitionist who for many years served as pastor at Shiloh Church in New York City. He died in 1882.

8. The 1870 federal census lists an Onesimus Futch, a fifty-year-old farmer. Mr. Futch and his wife Mary had five children ranging in age from twelve to twenty-seven, all of whom apparently lived at home. A second Futch family was headed by Laura Futch, who had seven children seventeen or younger. Her husband apparently had died.

9. The *Ladona*, a steamship from New York bound for New Orleans, ran aground on shore during a storm on August 17, 1871. Cummings also writes about the ship in his article "The Florida Wreckers" (chapter 2).

10. Mosquito netting. Cummings frequently mentions mosquito bars in his Florida articles.

11. As noted above, Campbell most likely was married to a Dummett daughter. In the 1870 census, Doctor Campbell is listed as a fifty-three-year-old mixed-race man from South Carolina.

12. Owned by Joshua Eaton, an early settler at Enterprise; see Michael G. Schene, *Hopes, Dreams, and Promises*, 60.

13. According to Ianthe Bond Hebel (*Centennial History of Volusia County*, 88), the name of the Hillsborough River was changed to Indian River to avoid confusion with the Hillsborough River on the Florida Gulf coast.

14. The camp got its name from the three generations of Swift family members who exported live oak logs back to Falmouth and New Bedford, Massachusetts, most likely for ship building. The business was started in the 1840s by three brothers, William, Rodolphus, and Obed Swift, and continued by their sons and grandsons, including Elija, Adolphus, and Oliver; see Eriksen, *Brevard County*, 91; Gold, *History of Volusia County*, 62, 86, 102; Hebel, *Centennial History*, 3; and Schene, *Hopes, Dreams, and Promises*, 55.

15. Mills O. Burnham established a plantation in the 1840s on the east bank of the northern Banana River east of the Cape Canaveral lighthouse and northeast of New Found Harbor (Eriksen, *Brevard History*, 43–44). The Burnhams and Dummetts were among the earliest families in the region.

16. It is likely that these shells were from shell middens left behind by the pre-Columbian and early colonial period Florida Indians. In the eighteenth century, William Bartram mentioned several such shell deposits along the St. Johns River. Later archaeologists have documented literally hundreds of similar shell middens containing freshwater snail and mussel shells, the remains of animals eaten by the Indians who gathered the mollusks from the river.

17. Hubbard L. Hart owned a stagecoach company that ran passengers, mail, and cargo from Palatka to Tampa. He also operated steamboats on the Ocklawaha River;

see Mueller, *Along the St. Johns and Ocklawaha Rivers,* 80–81, 89; and Noll, "Steamboats," 10–13, 15–22.

18. This may have been Koert DuBois, father of Henry K. DuBois, a New York City physician who had a grove in the area in 1877 (Gold, *History of Volusia County,* 467–68).

19. DeBary, Florida, is named for Frederick de Bary, the "champagne king," who wintered in Florida from 1870 or 1871 until his death in 1898. De Bary was a New York wine merchant and shipping mogul who was the U.S. distributor for Mumm champagne after 1840. A wonderful account of de Bary and his Florida home, DeBary Hall, can be found in Edith G. Brooks's *Saga of Baron Frederick deBary and deBary Hall, Florida.*

20. The acetylene gas (see Brooks, *Saga,* 32) almost certainly was manufactured by mixing carbide and water. Its use in Florida at this early date would have been uncommon.

21. This may be one of the sulfur springs described and footnoted in Cummings's article "Florida's Indian Mounds" (chapter 8).

22. Mr. Rossiter also is mentioned in Edith Brooks's account of DeBary Hall (*Saga,* 46).

23. Henry Shelton Sanford, who received a commission as major general from the Minnesota militia at the outbreak of the Civil War, was appointed as a United States diplomat to Belgium in part to keep an eye on the intentions of European nations and monarchies during that conflict. After the war in 1870, he moved to Central Florida and founded the town of Sanford. He caught the orange fever and arranged to bring in Swedes to work his groves. He also employed Italian immigrants.

24. Jacob Brock was owner and operator of one of the major St. Johns River steamship lines. Later his son, Charles, took over the business (Gold, *History of Volusia County,* 85, 95).

25. Margaret Summers of Enterprise, age twenty-nine, is listed in the 1870 federal census. She had a young daughter and probably was a widow. Value of her real estate was $10,000, which, relative to that of her neighbors, was huge.

26. This may have been Thomas "Starke," listed in the 1870 federal census as a farmer, fifty-eight years old. His real estate holdings were valued at one-fifth of those of Margaret Summers but still were relatively high.

27. John W. Harvey, age sixty-five, is listed in the 1870 census as a house carpenter.

28. There are three families of Feasters at Sand Point in the 1870 census, all headed by male farmers: John W. (sixty-four), Jacob N. (forty-eight), and E. H. (forty-six).

29. The small settlement of Sand Point later became Titusville.

30. Francis L. Dancy, who graduated from West Point in 1826, supervised the construction of the St. Augustine sea wall in the period 1836–39, served two terms as mayor of the town, and fought in the Second Seminole War. His farm was called Buena Vista. I am indebted to Clara Waldhari of St. Augustine for helping me to unravel his name, which was unreadable in the microfilm.

31. Andrew Anderson's grove, described as twenty acres in extent, was on the west side of town at Markland, the family home. Dr. Anderson's father, also Andrew Ander-

son, was exporting oranges from St. Augustine in the early 1830s. He died in 1839, the same year his son was born; see Brinton, *A Guide-Book*, 70, and Graham, *The Awakening of St. Augustine*, 36–39, 53, 147.

32. Senator Abijah Gilbert, a native of Otsego County, New York, moved to St. Augustine from New York in 1865. He served in the Florida Senate as a Republican from 1869 to 1875.

Chapter 2. The Florida Wreckers

1. Haulover Canal allowed small boats to go from the Mosquito Lagoon into the north end of the Indian River at the north end of Merritt Island. At low water, boats could be "hauled over" the small strip of land. It is likely that the Florida Indians used the same haulover in earlier times.

2. One wonders if this person was one of the Swedes whom Gen. Sanford had brought to Florida to work in his groves and about whom Cummings wrote in "Florida's Orange Groves" (chapter 1). See more about Lake Worth in Cummings's article "Adventures in Florida" (chapter 13).

3. The *Ladona* is mentioned by Cummings in his article "Florida's Orange Groves" (chapter 1).

4. I wonder if this were actually a Summerlin, a relative of the Florida Summerlin family involved in cattle raising in Florida.

5. An "old cove" is an old chap. Harris may be Ebon Harris, a sixty-year-old native of Georgia who, with his wife and two children (ages eight and sixteen), were living in Volusia County at the time of the 1870 federal census.

6. Frank Sams bought the Ocean House hotel in New Smyrna from E. K. Lowd, who had built it. Under Sams, the hotel was enlarged (Schene, *Hopes, Dreams, and Promises*, 105).

7. Dr. Benjamin F[rank] Fox (Schene, *Hopes, Dreams, and Promises*, 105).

8. I believe this was piping, in this case a long, narrow band of leather that was nailed along a wooden seam, such as on a barrel.

9. Henry T. Titus moved to the small settlement of Sand Point following the Civil War. During that conflict, he had been a blockade-runner for the Confederacy. Prior to the war, he had led proslavery forces in Kansas and had been with William Walker in Nicaragua from 1856 to 1860. Sand Point was later named Titusville in his honor (Eriksen, *Brevard County*, 65).

10. George J. Alden (see Schene, *Hopes, Dreams, and Promises*, 82, 136) is further identified by Hebel (*The Dummetts*) in her documentary study of the Dummett (Dummitt) family as collector of customs in New Smyrna.

11. I think Cummings means Harris, not Harrison. I could find no Scoveys in the 1870 census, though a twenty-one-year-old man named Duncan Scobie with "no occupation" was living in St. Augustine at that time. I doubt he was the "wrecker."

12. A firkin is a small wooden cask.

13. A boat, generally small, used to resupply larger ships.

14. Clay MacCauley's 1880 Seminole Indian census lists Young Tigertail as family

head of a Mikasuki-speaking household on the Miami River (see Sturtevant, "MacCauley's 1880 Seminole Census").

Chapter 3. The Florida Alligators

1. George M. Barbour (*Florida for Tourists*, 30) describes the *Volusia*, a steamboat that plied the St. Johns River captained by Lund, as "old, small, odd-looking but excellent."

2. Cone, the alligator hunter, also figures prominently in Cummings's article "Florida's Indian Mounds" (chapter 8). A William Cone (forty years old and a farmer), his wife, and five children (ages two through eighteen) appear as residents of Volusia County in the 1870 federal census for Florida. All but the youngest child were born in Georgia.

3. Frank Sams also is mentioned in Cummings's article "The Florida Wreckers" (chapter 2).

4. The Ocean House; see "A Tropical Wilderness" (chapter 7).

5. In "Florida's Indian Mounds" (chapter 8), Cummings says that Tom Reeves is a New Yorker who moved to Florida for health reasons. I could not find him in the 1870 census.

6. Frank Kerns, age thirty, and his spouse, Hannah Kerns, age twenty-five, are both in the 1870 New York census as residents of Manhattan (both were natives of Pennsylvania). Their occupations are listed as actor and actress.

7. Frederick de Bary; see Cummings's article "Florida's Orange Groves" (chapter 1).

8. This may have been J.P.C. Emmons, who served as Governor Harrison Reed's attorney during the attempt to impeach him.

9. Douglas Dummitt is mentioned in several of Cummings's articles, for example, see "Florida's Orange Groves" (chapter 1).

10. Frank Fox; see Cummings's "The Florida Wreckers" (chapter 2).

11. William B. Watson, whose father was Jerry Watson, was the captain of the steamboat *Hattie*.

Chapter 4. The Trouble in Florida

1. Warren S. Bush was tax collector and a member of the Columbian County legislative delegation in 1873–74. I could not confirm that he also was Columbia County sheriff at that time (see Keuchel, *A History of Columbia County, Florida*, 128, 229).

2. A Republican.

3. Governor Reed, a Republican, served as Florida governor from 1868 to 1873. A native of Massachusetts, he moved to Fernandina from Wisconsin in 1863.

4. Samuel T. Day (Keuchel, *A History of Columbia County, Florida*, 124). Day's signature, as assistant marshal, appears on the 1870 Columbia County federal census forms.

5. William D. Bloxham was the Democratic candidate for governor against Ossian Bingley Hart in 1873. Though he lost that election, he later won the governorship in 1881 and again in 1897.

6. Jonathan C. Gibbs was appointed to office during Reconstruction in 1868, serving

until 1873. He was Florida's first African-American secretary of state.

7. Waldron, whose age on the 1870 federal census was given as twenty-five, and his father, George W. S. Waldron, were, according to the census, among the wealthiest individuals in Columbia County.

8. Ossian Bingley Hart, a Republican, became governor of Florida in 1873 but died in office in 1874. During the Civil War he was a Unionist.

9. A Willie(?) W. Moore, thirty-eight, is listed in the 1870 census. He owned real estate even more valuable than that of the Waldrons. Moore's occupation is listed as printer.

10. In the census the last name is Keen, which is correct. George Keen's reminiscenses of his life in Florida are recounted in Denham and Brown, *Cracker Times and Pioneer Lives*. Though Keen mentions many of the people who appear in Cummings's three articles, only one paragraph is devoted to the Lake City outrage (75–76).

11. Joseph F. Baya (Keuchel, *A History of Columbia County, Florida*, 132–33, 144, 152).

12. The ex-congressman was Silas T. Niblack, a Democrat representing Pinellas County. In January 1873, he successfully contested the congressional election of Josiah T. Walls, an African-American elected in 1871. Niblack served the remaining two months of Walls's term.

13. This may be Glen H. Hunter, a merchant, who appears in the 1860 Columbia County census (Keuchel, *A History of Columbia County, Florida*, 87, 220).

14. Possibly Duncan McLauren, who appears in the 1870 census.

15. Possibly James Young, who is listed in the 1870 census.

16. Most likely this is the person listed in the 1870 census as John Meckler, thirty-four, whose occupation was retail sales.

17. Probably Thomas C. Griffin, age forty-nine, listed in the 1870 census.

18. Alex Davidson, a well-to-do merchant, listed as age forty-five in the 1870 census.

19. Jones is identified in the *Tri-Weekly Florida Union* articles as an African-American man. This may be Gabe Jones, identified in the 1870 federal census as a laborer for the railroad and a resident of Lake City. In 1870, he was twenty-five years old.

20. Thomas McMurray, who appears in the next Cummings article and also in my epilogue to chapters 4–6.

21. John P. Varnum, son of Revolutionary War general James M. Varnum, served in that post from 1870 to 1877.

22. Based on the 1870 census, I believe this last name is Bethea, a family surname found in Columbia County at the time. In the Jacksonville newspaper account cited in the epilogue to these three articles, his name is given as Tussy Berthay.

23. The 1870 census lists a Michael King, age sixty-eight, of Suwannee Shoals.

24. Almost certainly this was Thomas T. Long, active in Columbia County politics during Reconstruction (see John Wallace, *Carpetbag Rule in Florida*, 11).

25. Elisha G. Johnson served in the state senate from 1871 to 1875 (Keuchel, *A History of Columbia County, Florida*, 228). He is listed in the 1870 federal census as a native of North Carolina.

26. Dan Watson is mentioned later in the article. I could not further identify him in the 1870 census.

27. Isaac Stephens, a fifty-year-old native of South Carolina, is listed as a laborer in the 1870 census.

28. John Anderson, another South Carolina native, is listed in the 1870 census as a twenty-six-year-old black man.

29. Francis Selph, a forty-five-year-old farmer from Georgia, is listed in the 1870 census as a resident of Lake City.

Chapter 5. The Trouble in Florida

1. Dr. Hunter was also mentioned in the first article titled "The Trouble in Florida" (chapter 4).

2. Elisha Johnson, mentioned in the previous article.

3. Barbour (*Florida for Tourists*, 94) describes the National Hotel as one of Jacksonville's "great hotels" along with the St. James, Windsor, and Carleton, which, during the winter season were "thronged with wealthy tourists from all parts of the world."

4. I believe this is Barry Rigell, who is listed as a twenty-year-old drug(?) clerk in the 1870 census.

5. There is no Duval Selph listed in the 1870 census from Columbia County, Florida. Most likely Duval was Francis (Frank) Selph's brother. Both were later indicted (see the epilogue that follows chapter 6).

6. This is likely the same individual recorded in the 1870 census as Samuel Ashton, a twenty-eight-year-old printer.

7. Reid was named managing editor of the *New York Tribune* in 1868.

8. I've not been able to further identify Gallagher. Cummings, however, apparently was a boxing fan. Scrapbook 4 of the collection of four in the New York Public Library contains several newspaper clippings about John L. Sullivan.

9. Samuel B. McLin, Democrat, served from 1873 to 1877.

10. Major-General John Newton led a Union division at Fredericksburg in 1863, for which he received the rank of major-general of volunteers. He also commanded divisions at Chancellorsville. After the Civil War, he lived in New York City. He probably was personally known to Cummings.

11. The 1870 census lists a Henry Connor or Connors, twenty-five years old and a native of England, living near the town of Tustenuggee. The town was about 15 miles south of Lake City near the present-day O'Leno State Park. I am not certain if he is the desperado.

12. In the previous article, the named was spelled as McMurray.

Chapter 6. The Trouble in Florida

1. Stealing or misusing money entrusted to one's care.

2. Samuel Barclay Conover, a Republican who moved south from New Jersey, served from 1873 to 1879.

3. Gleason had moved south from Wisconsin shortly after the Civil War. He was

elected lieutenant governor and served from 1868 to 1870. At one point, when efforts were under way to try to oust Governor Reed from office, Gleason declared himself governor. But Reed survived, and Gleason himself was removed from office. He later was elected to the U.S. House of Representatives, serving from 1871 to 1874.

4. Israel M. Stewart.

5. E. T. Sturtevant. This incident and others Cummings mentions are covered in Wallace, *Carpetbag Rule in Florida.*

6. William D. Bloxham, a Democrat, would twice be elected governor of Florida, serving from 1881 to 1885, and from 1897 to 1901. Previously, he served as Florida's secretary of state (1877–80).

Chapter 7. A Tropical Wilderness

1. As noted in "Florida's Orange Groves" (chapter 1), the name of the Hillsborough River was changed to the Indian River.

2. Cummings several times compares what is today the Indian River to that New Jersey bay; for example, see "Florida's Orange Groves" (chapter 1).

3. This was the Ocean House, built by E. K. Lowd. According to an 1887 account, the hotel "has for many years been a favorite resort for sportsmen and tourists" (in Gold, *History of Volusia County,* 125). The hotel, built about 1867 (Hebel, *Centennial History,* 85), charged three dollars per day or fourteen dollars per week for room and board (Ziska in Rambler, *Guide to Florida,* 142).

4. Gold (*History of Volusia County,* 87–88) mentions a Wickwire family who settled on Spruce Creek about 1859. Henry Wickwire, a farmer from Vermont, age sixty-two, was living near Port Orange with his wife and four unmarried daughters, ages twelve through twenty-one, at the time of the 1870 federal census.

5. Frank Sams is mentioned in other Cummings articles.

6. According to Gold (*History of Volusia County,* 62, 80, 89), Pacetti took up residence at Mosquito Inlet following the Second Seminole War (he served in the 3rd Florida Regiment). The land on which he lived was owned by his brother Gomezinda Pacetti, who lived in Cuba. Bartolo "Pacetty," age forty-eight, his wife, and five children are listed in the 1870 census, living near Enterprise. A large number of Pacetty and Pacette families are recorded in that same census as residents of St. Augustine.

Chapter 8. Florida's Indian Mounds

1. Le Baron (*Map of Brevard County*) places De Soto Groves on the east shore of the Banana River about halfway between False Cape and Cape Canaveral. Today it would lie within Cape Canaveral Air Force Station.

2. As noted earlier, the name of the Hillsborough River was changed to Indian River in 1901 to avoid confusion with the Hillsborough River on the Florida Gulf coast.

3. Dummitt (or Dummett) is mentioned in several other of Cummings's articles.

4. A Dr. G. M. Wallace was elected to the Daytona Beach City Council when the town was incorporated in 1876; see Hebel, *Centennial History,* 92. The next year he was elected mayor (Gold, *History of Volusia County,* 107). At about the same time, a Dr. George Wallace was a medical doctor and resident of Daytona (Schene, *Hopes, Dreams,*

and Promises, 103). I am uncertain if Dr. George Wallace and Dr. G. M. Wallace are the same individual.

5. Most likely this is the Castle Windy site, 8Vo112, visited by Charles B. Vignoles (*Observations upon the Floridas*, 40); see also Goggin (*Space and Time*, 95). By the time Ripley P. Bullen and Frederick W. Sleight excavated the site in the late 1950s, the "house built on this high eminence . . . was demolished and a considerable amount of shell was removed" (Bullen and Sleight, *Archaeological Investigations of the Castle Windy Midden*, 1). The site appears to be entirely from the St. Johns II period.

6. Mills Burnham is mentioned in other of Cummings's articles.

7. Rouse (*A Survey of Indian River Archeology, Florida*, 192–94) correlates this mound with the Burns Mound, 8Br85, and provides important information about it, including the results of subsequent investigations. The mound dates to the Malabar II period, the equivalent of St. Johns II. For information on the Indian River/Malabar archaeological region, see Milanich (*Archaeology of Precolumbian Florida*), and Rouse (*A Survey*).

8. This refers to St. Johns Check Stamped pottery, an Indian ceramic type common in East Florida during the St. Johns II period.

9. The doctor also is mentioned in other of Cummings's articles.

10. This mound has not been identified. Le Baron ("Prehistoric Remains in Florida," 783) notes a mound near the head of New Found Harbor (probably site 8Br65), but it is doubtful that it is the one mentioned here.

11. These artifacts are commonly called plummets. For more about how they may have been used in coastal settings, see Walker, "Material Culture."

12. Most likely this was actually heat-treated (thermally altered) Florida chert; see Purdy, "Investigation Concerning the Thermal Alteration of Silica Minerals."

13. I believe this should be South Lake just west of Titusville. Le Baron ("Prehistoric Remains," 779) notes a sand mound in the woods about 0.5 miles northwest of Titusville. Though unseen at the time, the mound nevertheless was recorded as site 8Br28 in the early 1950s. It probably no longer exists.

14. The extensive shell middens near Enterprise on Lake Monroe, site 8Vo55, were investigated by famed Harvard Peabody Museum archaeologist Jeffries Wyman, who published two monographs that contain reports on his work at that site: *An Account of the Fresh-Water Shell-Heaps of the St. Johns River, East Florida* (9–11) and *Fresh-water Shell Mounds of the St. Johns River, Florida* (18–21). Much more recently, an archaeological team led by Barbara A. Purdy of the University of Florida excavated in a portion of the site that proved to be as old as 4,000 B.C. Results of those excavations have been published in several papers by Purdy and her colleagues in *Florida Anthropologist* 47 (December 1994).

15. The sulfur spring was one of two near the site whose oddity did not escape early visitors. In an 1843 letter, one such visitor to Enterprise, Florida, wrote: "I must not omit something of the Mineral springs. There are two, known as the Salt and Basin Spring. The first is situated seventy to eighty yards from the margin of the lake (Lake Monroe), is one hundred and twenty yards in circumference, and sends off a cold stream, which flows into the lake; the other, the Basin spring, is two hundred or more

yards in rear of Salt spring, in circumferences eighty or ninety yards, perfectly transparent, and of great depth; the stream from it united with that of the Salt spring. These waters have never been analyzed; they are, however, certainly strongly impregnated with sulphur" (in Dodd, "Letters from East Florida," 58–59). One of these may be the same spring mentioned in "Florida's Orange Groves" (chapter 1).

16. Cone is also mentioned in "The Florida Alligators" (chapter 3). The human skeletons found by Cone were most likely Seminole Indian burials whose graves were dug into the earlier shell midden.

17. Possibly these are the Thornhill Lake Mounds I and II (8Vo58, 59), if by the right bank of the St. Johns River the east side is meant. Clarence B. Moore excavated the mounds in 1893 and 1894 ("Certain Sand Mounds of the St. John's River, Florida," pt. 1, 88–89; pt. 2, 167–73). Moore found stone beads in both mounds, which subsequently have been identified as red jasper (Goggin, *Space and Time*, 52).

Chapter 9. The Farming in Florida

1. Gold (*History of Volusia County*, 102) mentions a James Sawyer, an early settler to the region who bought land near Port Orange and was from Fond du Lac, Wisconsin.

2. The Ocean House; see "The Florida Alligators" (chapter 3).

3. Probably this is Captain Charles Brock, son of Jacob Brock, who is mentioned in "Florida's Orange Groves" (chapter 1).

4. See "Florida's Orange Groves" (chapter 1).

5. See "The Florida Wreckers" (chapter 2).

6. See "Florida's Orange Groves" (chapter 1).

7. Dr. William Wittfeld; spelled Whitfeldt on pp. 112 and 119. Some contemporary accounts (for example, Rambler, *Guide to Florida*, 137) spell his name as "Wittfeldt." In the 1870 federal census of Volusia County, William "Whittfield," is listed as a forty-year-old native of Germany. Dr. Wittfeld's home was on southern Merritt Island. The doctor gave his name to nearby Lake Whitfield, also known as Honeymoon Lake (Eriksen, *Brevard County*, 119). He is mentioned in other Cummings articles.

8. General Duncan L. Clinch served in Florida during the Second Seminole War. In 1836, he resigned his commission and moved to Georgia, and later was elected to the U.S. Congress. He died in 1849.

9. Dr. Frank Fox; see "The Florida Wreckers" (chapter 2).

10. See "Florida's Orange Groves" (chapter 1).

11. Judge Paine also is mentioned in "Adventures in Florida" (chapter 13), and see "The Shore of Okechobee" (chapter 12). I believe the "judge" is Henry J. "Payne," age sixty-one (sixty-seven?), listed as a resident of Fort Capron in the 1870 federal census.

12. In the 1870 census, Thomas "Payne," then fourteen years old, is listed as a son of Henry J.

13. Benjamin Franklin Butler, a Massachusetts politician before the Civil War, served as a brigadier-general of the Massachusetts militia during that conflict. He was famous—some might say infamous—for actions during the Union occupation of New Orleans. After the war, he returned to Congress, this time as a Republican, and later led the prosecution's impeachment proceedings against President Andrew Johnson. The

"Beast of the South," a name he earned in New Orleans, was said to be so hated by southerners that his picture adorned the bottom of chamber pots well after the war.

14. Gov. William H. Gleason; see "The Trouble in Florida" (chapter 6).

Chapter 10. A Railroad in Florida

1. Articles in several old newspapers I found online indicate foot-and-mouth disease, an epizootic disease affecting horses, mules, and other animals, was present in the United States during the period 1873–75. One result of the disease is that animals slobbered a great deal. I am not certain if Cummings is saying the horses actually had the disease, or if he is using epizoot to describe tired and slobbering horses.

2. Gilbert began serving in the U.S. Senate in 1869; see "Florida's Orange Groves" (chapter 1).

3. Goad.

Chapter 11. The Fishing in Florida

1. Domingo Acosta claimed land on the east side of the St. Johns River in Volusia County during the period 1816–21 (Gold, *History of Volusia County*, 38), but I do not know if he was a relative (father?) of George Acosta.

2. Also mentioned in "The Farming in Florida" (chapter 9).

3. Cummings provides much more information about this famous shell mound archaeological site in Volusia County in "Florida's Indian Mounds" (chapter 8).

4. Cummings, writing as Ziska and quoted in Rambler's *Guide to Florida* (144), places Pepper Hammock on Banana Creek, which connects the Indian and the Banana rivers at the north end of the latter. Le Baron's 1885 map shows Pepper Haulover on the coast at the east side of the creek.

5. Fort Capron was opposite the Fort Pierce Inlet, according to Le Baron's map (*Map of Brevard County*). In the past, that inlet was called Indian River Inlet. The military outpost there was originally established in 1849 (Barbour, *Florida for Tourists*, 179).

6. A type of harpoon with a detachable head.

7. Cape Florida is on Key Biscayne.

8. At the mouth of the New River at Ft. Lauderdale.

9. Rudolphus S. Sheldon (Gold, *History of Volusia County*, 90), "Dolph" is also mentioned by Cummings (writing as Ziska and quoted in Rambler's *Guide to Florida*, 141) as a "trustworthy" fishing guide, as are Frank Sams, Dr. Fox, and C. Pacetti, the latter probably Bartolo C. Pacetti (see "A Tropical Wilderness," chapter 7). Dr. Frank Fox and Captain Frank Sams are mentioned several times in Cummings's articles.

10. The cow-nosed ray, *Rhinoptera bonasus*.

Chapter 12. The Shore of Okechobee

1. A predecessor of the American Geographical Society.

2. Frederick Ober refers to Van Boskerck as "Van Buster."

3. This bay on the coast of New Jersey is mentioned by Cummings in other articles, for example, "Florida's Orange Groves" (chapter 1).

4. Aaron Jernigan (not "Jernegan," as Cummings spells the name) settled near Fort

Gatlin, a small outpost that later became Orlando. His once glowing reputation as a founding father has dimmed as historians have taken aim at him and his exploits. In late 1851 or early 1852, he led a small group of cowboys into the headwaters of the St. Johns River where they raided a Seminole Indian encampment killing some of the Indians, slaughtering their livestock, and stealing 120 hogs. Actions such as the raid by Jernigan were in part responsible for the Third Seminole War (1855–58). In that war, Jernigan served as captain of a company of mounted militia, though his record as a soldier was none too sterling. In 1856, an army officer wrote about Jernigan: "during the past three months he has either been drunk or sick (hangover)." According to the officer, residents of Central Florida felt Jernigan and his militiamen were more "dreaded than the Indians" (in Covington, *The Billy Bowlegs War, 1855–1858,* 23, 37, 56; historian Chris Kimball steered me to this information, which is contained in his Web site on the Seminole wars: http://tfn.net/~cdk901/). One of the militiamen serving under Aaron Jernigan was his nephew Elias, an enlisted soldier. Elias "Journegan," a thirty-four-year-old farmer, is listed is the 1870 federal census as a resident of the Fort Capron area.

5. According to Ada Coats Williams (in *A Brief History of St. Lucie County*), the Paine family were early residents of that area. She quotes an 1880 visitor as saying, "The only inhabitants of Saint Lucie . . . are members of the Paine family." One Paine was the postmaster, another the tax collector, and the family ran a boardinghouse as well. Several families of "Paynes" are listed in Fort Capron in the 1870 census. The Paynes also are mentioned in "Adventures in Florida" (chapter 13) and "The Farming in Florida" (chapter 9).

6. Fort Bassinger is actually only about twenty miles from Lake Okeechobee.

7. With tongue in cheek, Cummings is referring to the unbelievable tales and travels recounted in the well-known *Adventures of Baron Munchhausen,* first published in 1785.

8. Also known as devil's dung, this gum resin spice has a sulfurous smell.

9. Using oars to row.

10. Gen. Zachary Taylor, later President Taylor, commanded U.S. Army forces in Florida during the Second Seminole War. As a colonel, he was involved in the Battle of Okeechobee with the Seminole Indians on Christmas Day 1837.

11. Brothers Arthur and Thomas Daughtery settled on the Kissimmee River in the 1860s (see VanLandingham and Hetherington, *History of Okeechobee County,* 12). Thomas's homestead is marked on the 1885 Le Baron map.

12. Louis Agassiz, the famed biologist.

13. Judge Charles P. Daly presided over the American Geographical Society from 1864 to 1899.

Chapter 13. Adventures in Florida

1. Seneca Lake, one of the New York Finger Lakes, is approximately 34½ miles long and 2 miles wide.

2. The 1850 census of Conneautville includes the members of the Hammond family. I suspect that Hiram L. Hammond, who was nine years old at the time of the census,

was the person who accompanied Cummings on this journey. Hiram would have been about thirty-three at the time. However, the person could also have been Hiram's father, C. A. Hammond, who would have been about fifty-six years old.

3. Moore is mentioned in "The Home of the Turtles" (chapter 16).

4. Judge Paine and his family owned much of the commerce of Fort Capron (see "The Farming in Florida," chapter 9). Several families of "Paynes" are listed in the 1870 federal census for Fort Capron.

5. Someone who followed the army and sold provisions to the soldiers.

6. An *arbor vita* is a hedge of evergreen shrubs.

7. The Fulton Fish Market is still functioning in lower Manhattan near the South Street Seaport, though it is soon to be moved across the East River.

8. The mouth of the St. Lucie River is near Stuart, Florida.

9. Also known as a limelight, the Drummond light provided an incandescent, brilliant white flame by using streams of oxygen and hydrogen to heat lime.

10. West of Jupiter Island; this passage is now part of the Intracoastal Waterway.

11. Gilberts Bar is on Hutchinson Island near Stuart, Florida.

12. In 1763, St. Augustine became a British colony under King George III. But there was no military action such as that described here by Cummings.

13. Some of the South Florida bromeliads do resemble pineapple plants.

14. Hobe Sound.

15. As noted in "The Shore of Okechobee" (chapter 12), a "white-ash breeze" means using oars to row.

16. The light keeper was James Armour. Built in 1860, the light can be visited today. It is owned and maintained by the U.S. Coast Guard.

17. Cummings and his companions were in Lake Worth Creek, today part of the Intracoastal Waterway.

18. The straight-line distance is less than eight miles.

19. The "Indian Camping Ground" possibly was a pre-Columbian midden on which later Seminole Indians camped. At one time many such middens dotted Southeast Florida.

20. *Furze* refers to the low scrub vegetation.

21. These mud terraces were destroyed by the dredging of Lake Worth Creek in the 1890s.

Chapter 14. Life in the Palmettoes

1. A photograph of the *Lollie Boy* is reproduced in Mueller's *Along the St. Johns and Ocklawaha Rivers* (90).

2. Bulow Creek flows into the Halifax River on the Atlantic coast in southeastern Flagler County.

3. Several families with the name Cochran (not Cochrane) lived in North Florida, according to the 1870 federal census, including one with two boys, ages fourteen and sixteen. But none lived near Bulow Creek in what is now Flagler County.

4. Frank Sams of New Smyrna is mentioned in several of Cummings's articles.

5. A slang word meaning "damned."

6. In a newspaper article apparently from the *Mayo Free Press* entitled "Lafayette County History, Seven of A Series," author Holmes M. Melton Jr., quoting from the diary of a soldier living in the Suwannee country, writes that the raiders were led by Major Campfield from Alabama (this and other clippings are collected in Melton's 1974 collection *Lafayette County; History and Heritage,* a copy of which is in the University of Florida's P. K. Yonge Library of Florida History).

7. A drumhead court-martial was a court-martial held in the field during military operations. Its name is derived from the practice of using the head of a drum as a table around which the proceedings took place.

Chapter 15. The Terror of the Pines

1. Governor Ossian Bingley Hart is also mentioned in the first article titled "The Trouble in Florida" (chapter 4).

2. Almost certainly King John of Saxony, who ascended the throne at age fifty-two in 1854. He died in 1873.

3. Cummings had made that journey, as we saw in his article "Adventures in Florida" (chapter 13).

4. As noted in other articles, Sand Point later became Titusville.

5. Charles Moore appears prominently in "Adventures in Florida" (chapter 13).

6. An unmarried mother—Jane Drawdy—with four children was living in Volusia County when the 1870 federal census was taken. That same census includes three families of Pagets in the Fort Capron area.

7. Jonergan may have been one of the many Jernigans in Central Florida at that time.

8. This could be either Lewis "Stuart" or Frank "Stuart"; both are listed in the 1870 census for the Fort Capron area.

9. Families of Savages, Hodges, Houstons, and Stuarts all are listed in the 1870 census in the Fort Capron area.

Chapter 16. The Home of the Turtles

1. The green turtle, *Chelonia mydas,* is an endangered species.

2. Pulse refers to legumes, plants that produce peas and beans. The turtles feed on sea grasses and algae, some of which have legumelike nodes.

3. Loggerheads, *Caretta careta,* are another endangered turtle species.

4. The shellback sea turtle is more commonly called the leatherback (*Dermochelys coriacea*). It, too, is endangered.

5. Trunk-backed turtle is another name for the leatherback.

6. It is possible that Castle Rag is a tongue-in-cheek reference to Mr. Moore's shabby circumstances. In the next article, Cummings refers to him as "an old salt."

7. The Minorcans, from the Balearic Islands (Minorca and Majorca), settled at Andrew Turnbull's Smyrna colony in 1768. When the colony failed, many relocated to St. Augustine, Florida.

8. Cummings either got the name of this turtle wrong or usage has changed over time. The turtle that we today call the leatherback is what Cummings refers to in this

article (see notes 4 and 5 above) as the trunk-backed turtle. The turtle with the soft shell he describes in this paragraph is the Florida softshell turtle (*Apalone ferox*). I am grateful to Dr. Wayne King, curator of herpetology at the Florida Museum of Natural History, for this identification.

9. The gopher tortoise, *Gopherus polyphemus*. In various southeastern states, it is a threatened or endangered species.

10. Dr. Frank Fox is mentioned in several other of Cummings's articles (for example, "The Florida Wreckers," chapter 2).

11. Dr. Wallace also appears in "Florida's Indian Mounds" (chapter 8).

12. For more on Bartolo Pacetti, see "A Tropical Wilderness" (chapter 7).

13. Doctor "Whittfeld" (Wittfeld) is mentioned in several of Cummings's articles.

14. See "The Florida Wreckers" (chapter 2) for more on the founder of Titusville, Florida.

Chapter 17. The Fate of a Stranger

1. Dr. Wittfeld is mentioned in a number of Cummings's articles. His homestead on the west side of Newfound Harbor at its mouth must have had a spectacular view east across the Banana River.

2. George Island was at the east side of the mouth of Newfound Harbor northeast of Wittfeld's homestead.

3. As noted in other articles, Titus would give his name to Titusville, which originally was Sand Point. Titus ran a hotel in the town. Cummings (writing as Ziska in Rambler, *Guide to Florida*, 143) notes he stayed at the "good hotel" a "day or two."

4. Brady Island was just north of George Island and south of Buck Point at the mouth of Newfound Harbor.

Chapter 18. The New Sugar Kingdom

1. Col. Zachary Taylor and U.S. troops fought what has been named the Battle of Okeechobee on Christmas Day 1837. Largely as a result of that engagement, Taylor was promoted to general.

2. Kreamer later was hired by the Lake Okeechobee Land Company to dredge a canal from Titusville to Lake Worth (see the Cummings article "The Shore of Okechobee," chapter 12). Work began along Lake Worth Creek in 1892, and then continued north through the saw-grass marsh. In 1896, work was halted. Two years later, Henry Flagler completed cutting the canal into Lake Worth. Today a portion of the Inland Waterway follows the canal.

3. The small town of Runnymede was east of present-day St. Cloud on Lake Runnymede in Osceola County. The town no longer exists.

4. St. Cloud plantation, the site of Hamilton Disston's first sugarcane factory, was at East Lake Tohopekaliga. Later, the name was transferred to a nearby settlement, St. Cloud, Florida.

5. Henry C. Warmoth was governor of Louisiana from 1868 to 1872. His administration is often cited as that state's most corrupt.

6. Spreckels, a native of the kingdom of Hanover (today Germany) came to the

United States in 1846, moving to San Francisco in 1856, where he was involved in a number of business ventures, among them sugar beet production. He also maintained sugarcane plantations in the Sandwich Islands (Hawaiian Islands). Various contemporary accounts describe him as "fabulously wealthy."

7. Summerlin, thought to have been born about 1820 in Bartow, Florida, was patriarch of a Florida family. He gained fame as a supplier of beef to the Confederate army during the Civil War and as a blockade-runner. Later, he helped build the small town that today is Orlando. Summerlin, often called the Cattle King of Florida and whose image was that of the consummate Florida Cracker, died November 4, 1893.

8. Ichneumons comprise a large family of parasitic wasps, mostly stingless, that prey on other insects.

9. I believe this name should be Ravenels, of which there were many in Charleston.

Chapter 19. Hunting with a Botanist

1. Smith is further identified in the introduction to "Another Botanical Hunt" (chapter 20).

2. Wilkes, promoted to commodore in 1862, commanded an expedition of six ships that sailed from Virginia in 1838 on a four-year, around-the-world voyage of scientific research. That expedition did not reach Japan, and it is very doubtful that Smith was on it, since, at the time it sailed, he was ten years old and living in Scotland. I could not find information indicating that Smith was a member of Commodore Matthew C. Perry's famed expedition that landed in Tokyo Harbor in 1853, nor could I ascertain that Smith was on the United States North Pacific Exploring Expedition, 1853–56, which also was in Japan. I think, based on the article that follows, that Cummings got the incident wrong. It was not Smith who went to Japan; rather, plants from Japan from the Perry expedition came to Smith.

3. Augustus H. Garland, a native of Tennessee and former governor of Arkansas as well as a former U.S. senator, served as attorney general of the United States under Grover Cleveland (1885–89).

4. The parade on April 27 involved ships from ten nations. It was held to celebrate the World's Columbian Exposition.

5. Keystone Bluff was the estate of Mary Packer Cummings and her husband, Charles H. Cummings. Mrs. Cummings was the daughter of Asa Packer, who built the Lehigh Valley Railroad, founded Lehigh University, and served as governor of Pennsylvania. She bequeathed the property to the St. John's Episcopal Cathedral of Jacksonville. At the time of her marriage in 1885, press accounts said Mary Packer Cummings was one of the richest women alive, with an income estimated at one thousand dollars a day. She also inherited the Packer mansion in Mauch Chunk, Pennsylvania. In the *New York Times* story about the Cummings's wedding (entitled "A Wealthy Bride"), Charles H. Cummings, whose name is give as "Charles P.," is described as a "self-made man" from New York who began working as a conductor on the Lehigh Valley Railroad and worked his way up to head of the New York end of the company.

6. Also known as sabal, or cabbage, palm, the tree is ubiquitous in Florida.

7. Louis Benoit van Houtte, born in 1810, died in 1876.

8. Today *Livistona australis.*

9. Today more commonly *Serenoa repens.*

10. *Sabal adansonii.*

11. Today *Rhapidophyllum hystrix.*

12. *Phoenix canariensis* is the Canary Island date palm.

13. Phoenix *reclinata,* P. *Spinosa* (which some authorities equate with P. *reclinata*), and P. *farinifera,* more commonly called *Phoenix pusilla.*

14. Built by Henry Flagler in 1889, the Alcazar Hotel today houses the St. Augustine City Hall and the Lightner Museum.

15. Cycas revoluta.

16. As noted in the introduction to this article, the murder of four people on December 11, 1891, occurred in a cottage owned by Frank J. Packwood.

17. John Lendrum Mitchell served as a United States senator from 1893 to 1899. He was the successor to Philetus Sawyer, who served two terms, from 1881 to 1893.

18. The Malabar Coast is in Kerala, India.

19. Today *Melocanna baccifera* (synonymous with *Nastus baccifera*).

20. *Senecio maritima,* which is synonymous with *Cineraria maritima.*

21. *Sarracenia* is the genus for many species and subspecies of North American carnivorous plants.

22. I believe Cummings is referring to *Narcissus thalia,* the thalia daffodil or jonquil, rather than to one of the *Thalia* sp., aquatic plants.

23. The southern prickly ash, *Zanthoxylum clava-herculis,* commonly called Hercules club, or the devil's walking stick, as well as the toothache tree.

24. Today the big-flower paw-paw is *Asimina obovata,* which is synonymous with *A. grandiflora,* the scientific name originally given the plant by William Bartram. The "dog banana" might actually have been *Asimina reticulata.*

25. *Asimina parviflora,* the dwarf paw-paw.

26. Also known as the coral bean.

27. Also known as the spotted pitcher plant.

28. The yellow pitcher plant.

29. Orange County, New York, is still a dairy area.

30. Also known as the parrot pitcher plant.

31. Also commonly called the purple pitcher plant.

32. A type of movable, defensive fortification most commonly made by attaching long spikes to a log or framework to obstruct cavalry.

33. There are five species of sundews native to Florida, several of which are threatened or endangered.

34. A number of butterworts are found in Florida and, like the sundews, most are threatened or endangered species.

Chapter 20. Another Botanical Hunt

1. Diven, an attorney who died in 1896, served in the Union army during the Civil War. It was during that war that he was promoted to general. He also served in both the

New York and United States legislatures. His Florida home was at Hazzard Bluff, later Empire Point, at the confluence of the St. Johns River and Arlington Creek.

2. The oak is still there.

3. Whitney, a prominent New York Democrat and financier, served as U.S. secretary of the navy from 1885 to 1889. He died in 1902. He is the same Whitney whose photograph (and those of six other politicians) was with the photograph of Cummings displayed in the introduction to this book.

4. Today more commonly *Cinnamomum camphora*.

5. The Crescent City is, of course, New Orleans.

6. *Psidium guajava*.

7. *Psidium cattleianum*, the strawberry guava.

8. *Trachelospermum jasminoides*, Confederate jasmine.

9. *Camellia sinensis*.

10. Today *Osmanthus fragrans*, also known as the tea olive.

11. Commonly called orange jasmine or mock orange, the plant is not related to the orange family.

12. Today *Tetrapanax papyriferus*.

13. Commonly called heavenly bamboo.

14. *Cryptomeria japonica*, commonly called Japanese cedar.

15. Also commonly called ramie, or Chinese grass cloth.

16. Frank P. Blair Sr., a native of Kentucky and supporter of Andrew Jackson, founded the *Washington Globe* in 1830. He had a country estate in Silver Springs, Maryland. Blair, who died in 1876, also was a speech writer for President Jackson.

References

Andrews, E., and C. Andrews, eds. 1945. *Jonathan Dickinson's Journal; or God's Protecting Providence.* New Haven: Yale University Press.

Anonymous [Frederick A. Ober]. 1873. Lake Okeechobee. *Forest and Stream,* November 20, 233.

———. 1874. Lake Okeechobee Florida. *Forest and Stream,* April 16, 153. (Includes a map of the lake attributed to F. A. Ober.)

Barbour, George M. 1882. *Florida for Tourists, Invalids, and Settlers.* New York: D. Appleton and Co.

Bartram, William. 1928. *Travels of William Bartram.* Edited by M. Van Doren. New York: Dover Publications.

Beverly, Fred [Frederick A. Ober]. 1874a. The Okeechobee Expedition. *Forest and Stream,* March 5, 49–50.

———. 1874b. Our Okeechobee Expedition. *Forest and Stream,* March 26, 105.

———. 1874c. Our Okeechobee Expedition. *Forest and Stream,* April 16, 145–46.

———. 1874d. Our Okeechobee Expedition. *Forest and Stream,* May 7, 193–94.

Brinton, Daniel. 1869. *A Guide-Book of Florida and the South for Tourists, Invalids, and Emigrants.* Philadelphia: G. Maclean; Jacksonville: C. Drew.

Brooks, Edith G. 1968. *Saga of Baron Frederick deBary and deBary Hall, Florida.* N.p.: Convention Press.

Brown, Canter, Jr. 1997. *Ossian Bingley Hart: Florida's Loyalist Reconstruction Governor.* Baton Rouge: Louisiana State University Press.

Bullen, Ripley P., and Frederick W. Sleight. 1959. *Archaeological Investigations of the Castle Windy Midden, Florida.* William L. Bryant Foundation, American Studies Report 1. Deland.

Covington, James W. 1982. *The Billy Bowlegs War, 1855–1858: The Final Stand of the Seminoles against the Whites.* Chuluota, Fla.: Mickler House Publishers.

Denham, James M., and Canter Brown Jr. 2000. *Cracker Times and Pioneer Lives: The Florida Reminiscenses of George Gillett Keen and Sarah Pamela Williams.* Columbia: University of South Carolina Press.

Dodd, Dorothy. 1936. Letters from East Florida. *Florida Historical Quarterly* 15:51–64.

Drennen, Marguerite. 1948. Celebrated Dummitt Grove. *Literary Florida* 5, no. 2:14–16.

Eriksen, John M. 1994. *Brevard County, A History to 1955.* Tampa: Florida Historical Society Press.

Florida Commission of Lands and Immigration. 1869. *Florida: Its Climate, Soil, and Productions.* Jacksonville: Florida Union and the Jacksonville Tri-Weekly Union.

Goggin, John M. 1952. *Space and Time Perspectives in Northern St. Johns Archeology, Florida.* Yale University Publications in Anthropology 47. New Haven.

Gold, Pleasant Daniel. 1927. *History of Volusia County.* Deland: E. O. Painter Printing Co.

Graham, Thomas. 1978. *The Awakening of St. Augustine: The Anderson Family and the Oldest City, 1821–24.* St Augustine: St. Augustine Historical Society.

Haynes, John Edward. 1882. *Pseudonyms of Authors, Including Anonyms and Initialisms.* New York: n.p.

Hebel, Ianthe Bond, ed. 1955. *Centennial History of Volusia County, Florida, 1854–1954.* Daytona Beach: College Publishing Company.

———. 1968. The Dummetts of North East Florida. Daytona Beach. Typescript; copy in the University of Florida Library.

Hicks, John. 1950. *Adventures of a Tramp Printer, 1880–1890.* Kansas City: Midamericana Press.

Keuchel, Edward F. 1981. *A History of Columbia County, Florida.* Tallahassee: Sentry Press.

Lanier, Sidney. 1875. *Florida: Its Scenery, Climate, and History, with an Account of Charleston, Savannah, Augusta, and Aiken, and a Chapter for Consumptives, Being a Complete Hand-book and Guide.* Philadelphia: J. B. Lippincott and Co.

Le Baron, J. Francis. 1884. Prehistoric Remains in Florida. *Smithsonian Institution Annual Report for 1892,* 771–90.

———. 1885. Map of Brevard County. P. K. Yonge Library of Florida History, University of Florida, Gainesville. Map 823. Photocopy.

Melton, Holmes M., Jr. 1974. *Lafayette County; History and Heritage.* N.p. Photocopy of newspaper articles.

Milanich, Jerald T. 1994. *Archaeology of Precolumbian Florida.* Gainesville: University Press of Florida.

———. 2002. The Historian's Craft. *Florida Historical Quarterly* 80:375–78.

Moore, Clarence B. 1893. Certain Shell Heaps of the St. John's River, Florida, hitherto Unexplored (Third Paper). *American Naturalist* 27:605–24.

———. 1894a. Certain Sand Mounds of the St. John's River, Florida. Pt. 1. *Journal of the Academy of Natural Sciences of Philadelphia* 10:4–128.

———. 1894b. Certain Sand Mounds of the St. John's River, Florida. Pt. 2. *Journal of the Academy of Natural Sciences of Philadelphia* 10:129–246.

Mueller, Edward A. 1999. *Along the St. Johns and Ocklawaha Rivers.* Charleston: Arcadia Publishing.

Noll, Steven. 2004. Steamboats, Cypress, and Tourism: An Ecological History of the Ocklawaha Valley in the Late Nineteenth Century. *Florida Historical Quarterly* 83:6–23.

Ober, Frederick A. 1874a. Lake Okechobee. *Appleton's Journal*, October 31, 559–64; November 7, 591–94.

——. 1874b. Natural History: Birds of Lake Okeechobee. *Forest and Stream*, April 23, 162–63.

——. 1887. *The Knockabout Club in the Everglades; the Adventures of the Club in Exploring Lake Okeechobee*. Boston: Estes and Lauriat.

O'Brien, Frank M. 1928. *The Story of the Sun, New York: 1833–1928*. New York: D. Appleton and Co.

Purdy, Barbara A. 1971. Investigation Concerning the Thermal Alteration of Silica Minerals: An Archaeological Approach. PhD diss., Department of Anthropology, University of Florida, Gainesville.

——. 1994. Excavations in Water-Saturated Deposits at Lake Monroe, Volusia County, Florida: An Overview. *Florida Anthropologist* 47:326–32.

Rambler [pseud.]. 1875. *Guide to Florida*. New York: American News Company.

Rouse, Irving. 1951. *A Survey of Indian River Archeology, Florida*. Yale University Publications in Anthropology 44. New Haven.

Schene, Michael G. 1976. *Hopes, Dreams, and Promises, A History of Volusia County, Florida*. Daytona Beach: News-Journal Corp.

Shofner, Jerrell H. 1974. *Nor Is It Over Yet: Florida in the Era of Reconstruction, 1863–1877*. Gainesville: University Presses of Florida.

Sturtevant, William C. 2000. MacCauley's 1880 Seminole Census. In *The Seminole Indians of Florida*, by Clay MacCauley, xxxvi–lii. Gainesville: University Press of Florida.

Sunshine, Silvia [Abbie M. Brooks]. 1880. *Petals Plucked from Sunny Climes*. Nashville: Southern Methodist Publishing House.

Turner, Gregg M. 2003. *A Short History of Florida Railroads*. Charleston, S.C.: Arcadia Publishing.

VanLandingham, Kyle S., and Alma Hetherington. 1978. *History of Okeechobee County*. Fort Pierce: VanLandingham.

Vignoles, Charles. 1823. *Observations upon the Floridas*. New York: E. Bliss and E. White.

Walker, Karen J. 2000. The Material Culture of Precolumbian Fishing: Artifacts and Fish Remains from Coastal Southwest Florida. *Southeastern Archaeology* 19:24–45.

Wallace, John. 1964. *Carpetbag Rule in Florida. The Inside Workings of the Reconstruction of Civil Government in Florida after the Close of the Civil War*. Gainesville: University of Florida Press. (Orig. pub. 1888.)

Williams, Ada Coats. 1963. *A Brief History of Saint Lucie County*. Fort Pierce: Theresa M. Field Office Services.

Wyman, Jeffries. 1868. *An Account of the Fresh-Water Shell-Heaps of the St. Johns River, East Florida*. Salem, Mass.: Essex Institute Press. (Reprinted from the *American Naturalist* 2 [8–9].)

——. 1875. *Fresh-water Shell Mounds of the St. Johns River, Florida*. Peabody Academy of Science, Memoir 4:3–94. Salem, Mass.

Index

Page numbers in *italics* indicate photographs or illustrations. Place names are in Florida unless otherwise indicated. Alternate spellings or meanings for the same term or name are separated by a slash (/).

Jerald T. Milanich is curator in archaeology for the Florida Museum of Natural History. He has been involved in archaeological investigations in Florida and Georgia for over thirty years. He is the author of more than a dozen books dealing with the native peoples of Florida and South Georgia, most recently *Florida Indians: From Ancient Times to the Present* (University Press of Florida, 2002).

Titles of related interest from the University Press of Florida

Al Burt's Florida
Snowbirds, Sand Castles, and Self-Rising Crackers
Al Burt

The Calusa and Their Legacy
South Florida People and Their Environments
Darcie A. MacMahon and William H. Marquardt

The Florida Journals of Frank Hamilton Cushing
Phyllis E. Kolianos and Brent R. Weisman

Florida's History through Its Places
Morton D. Winsberg

The Great Journey
The Peopling of Ancient America, Updated Edition
Brian M. Fagan

Grit-Tempered
Early Women Archaeologists in the Southeastern United States
Nancy Marie White, Lynn P. Sullivan, and Rochelle A. Marrinan

How to Do Archaeology the Right Way
Barbara A. Purdy

Interpretations of Native North American Life
Material Contributions to Ethnohistory
Michael S. Nassaney and Eric S. Johnson

The Lost Florida Manuscript of Frank Hamilton Cushing
Phyllis E. Kolianos and Brent R. Weisman

Orange Journalism
Voices from Florida Newspapers
Julian M. Pleasants

Pioneer in Space and Time
John Mann Goggin and the Development of Florida Archaeology
Brent R. Weisman

Seasons of Real Florida
Jeff Klinkenberg

Sunshine States
Wild Times and Extraordinary Lives in the Land of Gators, Guns, and Grapefruit
Patrick Carr

Up for Grabs
A Trip through Time and Space in the Sunshine State
John Rothchild

For more information on these and other books, visit our website at www.upf.com.